PEOPLE WAGING PEACE

People Waging Peace

Stories of Americans striving for
peace and justice in the world today

Elizabeth Anne McGuinness

Photographs by the author

Alberti Press

Library of Congress
Catalog Card Number: 87-73030

ISBN: 0-944758-10-X
ISBN: 0-944758-11-8 pbk.

Library of Congress Cataloging-in-Publication Data

People waging peace.

    Includes index.
    1. Pacifists—United States—Biography.
I. McGuinness, Elizabeth.
JX1962.A2P46 1988   327.1'72'0922 [B]   87-73030
ISBN 0-944758-10-X
ISBN 0-944758-11-8 (pbk.)

To Marge Roberts

CONTENTS

Preface

ILLUSTRATIONS

PREFACE

During the Vietnam War, the peace movement was the darling of the headlines. It was raucous and rowdy; it dared to throw its fist in the air, aimed in the general direction of Washington. While the rest of us worriedly wondered if the government could be right, if the next domino might really crash down upon us . . . the peace movement shouted, "No!" And finally, it was a movement that played a major role in moving the United States out of a debilitating and undeclared war.

As that unhappy war progressed, media tagged along after public opinion—at first, aghast at the peace movement's brazen politics, its barely-mentionable lifestyles; then, as the war lost popularity, discovering that those long-haired young people had some sense, after all. Today, media look back on that movement with all the affection of a kindly uncle: Those kids were able to teach us something, weren't they.

But when it comes to today's peace movement—not the one "back then"—the media take another tack. That reaction can be summed up in a two-word question: "What movement?" Look through any of the nation's daily papers. There's a choice of stories about war preparations, military buildups, flashpoints of tension that could lead to World War III. Yet, try to find even one story about today's peace movement. Once in a while, there will be one. Maybe even a glowing one. But seldom one that suggests a strong, nation-wide reach toward peace . . . no recognition of a peace "movement."

And yet, thousands of people across the nation already are working to turn this country away from its death dance with war. These Americans already are committing their time and inspiration and energies. They are people waging peace.

The fact that there seemed to be a good story out there—one that the media weren't covering—was a major reason I began this book. I've been a journalist most of my working life, writing for a variety of papers, most recently The Los Angeles Times, and teaching at Golden West College in Huntington Beach, Calif. Researching and writing this story would be a professional challenge.

Beyond that, it seemed this was a story that needed to be told. Headlines today are full of plans and possibilities for war—war that could mean the end of the this world as we know it. With a threat that huge, problems so mind-boggling, it's tempting to shrug our shoulders and rationalize our inactivity: "What could one person do anyway?" Maybe, I felt, those in the peace movement could answer that question and suggest alternatives. Maybe they could offer models for the rest of us, including me. This would be a personal quest as well as a professional one.

The search to find those people led to two long swings through the nation, connecting with peace and justice groups, and talking with individual members. About 50 of those people appear in the pages that follow.

Their stories brought some surprises. For one, they showed a movement much more complex than I had anticipated. Starting out, I thought that if the goal of this movement was peace, then the focus must be anti-war, or perhaps anti-nuclear. But this movement has bigger dreams. Many individuals, in fact, no longer speak of a "peace" movement; for them, it has become a "peace and justice" movement. They are not only opposing weaponry, but also trying to change the world in such a way that weaponry will not be needed.

Many focus at least part of their efforts on serving human needs: working with refugees, the hungry, and the disenfranchised. Some of those efforts are touched with heroism. Marge Roberts, with whom the book begins, is a good example: a gentle 57-year-old from Denver who took chances with her own life to help protect a young Guatemalan woman whose sister already had "disappeared."

All stories tell of personal commitment and a willingness to take responsibility. Sharna Sutherin, a Baptist minister working with students at the University of Montana at Bozeman, was one of those who spent their own money to travel to the Soviet Union, for instance, seeking human connections where governments seemed unable to make official ones. Others traveled to Japan, Europe, Central America.

Some have left both homes and jobs, making the peace effort their full-time occupation. Among these were two Beyond War families—the Ed Thomases and David Smiths, both of Palo Alto, Calif. The Thomases were living in Des Moines, the Smiths in Atlanta, both couples at their own expense, to encourage other Americans to move beyond the thought of war.

All of that—and the rest of what's out there—adds up to an idealistic effort. It is also, for many, a spiritually-sustained one. The strength of that spiritual connection was another development I had not anticipated. No intensive look at the spiritual angle was planned as my research began; yet, that inspiration now claims a major role in the book, even running through many of those chapters not specifically noted as "spiritual."

This movement, of course, must also be described as a diverse one. That means it is often hard to tie down, to categorize. And that leads back to another explanation for media disdain. Editors like the quick, well-focused story, the event that makes pictures, the report with a recognizable beginning and end. That means the media is happy enough to cover a peace movement event now and then—a demonstration, perhaps, especially if a movie star is getting arrested; or, perhaps, a talk by Carl Sagan or Benjamin Spock. But the movement in general? They're not interested. Besides, as far as most are concerned, the "movement" ended along with the

Vietnam War.

That, however, is not the case. There is a movement today. It has roots reaching back to the Vietnam era and beyond, but has developed its own personality. Maybe it's a movement that is trying too much; maybe it's one that needs to get its act together and go after one major goal; maybe it needs to learn its own lessons about media manipulation.

Or maybe the real problem is that the rest of us need to listen.

Most of the people whose stories follow will be unknown to readers, although almost all are recognized leaders within their own communities—and some, across the nation. Peace activism is seldom a magic key to recognition and approbation; this late 20th century reserves its praise for those with other values, although the search for peace is arguably the most important challenge facing mankind today.

Sometimes I reached these people through references given me ahead of time; otherwise, I would look through a pair of peace directories at each stop, call groups that had not been represented, and ask them to suggest one of their members. A majority of those who were suggested appear in the book.

Research, interviews and writing began in late 1984 and lasted through most of 1987; the stories reflect what was happening in people's lives at the time we talked. All of these are people to whom I am indebted for sharing their lives and dreams.

Individual thanks go to several people, including Kay Mortenson, a wonderfully-talented art teacher at Golden West College, who asked, "Why can't you?!?!" so many times that I finally realized I could leave both teaching and reporting to take a chance on writing this book. Next, my publisher, Kerry Burtis, whose support, advice and faith made it come together, although there were times when it seemed that would never happen. Within the peace movement, to Jean Bernstein and Tim Carpenter of the Alliance for Survival, whose stories are included and who first offered major inspiration. Also, to Bob and Karen Brytan of Beyond War, next-door neighbors who not only helped me recognize the breadth of this movement, but who listened patiently as I tried to sort out the beginnings of this project. And finally, to Marge Roberts, whose story both begins and ends the pages that follow, and whose life exemplifies the depth of commitment that is growing within this movement.

Vigil at Rocky Flats

I

PEACE . . . AND JUSTICE

1. MICROCOSM OF A WORLD AT RISK

> *Each of us is called on to do something that no*
> *member of any generation before ours has had to*
> *do: to assume responsibility for the continuation of*
> *our kind—to choose human survival.*
> —Jonathan Schell

Rocky Flats lives up to its name. It is a barren, windswept stretch of land northwest of Denver, Colo. On this overcast, October Sunday afternoon, low white gates close off the two entry drives that lead across the flats to the Rockwell International plant—a plant that manufactures triggers for America's nuclear weapons. Two security cars wait a short distance inside the gates, one with its engine running. Two black-uniformed guards stand nearby, talking to each other with what seems forced joviality. Walkie-talkies hang from their belts.

Just outside the gates, a dozen or so people sit in a circle on the patch of gravelly ground between two driveways. They are silent, in meditation. The dozen include Marge Roberts, a soft-spoken woman whom friends describe as a "good hugger"; Peter Ediger, minister of Arvada Mennonite Church, plus one or two others from the Mennonite community; three or four from the Catholic Worker House; a couple of others with no special affiliation.

Those on both sides of this desolate stage are taking part in a small bit of drama that has played out every Sunday afternoon since 1979, through hot summers and icy-winded winters. It is a basic confrontation of ideals and values, one that questions fundamental assumptions of society. Those sitting outside are acting on their belief that nuclear weaponry is wrong, that the plutonium this plant has released into the air is wrong, and that somehow Rockwell, Rocky Flats and the whole world must change; those inside have been hired to make sure this particular morality play stays outside the gates so the American weapons-production machinery can move forward undeterred.

While there is no script for this drama, there is still an audience of sorts. That audience, riding in cars passing by, sometimes gets into the action by honking a horn or by shouting support or opposition.

This day, two cars actually stop briefly, and two women and a couple of children join the quiet circle for several minutes.

Then, suddenly, the mood changes as one of the meditators jumps up and dodges across the highway, carrying a camera. On the other side of the fence, the two guards drop their casual pose and tense for action. Both pull out their walkie-talkies; one hurries to his car and speeds off toward the plant. That photographer could signal trouble—perhaps that the meditators are about to start one of their rare fence-jumping episodes; it could mean more officers are needed to secure the plant and handle arrests.

But this time the incident is innocuous: The photographer takes a few pictures; the meditators stand, link arms around each other and join in a verse of "You Are My Sunshine," then walk to their cars and leave. The remaining security guard relaxes, and Rocky Flats goes back to "normal" for another week.

———————————

That Rocky Flats vigil—an uneasy drama played out between law enforcers and citizens—represents more than a continuing minor headache for Rockwell International near Denver, Colo. It also serves notice to the nation that many thousands of its citizens already are at work, encouraging change that could make this a different kind of nation . . . a different kind of world. For this is the contemporary peace movement. It is not the one "back then"; this is a movement that deals with today's problems—a whole range of issues, including nuclear weaponry's potential to fulfill the ancient apocalyptic warnings of a sudden, violent end to the world.

These people are not alone, of course, in worrying about weapons buildups, in wishing for world peace or in wondering why politicians don't seem able to do something about it. All of those are major concerns for most Americans—often for children as well as adults.

However, most of us look at the immensity of the problems and ask, "What can one person do?" We shrug our shoulders and rationalize, "It's too complex for us to understand; we'd better let the experts and the politicians deal with it. After all, it's their responsibility, and they must know what they're doing."

But people like those at the Rocky Flats vigil disagree. "No," they say, "the politicians and experts don't know the answers. Besides, responsibility lies with the individual as well as the politician or expert. And yes, one person can make a difference." Their actions, based on those beliefs, are what make up today's peace movement.

Yet, in spite of the impressive numbers of Americans who support peace movement goals and in spite of some truly significant accomplishments, this is a movement that still seems best chronicled in the stories of its individual members, for most other Americans don't see this as an organized effort. The peace movement? That was in the '60s, wasn't it? Peace activists? They're mostly kids, aren't they? And as far as those people who go to demonstrations today . . . most of them are a little strange, aren't they?

There was, of course, a peace movement in the '60s, and there are connections that have lasted from that period; but this is a

different time and a different movement. And no, the people who
are active today don't fit into one neat category. Those I spoke with
during two lengthy trips around this nation ranged in age from teens
to seventies. There were pragmatists seeking concrete goals and
philosophers dealing mostly with ideas. Some were poor, some
were well-off and most were in-between. Their major "strangeness"
was that they were willing to put their beliefs into action—sometimes
into actions that would make the rest of us uncomfortable. My
sampling turned up a senator's wife, a judge's wife, a former Marine
Corps general, a Jesuit priest, a computer programmer, a school
counselor, a high school student, an accountant, a mayor, and many
more.

One of them—a woman whose story tells a great deal about
today's movement—was Rocky Flats' Marge Roberts.

2. WHERE THERE IS NEED
Marge Roberts, Denver, Colo.

> *If we all can persevere, if we can in every land and office look beyond our own shores and ambitions, then surely the age will dawn in which the strong are just and the weak secure and the peace preserved.*
>
> —*President John F. Kennedy*

The scene was a deserted street in Guatemala. The time was late evening. The young woman who entered the street was a university student, heading home from a class.

Suddenly, a carload of men pulled up behind her. For a block or two, they followed along, moving faster as the young woman began to hurry.

Then they gunned their car past her. As she shrank against the nearest building, the young woman got a quick look at the car. Its windows bristled with machine guns. All were pointed at her.

The men didn't shoot, but their message was clear: Next time you might not get off so easily. The young woman was panic-stricken.

She dropped out of the university; she feared ever to leave her home; she began searching for a way to leave the country. Yet, sometimes—in spite of her terror—she had to go out.

And soon there was a bodyguard to protect her. But this was no muscular young guardian, no well-trained, well-armed security expert; this was Marge Roberts—unarmed, 57 years old, a "good hugger" from Denver, Colo. When the need was so great that the young woman had to go out, Roberts put an arm around her waist,

Marge Roberts

held her hand, and went with her.

Roberts had come to Guatemala just a couple of weeks earlier as a volunteer with GAM—Grupo de Apoyo Mutuo (Mutual Support Group). GAM represented families in danger of retribution—those who opposed government intimidation and brutality, or those with members who had "disappeared" after being identified as government enemies. Since the Guatemalan government did not want to offend the United States or Canada, GAM reasoned, North Americans accompanying threatened individuals might be able to save them from attack.

Roberts had signed on. In spite of the real personal danger to herself, "a nonviolent bodyguard just kind of appealed to me," she said later. "I kind of liked the idea."

All of her assignments were with women. The first two were GAM leaders. A bodyguard seemed prudent at the time, said Roberts, because two other leaders had been killed not long before. It was hard to realize what she really was doing, Roberts said: "It was just an ordinary, middle-class life. And yet you would be aware sometimes of being watched. There would be people watching you, following you."

Her third assignment—the university student—was the daughter of another GAM leader. Roberts, who spent two and a half weeks with her, remembers two times they went out.

Once their destination was the migration office. "She had to go there to get her passport," said Roberts. "No one can do that for you. So she and I and her father took the bus, and I walked with her, with my arm around her waist and my hand gripping her other arm. She was scared to death, but just did what she had to do."

All three were wary and nervous, Roberts recalled. "We had to wait for an hour outside the migration office, and truckloads of soldiers were driving up and down the street. During that time, she had her back against the wall, and her father and I both just stood in front of her."

But that trip ended successfully. And so did the other, as Roberts walked with the young woman to the Canadian embassy, which not only agreed to welcome her to Canada, but to loan her money for her plane ticket and to arrange registration in a Canadian school. The day after Roberts left Guatemala, the young woman was on her way, as well.

That journey was Roberts' second into Central America. The year before, she had headed for Nicaragua, with plans to work on her Spanish and to find out for herself what was going on down there. She had returned home feeling incensed about "my government's attempts to destabilize this tiny nation."

But now, as we talked on the day of the Rocky Flats vigil, Roberts was back from both trips. She had a job with the Catholic archdiocese's peace and justice committee, she had renewed old contacts with the Rocky Flats group, she was back volunteering at the Catholic Worker soup kitchen.

It was a life that seemed to fit as comfortably on Roberts as the sweatshirt, jeans and moccasins she was wearing for the vigil. She was soft-spoken with an easy smile, one of those women often described as ageless.

She had been leery about talking to a reporter; you never knew if they'd tell what you "meant," not just what you said. But she'd decided to take a chance, and suggested that I go along on the Sunday afternoon vigil. As she piloted her aging car toward Rockwell's west gate, Roberts began her story. There was no time to finish during the vigil, so she picked up the tale again as we returned to Arvada Mennonite Church, our starting point, and then moved to a log at the side of the parking lot, talking and watching the sunset.

"The Sunday afternoon vigils started early in 1979," Roberts recalled, and since then they've gone on year-round, straight through the winter. "Oh, it gets very, very cold. Sometimes they get pretty short—15 or 20 minutes is all. But we feel it's important to be here."

Actually, the vigil's roots go back a year earlier, when a group of young people set up a tepee on the railroad tracks leading into the plant and stayed there round the clock for nine months. "When the train came through," Roberts said, "the company would take the tepee down and arrest the people on the tracks. The next day, or even maybe a few hours later, the tepee would be back up and there would be more people out on the tracks." Maybe 80 in all were arrested that year.

After that, the weekly visits began, with Roberts there from the beginning.

Roberts, herself, has been arrested more than once at Rocky Flats. When she does, it's intentional: It happens when she feels there is a statement that demands action, not just silent vigiling. And so she goes over Rockwell's fence.

Once it was during during Holy Week, when she and a friend went across carrying a dogwood tree and copies of a parable, the "Legend of the Dogwood Tree," telling of sadness felt by the tree chosen for Jesus' crucifixion. It was to be a symbolic action—planting the tree and handing out the parable on this site of war preparation. And the symbolism remained, they felt, even though they were arrested before the the tree was planted. "We gave it to one of the security people that we know," said Roberts.

Those who know Marge Roberts say they're not surprised when she jumps into action. It all seems natural for her. Yet, she said, her road toward involvement was not always an easy one. It began, perhaps, during World War II—her high school years—when "I would see movies and newsreels and pictures in the paper of people getting shot up and whole cities being destroyed. And I just couldn't fit that together with what I'd learned about our being supposed to take care of each other." But, said Roberts, "I didn't know anybody who felt as I did." So she grew up thinking there must be "something wrong with me."

She kept trying to fit in—even later, when she married. "I was working at being a typical housewife. I played the role for a long time, and pushed things away that didn't fit."

Then in 1968, after the family moved to Denver, Roberts attended a conference that helped redirect her life. She was representing the Arvada Police Department, where she had found a job. The subject was police and community relations.

Suddenly, "There were many people who thought like I thought—the first time that I really met anybody I could talk with and get affirmation. It was an excitement that broke everything loose for me."

During that Vietnam era, Roberts worried about what was going on at the nearby Air Force Academy. "I saw us teaching people to deaden their own spirit of what it means to be alive and to be human and to care for each other. We have to do that before we can teach people to kill." So, she was excited when the Academy agreed to enter a dialogue with the peace community.

Then the Air Force backed out. So, recalled Roberts, "we made some quick changes of our plans." That Sunday, Roberts and her friends joined the congregation at the Academy's chapel, standing during the service. Every five minutes one of them walked out— "signifying a certain number of deaths that had happened during that five minutes in Vietnam." The idea was similar, in a way, to the Holy Week fence-jumping at Rocky Flats. Some messages require direct action.

Meanwhile, however, as Roberts' activism gained depth and meaning, her marriage was raveling. She had married a conservative man, one who found it difficult to accept his wife's beliefs and actions. "We tried, worked really hard to come to some adjustment between ourselves," Roberts said. "Yet I feel that my husband never really forgave me for not being the person that he had thought I was all that time." The marriage broke up in 1983.

There were other troubles, as well. Roberts had interrupted her first trip to Central America following a call from her daughter Christy. The news was bad. Although Christy earlier had fought— and seemingly won—a battle against cancer, the illness had returned. Roberts flew home, staying with Christy through her daughter's death two months later.

Then, knowing that for her, the best way to fight grief was to get busy helping others, Roberts soon left for GAM and Guatemala.

With that behind her, she had returned to Denver and rebuilt a life that was both busy and dedicated. But somehow, something was still missing; she already was thinking of moving on. Once again, Roberts was feeling the pull of Central America. There was so much to be done in that part of the world. She had learned of a Jesuit refugee camp in El Salvador that desperately needed long-term volunteers. Maybe they could use her there.

As dusk settled over the small Arvada church and its grounds, Marge Roberts spoke softly, looking inward more than at me. "I am feeling really drawn."

So what does a Marge Roberts—who moves from weapons protests to soup kitchens to Central America and more—suggest about today's peace movement? Most significantly, perhaps, that this is more than a "peace" movement; a majority of those I spoke with now consider it a "peace and justice" movement.

People who last year—or last week—were holding candles outside a weapons conference are working in political campaigns, protesting apartheid, or working with refugees.

Those—and many more—are areas we must address if we are to have true peace, they argue. The bomb? Of course, we must control it. But even if you get rid of it now, it can always come back if we don't change the world.

It turns out, however, that there were some big advantages to having simply a "peace" movement—at least as things worked out during the Vietnam era. Back then, with one major goal—getting the United States out of an unpopular war—there was no problem getting public recognition. Nobody ever asked, "What movement?"

And that movement had one other advantage, if you want to call it that: It was pretty easy to recognize those who were involved—

or at least, we thought it was. They were young people, hippies, kids who rejected the world of their parents, weren't they? Of course, there were others, as well. But that's the way it seemed, and that, too, helped the rest of us identify a "movement."

Today there's no easy stereotyping. Peace people, when you meet them, seem about like the rest of us. They shop at local supermarkets, work in nearby businesses, join area clubs and attend neighborhood churches. They range from the young to the elderly, although a majority are middle-aged. They represent all economic levels, although most are middle class and live in typical middle-class communities. They include all races, although a majority are anglo.

The result? This is a movement that fights invisibility.

And so, government officials, who make decisions about both bombs and human needs, do not take it seriously. Media, who have no trouble at all identifying stories about weapons buildups and international conflicts, pay little attention. Other citizens, whom activists would like to enlist in their causes, simply turn away.

Yet, these people deserve better. Even if they don't have a single path, they are confronting issues and offering options. And their stories reveal strong threads of shared interest—threads that carry the potential for causing change.

In the chapters that follow, we'll look at some of those threads. And we'll try to discover something about these people: Who are they? What inspires and sustains them? How do they think humankind can survive in this nuclear age? Can they offer possibilities for the rest of us?

Some of those we'll meet are sturdy "old-timers" who got involved before World War II; others became active during Vietnam; some joined during the nuclear freeze campaigns in the early '80s.

There is Peter DeMott of Baltimore, who tried single-handedly to put a Trident submarine out of commission; Renny Golden of Chicago, who led the organization of Sanctuary's "underground railway" bringing Central American refugees to the Midwest;

Howard and Alice Frazier, of Woodmont, Conn., who organize friendship tours to the Soviet Union and encourage Soviets to visit here; Wes Sanders, member of a Cambridge, Mass., theatrical troupe that offers its challenging messages in skits and stories. And many more.

All are Americans committed to helping stitch back together a world threatened with extermination.

3. MAKING CONNECTIONS
David Meyer, Brookline, Mass.

The era of armaments has ended and the human
race must conform its actions to this truth or die.
—President Dwight D. Eisenhower, 1956

Every teacher knows a kid like David Meyer: almost too bright for his own good, scrappy, argumentative. Meyer was the one who would wait until his teacher had given the class instructions for the next day; then he would announce in a loud voice, "That's a dumb assignment." He even tried to "impeach" his fifth grade music teacher on grounds of incompetence.

Now 26, Meyer is still bright, scrappy and argumentative. He still challenges authority. But today all those traits are pluses in his role as researcher, analyst, speaker and writer—focusing on international security studies and U.S. nuclear policy—at the Institute for Defense and Disarmament Studies in Brookline, Mass. The institute has a reputation as the "well-regarded nonestablishment scorekeeper of the statistics of the nuclear arms race." It deals knowingly with military and arms control policies; it argues national weapons budgets with facts, figures and logic.

Meyer's boss at the institute is Randall Forsberg, the woman who first proposed a nuclear freeze, calling on both the United States and Soviet Union to end the nuclear arms race. That effort saw 70% of Americans approving the idea. But their support never translated into national policy, and so Forsberg changed tactics. While the Freeze opened separate offices in Washington, D.C., her institute concentrated on research and education. It was an operation that attracted young, committed workers like David Meyer.

Although Meyer these days also teaches college classes at North-eastern University and is working on his Ph.D. in political science at Boston University, he could still pass as an undergraduate, himself. This day, his shirtsleeves are rolled up; his enthusiasms spill out eagerly.

One of those enthusiams is for the work he's doing at the Institute. His role here involves helping seek answers to some fundamental questions: How the world's big powers can avoid war by means other than threatening global annihilation as the penalty . . . How nuclear weapons can be abolished . . . How all this can be done before the world is destroyed in a nuclear holocaust.

Meyer, who has been working at the Institute for the past year, began his search for answers with a full-time study of the history of American missiles. Then, as he entered his Ph.D. program, he pulled back to one day a week, "doing a little more analysis and some writing and some public speaking." But his dissertation, on which he now spends most of his time, is closely related; its topic is the freeze.

That life track is not the one charted out by parents and teachers. By junior high school, Meyer knew his parents were planning for law school. But he already had different ideas: "In 1972, as a junior high school student, my first political action based on national issues was wearing a black armband to school the day after Richard Nixon was re-elected."

Meyer already was taking on major issues during his teen years—especially concerning morality. He also was an avid reader—"and every time I read something, I wanted to try it if it made sense to me." One book that made sense then and still carries an impact was Dalton Trumbo's "Johnny Got His Gun."

"It's a terrifying book about a young man who comes home from World War I without arms or legs or a face," recalled Meyer. "It's the diary of his thoughts in a hospital . . . There's this impassioned plea at the end, 'Tell them, don't let them do this again.'" Another such reading was Thoreau's essay on "Civil Disobedience."

David Meyer

"The base of it, to me, was that you have to try and live your convictions . . . live your values and believe that you can have an impact."

Later, he found similar inspiration in some college classes, including one first-year religious studies course, "Expressions of Contemporary Prophecy."

"We heard all about Daniel Berrigan and Malcolm X . . . I couldn't read those things without trying to apply them to my life."

Meyer soon began to apply those lessons through a local drive to organize migrant farm workers. "I was a really bad organizer, because I was 17 and just 'knew' what these people needed," he said. "I was not a good listener." Still, "I learned a lot."

He took some of that knowledge on to a community organizing project in Somerville, a working-class city nearby. It is a town that has since become something of a symbol for Meyer, for it was where he first tasted real success in grassroots work. The goal at the time was to replace a state senator. Members of various groups had joined together to support one candidate, Sal Albono. Although Albono lost the Democratic primary, he and his supporters went on to push a write-in campaign. He won by 212 votes.

"I know," said Meyer, "it was the efforts of people, of grassroots activists, that put him into office. Now, electing Sal Albono instead of some slime to the state senate is not going to change the world, but you change a little piece of it, and that becomes a contagious thing."

That election, in a way, sums up Meyer's current view of how the whole nation could be turned around: through grassroots work and the "contagious" effects of moral courage. A successful effort would mean connecting a whole variety of groups, he said: those into social justice as well as those involved in anti-nuclear efforts.

"It has to reach large constituencies of people who've not been reached by the freeze movement. That means addressing issues that people care about desperately.

"Nuclear destruction is certainly something that people care

about, but terrifying them doesn't mobilize them for long periods
of time and doesn't provide the analysis necessary to bring about
change." The things people do care most about, he said, are "bread
and butter issues." They were what brought success in Somerville;
they are the issues—when people see how they are connected to
both peace and social justice—that could bring people into the
current effort.

"I honestly don't know whether we're going to win or not,
whether things are actually going to change or not," he said.
"Sometimes I'm very pessimistic. But I do know that the only way
you can live is to believe that you can make a difference." History
has stories of how great changes came about, he said: the civil
rights movement, for instance, and the abolition of slavery. "You
find those people who were just wistfully whistling into the wind,
just on the sheer hope that things can possibly change in some sort
of way . . . who actually wind up making a difference."

Meyer recalls that back in the fifth grade, there were those who
said, "When you're older, you're going to realize that [your teachers]
were right; that you should have done what they said."

"I still haven't realized that," he said. "It's always wrong to submit
to injustice." And, when some people are willing to take a stand,
he believes, others follow. When that happens, there is hope: "Great
things may become possible."

———————

My original appointment at the Institute had been with another
member of the staff, Matt Goodman, editor of the newsletter.
But when I arrived, Goodman was on his way out; he apologized,
explaining that he'd forgotten a promise to join a Witness for
Peace protest against the contra appropriation just passed by the
Senate. However, my lost appointment proved a point, Meyer suggested: "You came to interview somebody on the disarmament
movement, and he's going to a demonstration on Central America.
If you treat these as discreet issues that are not part of a picture,

then you're always going to have divided efforts and you're never going to get enough people to get anything done. When you start putting issues together and realizing they're part of a coherent whole, things become possible."

4. ONE HAWK FOR PEACE

Major Gen. William T. Fairbourn, U.S. Marine Corps (ret.), Salt Lake City

> *Global war has become a Frankenstein to destroy both sides. No longer is it a weapon of adventure—the shortcut to international power. If you lose, you are annihilated. If you win, you stand only to lose . . . [War] contains now only the germs of double suicide.*
> —*Gen. Douglas MacArthur, 1961*

The road from Los Angeles to Salt Lake City heads out through the Mojave Desert, cuts through Nevada and Las Vegas, snips off a corner of Arizona, then curls upward to St. George, Utah, before heading on to Salt Lake City. On the fall day I made the trip, the desert was a masterpiece in pastels. The lighting had a bleached quality, one that seems special to certain desert days. Pale mauves, greys and beiges of ground and brush met a washed-blue sky. Only the occasional red truck or car pulled in the full energy of the sun.

That muted loveliness only made the entrance to Utah all the more spectacular, as earth colors became boldly orange-red, defining the stark drama of the state's desert bluffs. St. George is the first town you hit, and it's enough to take your breath away—a whole town looking like a toy village under those magnificent walls of red. You wonder if the people who live here get up every morning and revel in the glory waiting just outside their doors.

Then you remember: St. George has one of the most disturbing recent histories of any city in the United States. It is a history recounted in frightening detail by John G. Fuller in his book, "The Day We Bombed Utah."

There have been many days of "bombing," actually, beginning in 1951 as the United States started nuclear weapons tests across the Nevada border, spewing radioactive waste into the air. Most of those tests were scheduled when air currents would carry the waste eastward toward St. George, Fuller reported; better there than Los Angeles or Las Vegas.

The first major suggestion that something was horribly wrong—in spite of Atomic Energy Commission reassurances that there was no danger—showed up following one 1953 blast, when fleece suddenly began falling off sheep in chunks and lambs began being born deformed, with strange potbellies or without legs. A total of 4,390 of the animals died.

By then, problems were showing up in people: First there had been red, itchy skin, and hair that fell out. Eventually leukemia and cancer began taking human lives.

Among those who may have been affected were Hollywood luminaries John Wayne, Susan Hayward, Agnes Moorehead and Dick Powell, all of whom came to the area not too long after that particular bomb test to make an outdoor action movie, "The Conqueror." All have since died of cancer. Wayne was the last of the four to go, and by the time of his death, 91 of the other 220 members of the cast and crew also had developed cancer, and half of them already had died.

Yes, some St. George area citizens have fought and won court action against the government. But the decision is still being appealed; damages have not been paid. And bomb tests still are being held at the Nevada Test Site.

For St. George and Utah, there can be no doubt about the horrendous danger of nuclear weaponry. Yet, that very knowledge puts the state in an excruciating quandary. For Utah also depends heavily on income from its military contracts. Without those contracts, Utah could face financial trouble.

Major Gen. William T. Fairbourn

Among those who have joined the battle to value lives over budgets is one native of Utah who, in an interesting turn of fate, was still building a military career as the St. George script began unfolding. In fact, Marine Corps Maj. Gen. William T. Fairbourn, now retired, was among the first military men who turned their attention to the future use of nuclear weaponry following World War II.

In those early days, he joined a Marine Corps committee studying how the new nuclear weapons would fit into the future of the Corps. The committee's final recommendation was to develop helicopter assault capability. The plan was adopted, and the Marines became "the first of the services to take into account both the support of nuclear weapons and the defense against them." At that time, Fairbourn saw the question in terms of strategy—and on that basis, he still applauds it.

The young officer went on to a distinguished career. He was a battalion commander in World War II, a regiment commander during the Korean conflict and a division commander during Vietnam.

Before he left the service, Fairbourn rose to the post of senior strategic planner for the Joint Chiefs of Staff. "I had 14 generals and admirals of the other services as my subordinates," said Fairbourn, still a bulldog of a man, with a voice that booms across to his listener. "I had a total of, I think, 176 officers, none below the grade of lieutenant colonel, about evenly divided among all the services." The job was a three-star post—one above Fairbourn's two stars—and he had been recommended for the new ranking.

But then, in 1968, Fairbourn quit. A nagging back injury was part of it. Yet, there was a longer story to it than that.

Along the way, Fairbourn—who still takes pride in his military accomplishments, who still stands tall as a Marine, and who proclaims proudly that "I probably am the biggest hawk that there is around"—developed serious questions about our nuclear dependency. "I'm hawkish about the things that contribute to our national security," he explained, "and nuclear weapons are not among them. Because they are weapons that can never be used."

To accept the potential use of nuclear weapons, said Fairbourn, means accepting one additional potential: "You must accept, really, the destruction of civilization." Because that, Fairbourn has come to believe, is where the use of nuclear weapons could lead. As a result, Fairbourn, who returned to his home state of Utah after 35 years in the Marine Corps, is active in two anti-nuclear groups: Utahns United Against the Nuclear Arms Race and the Washington D.C.-based Center for Defense Information (CDI).

Utahns United has been described as "an educational organization aiming to raise public consciousness about the arms race." Its current major project, said Fairbourn, is developing a school program of 12 lectures making up "An Introduction to Nuclear Concerns." He expected the first series to be offered the following spring through the nearby Granite School District's community education program; he would be in charge. The lectures would cover nuclear power and nuclear waste disposal, as well as nuclear weapons, said Fairbourn.

These topics, he added, have immediate concern for Utahns: a nuclear waste dump has been proposed in the southern part of the state; the arms industry ranks among the state's top employers. "Our goal," said Fairbourn, "is to see that both sides of the story are objectively and truthfully portrayed. Then the public will make up their minds."

The other group, the CDI, has a national perspective as an "information center on U.S. and major powers' military technology, weapons development and military policy." It is an impressive group; like Fairbourn, all of its leaders once held decision-making positions in the military. The director is Gene R. La Rocque, rear admiral, USN (ret.); the deputy director, Eugene J. Carroll Jr., rear admiral, USN (ret.). Associate directors are Fairbourn; Kermit D. Johnson, major general, USA (ret.); James A. Donovan, colonel, USMC (ret.), and James T. Bush, captain, USN (ret.). All are concerned about where the nuclear arms race is taking the nation.

Since the headquarters are on the East Coast, Fairbourn handles much of the work in the West. He would be leaving soon after our meeting to give a speech, "Some Thoughts on the Strategic Defense Initiative," before the Regina Coalition for Peace and Disarmament in Regina, Saskatchewan, Canada.

In a draft of the speech, Fairbourn challenged the contention that the Strategic Defense Initiative—or Star Wars—could protect the United States: "From the outset, proponents of the Strategic Defense Initiative have acknowledged that an airtight defense through which no weapons can successfully penetrate is not within the realm of possibility." He called for serious negotiations with the Soviets to identify mutual interests as "the first step in development of a stable relationship between the United States and the Soviet Union." Since both sides recognize "the catastrophic and uncontrollable character of nuclear war," said Fairbourn, "preventing nuclear war and shaping the strategic balance to that end with the aid of arms control has been accepted as one of the few areas of mutual interest even under the present harsh circumstances."

In spite of such opinions, Fairbourn unequivocally rejects the title of "peacenik." He does not support activists who sit in front of trains transporting weapons or who climb fences at defense plants or military bases . . . and he does not mince words telling his opinions about such actions; they are, he said bluntly, "utterly stupid" and "a damn nuisance." Instead, he suggested, the demonstrators should put their efforts into working "through the ballot box."

Likewise, he does not propose elimination of nuclear weapons: "You can't. Nuclear weapons are a fact of life." Since the technology is out there, and since the Soviets have nuclear weapons, the United States must have them, too. But nuclear stockpiles could be dramatically reduced by both superpowers, he argues. "We've got enough nuclear weapons to destroy the Soviet Union 17 times."

Fairbourn's military expertise tells him twice the knock-out strength is plenty. "What we need right now in nuclear weapons is 800 weapons, or 800 megatons, and that's the same amount the Soviet Union needs," he said. "Four hundred megatons delivered on the Soviet Union would render the Soviet Union militarily impotent; a similar amount delivered on the United States would render the United States militarily impotent. So, give each country twice that amount, which means they could use that amount of megatonnage to protect the megatonnage that IS needed; that's just a good conservative cushion to have, 100% replacement for your weapons. And that's all you need." Especially, he implied, for a game of bluff.

Fairbourn believes in putting his convictions into action: He campaigned vigorously for the nuclear freeze; although he strongly supported Ronald Reagan in the first campaign, he strongly opposed Reagan's re-election; he argued outspokenly that the United States should seriously consider the Soviet's proposal to end arms testing—and suggested that the United States make a similar offer. The Soviet Union's moratorium underway at the time of our talk could be partially traced to a CDI letter sent to both Reagan and the Soviet's Mikhail S. Gorbachev proposing just such an action, Fairbourn believes. Soon after that, in August 1985, Gorbachev announced the moratorium and a proposal to end testing; Reagan, on the other hand, replied that "he lauded our intent" but could not accept the proposal—more testing was necessary.

Meanwhile, the arms race is threatening the nation on another front, Fairbourn argues: It is eating away the economy. "We're profligates in our money, our resources and our manpower," he said. "We're spending the wealth that belongs to generations yet unborn." Fairbourn said he and other CDI members are convinced that the ultimate danger of the arms race could be economic: "We've all decided there's going to be an economic failure, and it's going to be serious enough to jeopardize the existence of the United States as a viable nation." He pointed to danger signs: Third World countries threatening to default on their debts, American money moving to foreign countries, corporations buying and selling each other based on tax advantages . . . while American people go hungry. Yet, he added, it is the civilian population that any country must depend upon. "That is really where your strength is, in a vigorous, viable, motivated population." Some people claim the arms buildup has led to "40 years of peace," the longest in world history, Fairbourn said. But, he countered, "Is this peace? I don't think so. Any situation that taxes you enough to deprive any part of your civilization of the bread of life is not peace in my judgment."

When I talked with friends outside the peace and justice movement, most were surprised that former military leaders would be involved in the anti-nuclear effort. Yet—as the list of leaders in the CDI testifies—there are a number of men with distinguished military careers who believe in a strong defense but disbelieve that ever more nuclear weapons or unlimited blank checks for weapons development are the best way to do the job. In 1982, Admiral Hyman G. Rickover stated, "The U.S. already has enough submarines to sink everything on the ocean . . . . We must expect that when war breaks out again, we will use the weapons available. I think we'll probably destroy ourselves. I'm not proud of the part I played."

Those who are most outspoken, naturally, tend to be those who already have retired from military service. Perhaps their opponents would argue that they speak against nuclear weaponry because their own careers were most involved with conventional, non-nuclear tactics; more true, it would seem, is that they know full well the horror that even conventional warfare can bring and are unwilling to throw the whole world on the table in the gamble with nuclear weaponry.

In a last minute phone call to confirm mailing information, I reached Mrs. Fairbourn, who told me the general had died in February 1987, shortly after suffering a light stroke. He was buried in Arlington National Cemetery.

5. JUMPING THE FENCE
Edwina Vogan, Tucson, Ariz.

> *Were half the power that fills the world with*
> *terror,*
> *Were half the wealth bestowed on camps and*
> *courts*
> *Given to redeem the human mind from error*
> *There would be no need of arsenals and forts.*
> *—H.W. Longfellow, "The Arsenal at Springfield."*

Edwina Vogan grew up a child of the boisterous, confident post-World War II period, when Americans saw the whole world as their territory. Her father, she recalls, was a construction engineer, a man who wanted to take in "a lot of life." He worked for the big companies, including Bechtel, and the family moved where the jobs opened up: New York, New Jersey, Illinois, Louisiana, Texas. They even spent a year in Venezuela.

Vogan's mother was Ecuadorean. So, at least on that side of the family, Vogan considers herself a first-generation American. She spoke only Spanish as a pre-schooler. Mostly, though, she was "raised as an anglo."

There wasn't much indication back then that Vogan—the lively, brown-eyed daughter of the ambitious construction engineer father and immigrant mother—would wind up in the 1980s in the sun-baked desert town of Tucson fighting nuclear weapons and nuclear power, defending Indian rights and wondering just how the world might regain its sanity. Or, that she would be one of those fence-jumping activists that Gen. Fairbourn might have considered "a damn nuisance."

That all evolved as Vogan, now 34, grew up in a changing American society, reacting to the struggle for desegregation in the South and the national self-torture over Vietnam. Vogan attended elementary school in Baton Rouge, La., moving in and out of schools three times as students were shifted around while the city tried to deal with segregation. It was a time when "blacks walked on one side of the street, and we walked on the other." But the family moved to New York City when Vogan was 10 or 11, and by her teen years, many of her friends were black. It was during that period that she began worrying about injustice.

She also became concerned about war, after signing up for a New York AM radio station's write-a-serviceman project. Vogan, then about 16, was paired with a soldier in Vietnam—"a California surfer." The whole thing, said Vogan, was probably "very naive." The idea was to say, "Here I am, this is what I do; tell me about what you're up to." When she really realized what her pen pal was up to, her concern became serious: "I saw the dramatic amount of death and tragedy that was happening in Vietnam—and I became involved in the anti-war movement."

Following high school, Vogan spent four years at Fairleigh-Dickinson University in Madison, N.J. She admits with a grin, "I spent more time participating in anti-war actions than I did in class. I went headlong into the fray."

Like many other students, Vogan took a break from classes following the invasion of Cambodia and headed for Washington, D.C., to join the protest. That experience is burned into her memory. The capitol "was an armed camp," she recalls. "There were tanks— tank after tank—lining the streets. It was like looking at Chile or Argentina. There were armed soldiers standing in all the government buildings, up in the windows with their M16s pointed at you. I'd yell up to the windows and say, 'Hey, what're you doing? We're the same age!'" The soldiers, she said, never answered. "I was just trying to make those human connections, because it was so surreal."

Even when the war ended, it brought Vogan little joy. "Basically,

I saw that we didn't achieve much." Feeling disillusioned, she decided to "take a couple of years off." Vogan, by then 23 years old, headed for Tucson. It turned out to be a good choice: "I came out here and I just felt renewed . . . the wide open spaces, the sunshine. I felt that 'this is a new start.' "

Where New York "felt so abstract and too much, too big," the city of Tucson appeared to be just Vogan's size. She first got involved in a food co-op. Then, discovering that nuclear waste was being transported through Tucson, Vogan lobbied hard, asking the city council to restrict such activity. They did. Later, after a local plant was caught releasing radioactive gas into the air, Vogan lobbied for a ban on nuclear industry within the city. Again, the council complied. "On a local level," said Vogan, "I can have some input."

But her goals today aren't restricted to Tucson. Vogan also is working with state legislators, seeking a Nuclear Free Arizona declaration opposing nuclear industry and weaponry statewide. She spends many hours fighting for Arizona Indians' rights. She holds a part-time job with Clergy and Laity for Central America, extending her interests across international borders. She is, of course, still involved in anti-war, anti-nuclear efforts. As far as Vogan is concerned, all those projects are related; all the problems they involve violate her sense of the sacredness of land and life.

Most of those activities today are a long way from the early days of confrontation and personal danger. Most of Vogan's work is among councilmen, supervisors, legislators and businessmen—contacts she has nurtured carefully to make her efforts more effective.

But in 1983, Vogan decided it was necessary to put herself on the line once again. Cruise missiles were being deployed in Europe, and the crews that would operate those missiles were being trained nearby at Davis Monthan Air Force Base. A civil disobedience action—with groups jumping the base's double row of fences—was planned by Tucson activists. Vogan worried about participating: How would it affect her working relationships within the Tucson community? "But I said to myself, 'What happens farther down the line when somebody asks me, "What did you do when those weapons were about to be deployed?" ' I had to put myself on the line."

Vogan became an enthusiastic participant. She and her affinity group built their own ladder to reach the top of the base's 8-foot fence; they found a mattress to put over the barbed wire on top; they even practiced jumping. That morning, they met for a potluck breakfast. The group included teachers, engineers, activists, students, a woman and her three daughters, a man from Britain, and an Indian friend with his three-month old baby.

And finally . . . "We crossed one fence; it was just a three-strand fence. Then we moved up to the 8-foot fence." There were soldiers with dogs on the other side. The soldiers were young, and they were "moving around crazy," said Vogan. "I started talking to them. I said, 'Hey, we're not here against you; let's stay calm.' " Eventually the dogs were taken away, and Vogan headed for the ladder.

"When I went over, it was just like a whole liberating feeling; it was like my whole spirit just moved out into the cosmos or the sky," she recalled, raising her arms upward and grinning. "I felt a liberation . . . this is my right time, this is what I needed to do."

Edwina Vogan is involved in a whole range of issues: anti-nuclear, Indians' rights, Central American intervention. Likewise, David Meyer has worked for candidates, bread and butter issues, and migrant laborers' rights. Gen. Fairbourn joins his opposition to weaponry to concerns about the economy and the ability of citizens to get food and jobs. Marge Roberts moves from weapons protests to humanitarian tasks like feeding the hungry or protecting a young woman who has been threatened in a foreign land. All see their own varied actions—and those of others—interlinked.

And that is typical. It is a situation that turns up again and again in the stories that follow. These Americans want more than just a country that no longer puts a primary emphasis on weaponry. They want a nation and world where human values matter most . . . where nuclear weaponry is not just controlled, but is no longer considered acceptable. A world, in other words, of both peace and justice.

II

TAPPING INTO POLITICS

Politics, it might seem, would be the natural, unifying tool of the peace and justice movement. Activists confronted the political process with furious enthusiasm in the 1960s—and helped end the Vietnam War. Activists used the political process to promote the nuclear freeze in the early 1980s—and changed national opinion about weaponry.

Yet, politics seems a tough pill for many of today's peace and justice people to swallow. Many are uncomfortable with politics and distrust politicians—or doubt that elected officials are the ones calling the shots anyway. Besides, while arms and disarmament is the "political" cause most often presented to activists, many question weaponry as the ultimate issue. Or, they are simply unwilling to switch from their own goals.

But the result is a serious one: Efforts appear fragmented. All the general public sees is a bunch of people climbing a fence here or sitting on a railroad track there. Those working for justice causes—in a soup kitchen, for instance—are seldom identified with the peace process.

And that situation leads directly to the devastating question, "What peace movement?" If there is no "movement," then there is little clout, meaning victories will be limited to local areas and specific occasions. Then it is difficult to pressure legislators to recognize a national swell of citizens demanding peace.

Growing numbers of activists are recognizing that situation and reclaiming their political rights. Gen. Fairbourn spoke out strongly for political action, admonishing activists to get things done "through the ballot box." Marge Roberts, David Meyer and Edwina Vogan all utilized political tactics at one time or another.

Six stories that follow show how differently activists are using the political process. They range from a California mayor who is trying to pull other local politicians into the peace process . . . to a South Dakota activist who hopes to alter his state's political power structure . . . to an Australian who became, perhaps, the United States' preeminent voice of the peace movement while urging Americans to get involved and get political.

6. LOCAL OFFICIALS, NATIONAL ISSUES
Larry Agran, Irvine, Calif.

> *A major fact in the politics of national security [is] that there is no effective political constituency with a national interest point of view in regard to arms control.*
> —Marshall Shulman, Carter era arms control adviser

Irvine, Calif., located in the middle of what once was a major farming, orange-growing area, now is a comfortable, upscale, planned community. Clustered "towns" of condominiums and single-family homes, most finished in soothing earth tones, gather snugly among the rolling hills that circle the University of California at Irvine. Industries nestle in enclaves, never intruding on the residential panorama.

Surrounding Irvine is California's Orange County—a county that boasts of Disneyland and yacht-at-your-doorstep living, as well as some of the world's best surfing beaches and some of the nation's most conservative politics. Unemployment here is among the nation's lowest. Irvine, itself, carefully nurtures the good life that draws high tech industries and their young, eager professionals.

Yet Irvine also is home to intense action seeking peace and social justice. And the basic premise is pragmatic: Get the grassroots involved, and get them into the political process. Irvine, it turns out, is birthplace of a politically-oriented organization that has since gone national: the Local Elected Officials (LEO) Project. LEO's goal is nothing less than changing the political agenda of the nation.

The man who got LEO started is attorney, college professor, city

Larry Agran

councilman and three-term mayor Larry Agran. He is something of an anomaly in conservative Orange County: a successful, progressive politician.

Early in his political career, Agran said, he recognized one big reason why communities never have enough money to deal with local problems: "The dollars are flowing out of the cities to Washington, D.C., to the Pentagon, and in many cases, overseas. And those dollars don't come back!"

Agran decided to share his dismay over that situation with other elected officials. The result was LEO.

Actually, LEO's birth was midwifed by the nuclear freeze campaign. Agran had been pulled into that effort because of a quirk in California law. Most other states looked benignly on advisory measures, such as the typical freeze referendums that simply made a statement in favor of ending the arms race. But California's constitution was fussier: A ballot initiative had to "do something," as Agran put it.

Local freeze supporters brought that problem to the Irvine attorney—and Agran came up with an initiative that would, indeed, require a small action: The governor would be directed to write the president, supporting the freeze. And that was the measure voters approved in California in November 1982, while Agran was serving his first term as mayor.

During the freeze campaign, Agran wrote every California mayor, asking for support. Without even a follow-up note, fully 16% agreed. "I took that to be a positive sign," said Agran. So, right after the 1982 election, Agran enlisted some 200 other California public officials and formed LEO.

Today Agran and LEO are reaching across the country to "a veritable army of local elected officials out there, a vast untapped constituency." There are more than 500,000 of them, he figures, if you add up all the mayors and council members, county supervisors and school board trustees, plus those who serve on water, library and sanitation districts.

Agran's goal is "to try to give them some sense of empowerment, showing them they can take charge of their own lives and
their own communities." Among other things, that would mean
seeking "a reversal of the arms race, a sharp reduction in U.S.
military spending and a conversion of these funds to more productive uses in our cities and towns."

For such officials, said Agran, it is easy to see the local effects
of the arms buildup. During public hearings in 1984 sponsored by
LEO in Irvine and in California's capital, Sacramento, testimony
described "the inability to build affordable housing because of
interest rates and the demand on capital that was being com-
mandeered for military purposes," said Agran. "We heard from
volunteers who provide social services, who told us of the hungry
and the homeless and the medically indigent. The testimony was
very moving."

Once LEO decided to expand, the first move was to Iowa, chosen
partly because that state traditionally held the nation's first presidential caucuses. Again, Agran sent out letters and got good response.
In January 1984, just weeks prior to the caucuses, LEO sponsored
a presidential candidates forum that drew national media attention.
And LEO began looking toward more states with "Main Street"
constituencies ready for organizing in the mid-1980s: New Hampshire, Massachusetts, Florida, Georgia, Alabama, and others in
the Midwest.

For Agran, all that activity means spending about half his time
on LEO. It means there are fewer hours left for his own law practice,
or for his occasional teaching stints at the University of California
at Irvine. So far, LEO has maintained only a modest payroll, but
as the group goes national, Agran hopes that may change. His goal
is to get the group on a sound financial footing, with a stable budget
and 3,000 to 5,000 progressive local elected officials as members.
LEO's main continuing activity is educational workshops conducted
for local officials around the country.

Those officials, Agran believes, can be a convincing force. "You know, we are really practitioners of grassroots democracy," he said. "There is a strong tradition of self governance in this country: no-nonsense, local self-governance. The national security state that we have built in Washington, D.C., is a contradiction of all that. It's an apparatus over which we have no control."

Yet, even when it comes to such a big issue as national security, "we have a special credibility as local officials," he said. For one thing, "We balance budgets." That is something, he added, the national government has not yet managed to do. Then, "we do resolve conflict without resort to violence."

"Could you imagine a local elected official talking about retaliating against a neighboring city for this or that or the other?" he asked. "You can generally go to sleep at night pretty confident that when you wake up in the morning you won't find your city is at war with a neighboring city."

It's too bad, said Agran, that nations cannot say as much.

Larry Agran has seen the political process work. "We have to acknowledge that there have been times in the last five to six years when things have really come together—for example, the whole freeze effort." That issue, he said, touched millions of people "who voted in various referendums, got educated about the horrors of nuclear weapons, and who, I think, in some sense have been per-manently converted."

But—and Agran believes this was a crucial shortcoming—there was no national political leadership to follow through. "We don't have a president, and we don't have Democratic leadership in Con-gress that really gives a voice to these concerns." Agran and LEO are working to help change that by marshalling the local political troops, working from the bottom up to cause national change. "It is happening!" he declared.

LEO members also are doing the grassroots work of letting their communities know the price they are paying for the military buildup.

"The American people, whether they want to or not, are going to have to be ready for radical alternatives," said Agran. "We can't go on spending $300 billion-plus a year for military purposes and driving ourselves deeper into deficit at the rate of $200 billion per year. The country will, in fact, be bankrupt."

His own experience has given Agran faith in Americans' openness to new ideas—when they make sense. Irvine may be in the heart of one of the nation's conservative bastions, yet on key issues the citizens are "moderate and very eager to have you present reasonable arguments about issues of public importance." Irvine was one of three cities within Orange County to approve the 1982 nuclear freeze initiative; more recently, it rewarded Agran—by then serving his third term as mayor—with a progressive majority on the city council.

When national politicians finally demonstrate leadership, Agran predicts, the peace and justice movement will be ready to join behind them. The movement may seem in disarray, but it is like a "sleeping giant," he said, ready to be kicked awake and to add its support to meaningful political action.

7. FROM POLITICS TO PEACE MARCH AND BACK AGAIN
Tim Carpenter, Irvine, Calif.

If five percent of the people work for peace, peace will prevail.

—*Albert Einstein*

Tim Carpenter was still a teenager when he had one of those experiences you hope to tell your grandchildren about some day. In spite of his youth, Carpenter was in charge of the Orange County Democratic Party office when it happened. He'd been volunteering for political candidates since the sixth grade, he explained, and it was summer, "when everybody really went on vacation," so they'd been happy to leave the dedicated young man in charge.

"One day, I was just kind of doing my thing on the phone," Carpenter recalled, "when a guy walked in.

"I said, 'I'll be right with you.' He said, 'That's OK, I'll just sit here and wait.'

"He took off his jacket and sat there, while I was running all over the place for about half an hour. I asked him, 'Do you want something to drink?' 'No, I'll be OK. I just need to talk to you when you get a minute.' I said, 'Fine.'

"So, about 45 minutes later, I sat down and said, 'Hi, I'm Tim Carpenter.' He said, 'Hi, I'm Jimmy Carter. I'm running for president.'

"I said, 'Oh, hi. What's going on.'" And then it sunk in: "Oh, God, this is great! A presidential candidate!" But, then as now, Carpenter was not one to let surprise ruin a good opportunity, so "I sat down and talked with him for over an hour and a half, just

Tim Carpenter

one on one."

Carpenter is still active in politics, although those interests long ago got linked to peace work. "I'm somewhat of a bastardized child of the peace movement" he said, laughing. "I came from electoral politics." As a result, Carpenter's story illustrates just how closely politics and peace intertwine in the lives of some activists.

For Carpenter, it began with a sixth-grade civics teacher who believed kids learn best by doing. She'd sent him off to the campaign offices of Senate candidate John Tunney. That's when Carpenter signed up for his first political job: envelope-stuffing. In the process, the youngster sensed the excitement of politics. He's been involved, one way or another, ever since.

The next year, as a seventh grader at St. Cecilia's in Tustin, Calif., Carpenter was working for presidential candidate George McGovern. "That's when the peace part of it began to enter into my psyche." But he continued in politics—on to Jerry Brown's campaign for governor and Tom Hayden's bid for the Senate.

Then, as a 19-year-old sophomore at California State University at Fullerton, Carpenter accepted a job with an Orange County supervisor. From there, he moved to the county Human Relations Commission . . . to a Coro Foundation internship (offered to encourage future managers and administrators) . . . and then to another job in county administration.

But by then Carpenter was deeply involved in the peace movement, and it became clear there was a choice to be made. He recalls—with typical Carpenter humor—how he told his family about his choice: "I called my parents and told them I was going to give up my job at the county and give up my apartment, take all my savings out and sell the car, and move into a garage in Orange and live with three lesbians and try to end the arms race. They were real good about it."

The group with which Carpenter intended to "try to end the arms race" was the Orange County Peace Conversion Project, which became the Alliance for Survival. He soon became co-director, and during the five years he served in that role, the scrappy, savvy Alliance grew "from no more than 20 to 30 people to an organization of over 4,000," he said proudly.

Like Carpenter, the group was serious, but with a sense of humor. One Christmas, they leafleted workers at a county weapons plant after dressing one member up in a plumped-out red suit—then enjoyed the spectacle of police officers uncomfortably arresting Santa Claus. During those years, Carpenter—scrappy and savvy, himself—was there as the Alliance, armed with candles and signs, challenged an international weapons show . . . as the Alliance protested at the San Onofre nuclear power station . . . as the Alliance demonstrated outside the Seal Beach Naval Weapons Depot.

Carpenter was the group's invaluable contact man. He knew whom to call and what to ask, how to pull in survival money when the bank account was dropping below zero, where connections could be made with other groups across the country, how to deal with media and law enforcement during demonstrations and civil disobedience actions. He handled that last job with such intelligence, wit and Irish charm that media soon began calling him . . . and two police officers who once helped arrest demonstrators became Alliance supporters. When police move in, he said, "We don't go limp and get dragged across the street; we talk and organize."

With the help of that Carpenter spark, the Alliance managed to gain respect along with numbers. It was THE peace group in conservative Orange County.

In the mid-'80s, however, Carpenter took a leave from the Alliance to handle the field staff for a new group called ProPeace (People Reaching Out for Peace). Their idea was to send a whole community of peace walkers from Los Angeles to Washington, D.C.—5,000 marchers who would pull the rest of the country after them, causing a groundswell demand for peace.

Although the march did eventually reach the nation's capital, and did prove life-changing for some who marched, it never did become the one envisioned in the original dream. The 5,000 people turned out to be more like 1,000, and that thousand argued about the march's goal—whether it was was to protest the bomb or just to live and walk together as a peace community. Beyond that, Pro-Peace was unable to raise the promised support money and finally, as marchers were stalled in the Mojave Desert, ProPeace dissolved in a sea of debt.

At that point, the marchers took control and renamed their trek the Great Peace March for Nuclear Disarmament. Carpenter tried to stick with them and to protect whatever money was left for the marchers. But he finally backed out when many of the marchers rejected him and other members of the old ProPeace staff . . . and when he suddenly stiffened up with a crippling bout of rheumatoid arthritis, a problem he'd lived with since his teen years.

In the past, Carpenter had been a master at covering up the pain and stiffness, but this attack left him walking like the rusty Tin Man in "The Wizard of Oz." He realized that the arthritis was telling him something about overwork and stress. And so he returned to Orange County, reserving time to rest, saying "No" to some requests, and choosing carefully before he said "Yes."

"I internally have a sense that I have a limited amount of time left," he said. "With that time, I really want to be effective."

He said "Yes" to two Orange County groups with which he had been active before the march, LEO and the Alliance—groups that brought Carpenter back to the mix that, for him, seemed to work best, combining activism, idealism and politics.

8. FROM WEAPONS CASINGS TO INDIANS' RIGHTS
Tim Langley, Watertown, S.D.

> *If we will have Peace without a worm in it, lay we*
> *the foundations of Justice and Righteousness.*
> —*Oliver Cromwell, speech, Jan. 23, 1656*

Symptoms of society's illnesses show up in various ways. In Los Angeles or New York, perhaps it's the street people . . . old, young and in-between . . . wandering, homeless, scrounging food. In Watertown, S.D., it's more likely the faces of farmers coming into town, or the "For Sale" signs dotting the side roads. Or the tale told by Dean Urban, a ranch and rangeland broker, and his wife Bev.

The Urbans, my bed and breakfast hosts, offered a bittersweet introduction to South Dakota in the '80s. Not that theirs hasn't been a good life; this state has been a fine place to raise a family. But now they're seeing their own financial base crumbling along with South Dakota's farm economy.

Sometimes farmers about to lose their land come in with tears in their eyes, hoping Dean can find a buyer. "We're the last resort," said Bev, "and we can't help." Dean has tried his best to get financing; he's written to investors as far away as California. Dean knows land and knows he's offering good value, but there are no takers.

For a broader look at South Dakota's troubles, one of the best people to talk with is Watertown's Tim Langley, who heads the South Dakota Peace and Justice Center. You can find him in the Center's sparely-furnished offices over the Coast to Coast Store.

The farm problem is just one of the major issues Langley deals with in his role as coordinator for the Center, an interfaith network of some 500 individuals and groups. His concerns reach out to American Indians, Central American refugees, the unemployed and the search for peace. "Though distinct," he said, "these issues are not ultimately separable."

Langley's territory is the whole state of South Dakota. It takes him from Watertown, near the Minnesota border, west through farm and ranch land to the mid-state capital, Pierre, and down to the Pine Ridge Indian Reservation, near the borders of Nebraska and Wyoming. It has given him a perspective—a picture of how all these problems interrelate—that might be less obvious in another state, under other circumstances.

It also has given Langley a mission: to encourage those South Dakotans who are victims of society's ills to get involved in the political process. "Our role is to educate people on issues and to organize people who are interested in being educated," he said. If Langley has his way, that could lead to dramatic change in South Dakota.

Langley does not have the look of a man bent on upsetting the status quo. Today, he's relaxing with a cup of coffee, wearing a flannel shirt, sleeves rolled up; a streak of grey is beginning to touch his hairline. You'd never pick him out from the other people walking down the main street of Watertown.

But behind him, as he sits at his desk above the Coast to Coast Store, a poster carries a picture of the rising sun and the reminder that "Each dawn is a new beginning." Those are words Langley takes seriously: He has some new beginnings of his own in mind.

His most dramatic plan calls for formation of a new political power base: a Nonpartisan League. It would be a non-aligned organization representing people's needs rather than a specific party. That way the league could work through all parties.

There is a historical model for Langley's league. A group with the same name was organized in the sister state of North Dakota in 1915. That one was started by farmers who had lost control to

Tim Langley

the Minneapolis rail and mercantile interests who handled their crops. The businessmen would set prices—and keep profits; meanwhile, the farmers were going broke.

That league, too, was organized as a caucus to operate within existing parties. Within three years, league members gained decision-making power in state government. They controlled, said Langley, "the governor's office and both houses of the legislature; it's history." They also chartered a state-owned grain elevator and a state-owned bank; they gave women the right to vote; they sent the state militia to protect striking miners, and they questioned whether the country should enter World War I.

The new league that Langley envisions would have equally striking goals, aimed at solving the multiple woes the Center has identified in South Dakota. One Peace and Justice flyer described that situation:

> Our system of decentralized, family-based agriculture is threatened with extinction, the future of our small communities is thrown into doubt, federal resources are shifted from human services to military hardware, and environmentally disastrous, low-wage business interests seek to exploit our vulnerability.

While the Peace and Justice Center would be involved in the organizational and educational work needed to start up the League, it would back off once things were in operation, Langley said, since the Center cannot be involved in politics. A major challenge the League is working on now is simply to convince people that the dream is possible, that it could happen again—the same people's power, but this time with farmers joined by Native Americans, women's activists, peace activists, educators, low-income advocates and environmentalists.

Today's farmers already are well aware of how their troubles tie into other segments of the economy, Langley said. There is lots of evidence, he suggested, citing one scene that was playing out in the city of Aberdeen, 10-plus miles to the northwest.

"They floated $4 million in industrial bonds to bring in a company that's going to manufacture casings for tactical nuclear weapons, and it's going to create exactly six jobs when it opens up," said Langley. "Meanwhile, people who are struggling to save farms can't get credit and are going out of business, banks are teetering. You see, you know where the money is and you know where the money isn't." When that happens, the peace issue IS the farm issue, he argued.

For farmers, Langley believes, the basic problem is one of national priorities: "The decision has been made that we don't care if people stay on the farms or not; what we care about is whether we're producing nuclear weapons." While the farmer can't get money, "look at General Electric Corporation or Westinghouse; they have hit the mother lode here. People are giving them checks and they get to write in the numbers."

"I don't think they want nuclear war, either; it would be terrible for business. They don't want to incinerate people . . . . It's just that they need to keep the money with no strings attached flowing . . . . All things being equal, perhaps, they would like to see their businesses do well and family farms prosper, too, and people in ghettoes get enough to eat. But if they can't have it both ways, they certainly have a priority for their own institutional survival."

That's a fairly common scenario, Langley suggested: the peace and justice people on one side, money interests on the other. That's the way it had worked earlier, too, during the nuclear freeze campaign. The Peace and Justice Center got the measure on the ballot, meshing the efforts of workers with all kinds of special interests. But the vote was lost. "We faced organized opposition with at least three times as much money for advertising in the last few weeks of the campaign as we had for the whole year," Langley recalled. Still, the freeze did get 48% of the votes, showing "serious support."

In the face of such overwhelming opposition, that was success, as Langley saw it. And it validated his idea about how people could make things happen when they worked together. Here was a "peace" proposal, yet the supporters represented many interests. Intriguingly, the highest vote for the freeze—67%—had come from the Pine Ridge Indian Reservation. Yet, if you go down there, "you won't find anybody that would identify him or herself as primarily an activist or an organizer of the peace movement," said Langley.

The reason? "One of the things is, there's 80 to 90% unemployment—you can underline that in your notes, so that later you won't wonder if you got it wrong—80 to 90% unemployment on the reservation. That's a typical figure. So people who are working and have the resources to be active are called on to wear so many different hats and they're confronted with so many immediate needs that they wouldn't have the luxury of being just a peace activist; that's only one of the items on their agenda."

"If people look for freeze activists like there are in white, middle-class communities, they won't find them in ghettoes or on reservations. But there are people who understand the connection and who are working on peace issues along with all the other things they've got to do."

It's exactly that kind of thinking, Langley believes, that will allow people to take charge of their own world. Then—whether it is helping farmers and Indians, or working for peace, or whatever—they can make it happen.

9. RETHINKING LITTLE BIG HORN
Gerald Clifford, Manderson, S.D.

> *My friend, I am going to tell you the story of my life . . . It is the story of all life that is holy and is good to tell, and of us two-leggeds sharing in it with the four-leggeds and the wings of the air and all green things; for these are children of one mother and their father is one Spirit.*
> —*Black Elk, a holy man of the Oglala Sioux, "Black Elk Speaks"*

Reservation driving—at least in South Dakota—is best left to those who live there or those who get their directions through divine inspiration. In the Rand McNally atlas, roads turn into grey lines without numbers; in that territory, road signs become about as helpful as Sitting Bull would have been to Custer on his way to Little Big Horn.

Tim Langley provided instructions for getting to Manderson, deep in the Pine Ridge Reservation, where I might find Charlotte Black Elk, a member of the Peace and Justice Center board, and her husband Gerald Clifford. Their work illustrated exactly what he meant about the need to combine peace with other issues—as well as how politics serves as a thread common to a variety of peace and justice issues.

As he saw me off, Langley warned, "Expect to get lost." I did, losing my personal battle at Wounded Knee, where I was supposed to make a turn. I wound up almost hitting the Nebraska border before turning back in the right direction.

This was the end of October. The few trees on the undulating prairie land already had shed their leaves. The fields were getting their final harvesting, and long stretches of land were mono-chromatic golden beige. Many farms between Watertown and Manderson had "For Sale" signs; some abandoned homes had empty windows gaping to the winds; tidied up pieces of farm equip-ment were on display near the roads with more "For Sale" signs on them.

Nearing Manderson, the land became raw, with little develop-ment. It is this part of the earth that is home to Gerald Clifford and Charlotte Black Elk . . . and has been, to their ancestors, for some 3,000 years, they believe. They offer a bit of folk history as proof: In ancient times, the Indians who lived and hunted on this land developed their own system of astronomy, naming constella-tions after the animals they knew. One constellation was named after the woolly mammoth—an animal long extinct.

That kind of knowledge is important to Clifford and Black Elk.

Their major project these days is one that they hold sacred to their Oglala Lakota Sioux tribe: a drive to regain Indian control of the Black Hills, land the Sioux retained in the Fort Laramie Treaty of 1868. But Clifford tells a sorry tale of what followed:

President Grant unilaterally abandoned that treaty in 1875, after gold was found in the Black Hills. Little Big Horn was just one of the conflicts that followed. And while the Indians won that one, they never did get back the promised lands. After studying govern-ment actions following the treaty, the United States Supreme Court declared in 1980 that "a more ripe and rank case of dishonorable dealing will never, in all probability, be found in our history."

What the Sioux ask now is the return of Black Hills land— although just 1.3 of the 7.3 million acres promised in the treaty. It would include only federally-owned areas—no private or state-owned land.

Mt. Rushmore, federal court houses, buildings, rights-of-way and military bases would not be affected. Clifford heads the joint Sioux tribes steering committee working to get that agreement. "We will

Gerald Clifford

do it," he said. "But it won't be easy."

Much of the Sioux campaign these days is handled from the angular, modernistic house that Clifford and Black Elk designed and built themselves on a hill above Manderson. It is home to the couple, their two daughters and son. As Clifford greeted me this day, his long black hair was pulled into a ponytail, his faded blue jeans were torn up the leg to allow boots underneath. We sat in his office, surrounded by the high tech tools he has brought into this ancient world: an Epson computer and printer, an IBM Selectric II typewriter, a Panasonic copier—tools to help regain the Black Hills.

For Clifford, Black Elk and the other Indians, that effort means more than recovering their spiritual home: It is part of a moral and ethical imperative that the Indians feel to protect the earth and all its creatures.

"The earth has a spirit," explained Clifford. "She is our mother. She has children, and we are one of those children. We have an obligation to protect our mother and to respect and protect our brothers and sisters . . . the winged peoples and the crawling peoples and the people that walk on four legs." And the timing, he believes, is important: "I know that this is a time of choice, and one way or another, choices will be presented to people."

"Maybe the choice will be to try to understand," he said, "maybe the choice will be peace . . . but the sum of all choices is going to determine, I guess, whether this planet survives." For Lakota people, the choice is clear, Clifford believes: "to reaffirm our respect for our traditions."

"In Lakota thought," he said, "we have a responsibility for the earth, for protecting the sacred places . . . and we also have a responsibility for keeping people from areas of the earth that, if disturbed, misused, could bring harm on the earth." For the Lakota, he added, the Black Hills are among those sacred places.

Clifford and Black Elk bring a unique blend of gifts and training to their task. For Clifford—whose name traces back to a non-Indian great grandfather—that training took a roundabout route. Most of his early education was at Holy Rosary Mission in Pine Ridge. Then he moved on to the South Dakota School of Mines and Technology at Rapid City, where he graduated in 1959 with a degree in general engineering.

With that, Clifford broke with reservation life, moving to Los Angeles. His jobs there included work on exit cones for Minuteman and Polaris missiles—tasks that, for him, involved no political objections at the time. Yet, even then, he soon developed "a general disgust that the 'bottom line' was the only principle that meant anything."

So one day in 1962, while driving along California's scenic Highway 1, Clifford—who had been raised a Catholic—impulsively turned off at a Camaldolese monastery. He talked with the monks there, and soon left the aircraft industry to become a contemplative hermit. He found he enjoyed that life—full of prayer and study, with its "emphasis on solitude." In the summer of 1967, he was among men sent to Rome for further study at the Benedictine College there.

But two events interrupted: Shortly after he arrived in Italy, his mother died of cancer; a couple of months later, his father's house burned down. "I came back here in April of 1968," said Clifford. "I built my father a house, and at that point made a decision just to stay."

By then, his Indian heritage was beginning to tug, and he "deliberately set out to find what it was to be an Indian."

"A group of people about my age, in their late 20s and early 30s, began to meet and ask ourselves those questions . . . what does it mean to be an Indian. We spent, I think, five weekends just dealing with those questions, and ultimately the group came out with sort of a program. Basic to it was the philosophy that in order to deal with all the problems on the reservation, we would have to recover the spiritual values of Lakota thought."

In 1969, he married Charlotte Black Elk, whose grandfather,

great-grandfather and great-great-grandfather all had been renowned Lakota healers and spiritual leaders—"what white men would call medicine men," said Clifford. Her great-grandfather, who is quoted at the start of this chapter, lived through the era of Wounded Knee, became a renowned medicine man and told of his life in the book, "Black Elk Speaks," written down by John G. Neihardt. Charlotte had been chosen by her grandmother to learn the Lakota oral tradition.

The Lakota religion had been considered illegal until the 1930s, said Clifford, and the American Indian Freedom of Religion Act was not passed until the late 1970s. Meanwhile, Indians were encouraged to become Christians. It was Charlotte who helped Clifford understand the Lakota spirituality that he values today. "I am still a Catholic, I'm a Christian, but I'm also Lakota," Clifford said. "I practice the Lakota way of praying and have accepted the Lakota philosophical view of reality."

Both Clifford and Black Elk also have become exceptionally sophisticated about how to make things work in white society. The couple, who commit most of their efforts to tribal causes, have established a small consulting service, hiring out to white or Indian groups needing expertise on a wide variety of Indian affairs. On the day I talked with Clifford, Black Elk was gone, fulfilling a consulting appointment. Such work pays the bills, said Clifford; the tribal council still can offer no salary.

The day we talked was a big one: A bill returning the land was just being introduced in the House of Representatives. A similar bill had been introduced earlier in the Senate, with part of the wording written by Clifford. Now, he said, "we're going to have to get somebody [on the Senate and House Indian Affairs committees] . . . to move it. And this is very difficult." Yet, he added, "we have been told through our ceremonies and prayers that we're going to get the Black Hills back."

Charlotte Black Elk explained the importance of that action in a July 1985 interview with the Indian Report newsletter: "We view

our struggle to maintain our religion, to keep the Black Hills, as
not just for ourselves, but so that everything in creation can live
and live well. That all the people may live well together. That the
earth, herself, can live."

As I left the reservation, cutting through the edge of Badlands
National Park, the late afternoon sun threw a starkly brilliant, golden
wash across the land with its dramatic Badlands outcroppings. It
was like a single-color moonscape, broken only by softly-colored
blue, pink and white clouds skirting the horizon. This, too, was
land the Indians had known as their own.

The next day, heading on west from Rapid City, I recalled Clifford's angry contention that mining in the area is an assault on the
Black Hills. Sure enough, just on the edge of town, great gouges
were dug into the red-clay earth—gouges that looked like huge,
bloodied sores on the land. A dirt bike trail had been worn into
one hillside, leaving reddened, monster fingernail scratches.

There is, it seems, a danger in talking to someone like Gerald
Clifford: It may change the way you see the world.

In a story datelined Hell Canyon, S.D., the Los Angeles Times'
Bob Secter reported on Aug. 30, 1987, that the Sioux lands once
again were embroiled in controversy. This time the Sioux had been
joined by some local ranchers to form the Cowboy and Indian
Alliance, which filed suit in U.S. District Court to block Minnea-
polis-based Honeywell Corp. from testing weaponry in Hell
Canyon. Honeywell already had been turned away in central Minnesota, where authorities cited environmental concerns for their
refusal to rezone the area to allow testing.

10. NO MORE TRIDENTS . . . NO MORE WAR
Albert Donnay, Baltimore, Md.

*With thousands of nuclear explosives in the world,
everyone must come to understand that a military
solution of any kind is not a solution at all.*
> —*Victor F. Weisskopf, physicist*

Baltimore's Albert Donnay would like you to think about an idea:

Granted, the world's powers have done a lousy job of controlling the nuclear threat. Well, what if cities, counties, states—even colleges, churches, whatever—around the United States and around the world decided individually that they wouldn't put up with any more nuclear nonsense in THEIR territories—no weapons, no manufacturing? Maybe even no contracts or investments with companies that are involved somehow in the nuclear business. Get enough of them and they would add up, right? Eventually: no more threat of nuclear war.

That's oversimplyfying the whole thing, but you get the general plan. Encouraging that particular variety of alternative political action is a full-time job these days for Donnay, co-founder and executive director of an operation called Nuclear Free America (NFA). NFA's adopted task is to serve as a worldwide resource and networking center, encouraging the growth of nuclear free zones.

Already, Donnay said, "there are 87 nuclear free zones in the United States, and 125 more campaigns are underway. Around the world, we're up to over 1,950 nuclear free zones in 16 countries."

"We're overwhelmed with work. We've heard from almost a new campaign every day since January."

Albert Donnay

Those zones, once they are declared, take a variety of forms, said Donnay. Some carry legal clout; others are only advisory. New York City's, for instance, has no legal power; it was declared in late 1984 as a protest against Navy plans to station the USS Iowa and its surface action group, armed with cruise missiles, at Staten Island. Amherst, Mass.; Hoboken, N.J., and Takoma Park, Md., all included provisions to ban municipal investments or contracts with industries involved in nuclear weapons production. That means, said Donnay, "no AT&T long-distance service, no IBM typewriters, no GE radios, no GM trucks, no Westinghouse light bulbs . . . "

One of the most-publicized zones is New Zealand's, which earned international headlines when its nuclear-free policy was invoked to prohibit the 1985 visit planned by a United States nuclear-capable ship. New Zealand's policy held up in spite of heavy Reagan-administration pressure. It proved to Donnay and other like him that the zones can, indeed, work.

Although Donnay, himself, is still in his mid-20s, he's already an old hand at taking personal responsibility for safety of the world. Like California's Tim Carpenter, he recalls his interest in political action reaching back as far as the sixth grade. He was attending an experimental school in the Washington, D.C., area at the time, and his class got a major assignment: They were to write a book. It was Donnay who suggested the topic—the environment. The title chosen was "How to Save the World." It was a title that would apply just as well to the life Donnay cut out for himself in the years that followed.

Shortly after Donnay completed that sixth grade class, his family moved to Canada, where his parents—both university professors and crystallographers—accepted posts at McGill University in Montreal. As a high school student there, Donnay volunteered with a local environmental group, STOP.

Then, moving on to McGill to work on a degree in mathematics, Donnay signed up with Greenpeace, that group of derring-doers who challenge big ships on the sea and weapons testers on land. "I was one of those Zodiac boat drivers who drove the little rubber boats in the Gulf of St. Lawrence to harrass the seal hunt," he said. It was a role that snubbed its nose at danger. "I got sprayed with firehoses from the deck of the ship and had sawhorses dumped into my boat," Donnay said. He also remembers being bumped by those sealing ships—"bumped, but not dumped."

The Zodiac boaters never were able to hold the ships inside the harbor, he said. "Greenpeace never looks like it's successful when they're doing something, but in the long term they usually win." Within five years, "we'd stopped the seal hunt; it's now completely finished."

About that time, Donnay also became concerned about asbestos in local schools. His interest was spurred by a newspaper article reporting that only a few small schools within the province, all in out-of-the-way locations, had any such problem. Donnay knew that was only part of the story: There was asbestos in his old high school; yet, it had not even made the list. "I said, 'This is just nuts; that's ridiculous.'"

During his senior year at McGill, Donnay won a grant to do his own study on asbestos, using his parents' crystallography lab—"that's exactly what they use X-ray crystallography for, to see whether a mineral is this or that." Donnay proved the presence of asbestos at his former school—"the whole ceiling!" The provincial government eventually did allocate another $30 million for elimination of asbestos in schools, although ironically, because of political maneuvering, his school did not get any of it.

After McGill, Donnay headed to Baltimore, where he worked on a master's degree in public health at Johns Hopkins University and studied radioactive waste disposal at the University of Maryland. During that period, he joined the drive to get the state to reject federal funds for civil defense, arguing—as many activists do—that civil defense simply would not work in a nuclear war. For one thing, he said, in case of attack, "this was people being asked to move from their own communities . . . to places they usually knew wouldn't want them. We were supposed to go to West Virginia. People in Baltimore understand that's ridiculous." Maryland was the first state to actually reject the funds.

While at Johns Hopkins, Donnay and other public health students also organized a chapter of Physicians for Social Responsibility, and that group spawned a number of other activities, including Nuclear Free America.

NFA was founded in 1982, after Donnay and a friend, Dr. Vikas Saini, noticed that cities in Maryland seemed willing to take anti-nuclear stands—actions such as approving nuclear free zones and a nuclear freeze. NFA was started to offer support. Donnay accepted his current full-time post as soon as he finished his work at Johns Hopkins.

"We're not the leaders and decision makers of the nuclear free zone movement," Donnay emphasized. "NFA is just a clearinghouse and a resource center." The group distributes information, answers questions, and tries to keep nuclear free zone advocates around the world in touch with each other. They also cooperate with other groups dedicated to encouraging more zones. Yet, mostly, the decisions to work for nuclear free zones seem to spring up locally, just through word of mouth, said Donnay. "We don't advertise."

And while interest seems to be growing, such zones have not always been able to stand up to higher authority or to changing local moods, Donnay admitted. Amherst's zone, which included a ban on production of nuclear weapons within the town, was over-ruled when the state proclaimed that such a zone, if duplicated throughout the country, "would constitute the balkanization of the nation, and result in the Government losing its control over foreign policy, and would deprive Congress of its war-making power." The city's Board of Selectmen responded by re-adopting the measures in the form of "policies."

The Hawaii County Council declared the nation's first nuclear free zone by ordinance in 1981, then three years later backed off under pressure to exclude compliance by the Navy. As originally written, the ordinance prohibited visits by ships carrying nuclear weapons. Although such a local ordinance had no real power over the Navy, which operates by federal authority, it did send out negative signals, said opponents.

Donnay recognizes critics' concern that the plan could add up to unilateral disarmament, since there is not much chance of developing similar zones in the Soviet Union. But he sees it differently, arguing that the major result of a strong movement would be to pressure the United States government into positive action—for instance, into taking negotiations more seriously. "They wouldn't give away the store."

Among his other duties these days, Donnay gets out the group's newsletter, The New Abolitionist. Its name, he believes, has special significance for the anti-nuclear movement—and especially for those who may think the dream of a nuclear free America is for poets or fanatics, not realists. In their day, Donnay explained, abolitionists "were considered fringe lunatics"; nobody believed slavery could be eliminated. Now, he said, there is a parallel situation: "A lot of people assume that war and weapons are a given, that they will never go away."

As Donnay sat in his cluttered NFA office this day, Good Friday church bells were pealing across Baltimore—a counterpoint to Donnay's summation of just how it could happen that the weapons really would disappear. Amazing things can be accomplished by small groups of people who make their minds up to do something, Donnay explained. Look, he argued, "you take away Trident submarines and you just took away General Dynamics . . . . There are maybe 50 companies that do [major military production], and they're very vulnerable, susceptible to our pressure. All you have to do is pull a few contracts and the whole house of cards collapses."

As slavery did end, said Donnay, so can the threat of nuclear war. All it will take is some dedicated people, plus a few cities and counties, some churches and schools; then a few more . . .

11. A NO-NONSENSE MESSAGE FROM DOWN UNDER
Helen and Bill Caldicott, Annisquam, Mass.

> . . . for it isn't enough to talk about peace. One
> must believe in it. And it isn't enough to believe in
> it. One must work for it.
> —*Eleanor Roosevelt, 1951*

Helen Caldicott doesn't look like the stereotypical fiery activist. She is petite, almost fragile-appearing. "In her pearls and pale pink knit suit," Los Angeles Times writer Elizabeth Mehren once wrote, "the 44-year-old mother of three looked rather like a refugee from the PTA." Yet, this is the same Caldicott who has become the thundering preacher of the anti-nuclear movement.

Speaking in front of a group, Caldicott is something to behold. The look is intense, the tone fervent, the words challenging.

"Now, we're going to drop a bomb right here," she told a hushed audience at Luther College in Decorah, Iowa. "It's going to be 20 megatons . . . five times the collective energy of all the bombs dropped in the Second World War . . . . [Within a six-mile radius] most people will be vaporized and will disappear . . . . If people reflexively look at the flash of the fireball, their eyes will melt. That happened at Hiroshima. People had their eyes running down their cheeks." And for those who do survive? No medical care, no world worth living in, she warned.

The talk enumerated contemporary nuclear ills in graphic terms: "More than half the scientists and engineers in this country today are working on producing the global gas oven" . . . "Nuclear war could happen any day . . . because the Pentagon computers keep

Helen Caldicott

Bill Caldicott

making errors" . . . "There are enough bombs in one Trident submarine to destroy every major city in the northern hemisphere, and America plans to build 30 Trident submarines."

Yet Caldicott's final appeal that evening was offered in the soft, consoling tones of a caring doctor: "When you go out, take a look at this beautiful sky tonight, the Iowa sky . . . . And the next time you see a rose, smell it, and realize how beautiful it is, and what the creation is all about. And the next time you see a newborn baby, look into its eyes and see the extraordinary innocence and the archetypal wisdom in those eyes, handed down from hundreds of generations. And remember that there aren't communist babies and capitalist babies. A baby is a baby is a baby. That's what this is all about. It's love that makes babies, and it's love that will assure the future of the human race."

It was a message that left some listeners in tears, something Caldicott had come to expect. If past experience were to hold true, it also would push some of those listeners into activism. For Helen Caldicott was by then America's most effective one-woman recruiting agent for the anti-nuclear cause. And she recruited more than individuals, for along the way it was Caldicott who almost singlehandedly revived the dormant Physicians for Social Responsibility (PSR), and who then went on to found Women's Action for Nuclear Disarmament (WAND)—now two of the nation's most influential groups.

It was, all in all, an amazing record—especially for one slim woman who also had built a prestigious career in pediatrics, and one whose roots were not in the United States at all, but in Australia.

Caldicott and her husband Bill, a pediatric radiologist, immigrated to the United States in 1977, after both accepted similar jobs: teaching at Harvard University and working on staff at Boston Childrens Hospital. By then, Helen already was committed to fighting nuclear weaponry.

It had begun for her as a teenager, she said: "I read 'On the Beach' when I was 17, and I've just never gotten it out of my mind." But it was the birth of her first child, Philip, in the early 1960s that pushed her toward action: "I suddenly learned what every mother must learn: That I would die to save the lives of my children, and that if they weren't going to survive, nothing else I ever did would matter. At that moment, I accepted personal responsibility for stopping the nuclear arms race."

That didn't mean she immediately zoomed to international anti-nuclear superstardom. Many other things had demands on her time in those days. Within three years, Philip was followed by a brother and sister; Helen was wife and mother to a growing family. Bill, meanwhile, was building his career. As soon as the children were old enough, Helen, too, began her pediatrics practice.

Yet, by 1971 the name Helen Caldicott was well-known in Australia. By herself, at first, she had begun a campaign to halt French atmospheric testing of nuclear weapons in the Pacific Ocean. In her first book, "Nuclear Madness: What You Can Do!" she commented, "At the time few Australians knew of the testing or were aware of its inherent dangers."

Caldicott, the pediatrician, went on television to explain just what the resulting radiation could do to humans. The message that worked then—the message she would continue to use—was her pediatrician's urgent warning to an ailing world.

"I'm talking as a physician practicing preventive medicine, trying to make sure you live a normal lifespan and die of natural causes—that you are not vaporized," was how she put it during a later talk in the United States. By then, of course, the focus was more than just testing; it was armageddon. "If we have a nuclear war, it will create the final medical epidemic," she told her audience. "We are facing the end of the earth."

Her reasoning had made sense to the Australians. First the public, then the governments of both Australia and New Zealand joined the protest. In late 1972, France announced the end of above-ground testing. It was Caldicott's first big victory.

Less than two years after arriving in the United States, Caldicott claimed two more major accomplishments: publication of "Nuclear Madness" and rebirth of PSR. Two years later she founded WAND. And a year after that she quit both Harvard and Boston Childrens Hospital to offer full-time leadership in the anti-nuclear movement.

In that role, she traveled the country, warning Americans that they must recognize the explosive end of the world toward which they were careening, and exhorting them to mend their ways. That mending, she told them in no-nonsense language, meant to "get off your tails and use your democracy." And that meant politics. As Caldicott sees it, elections are more than just routine voting rituals—each one is a "referendum on the fate of the earth." And each one offers a chance to force government to sit up and listen. That was what she set out to make happen.

In the process, women became her special targets. And with them, she aimed straight for the jugular.

"Do you want to be the last generation and never have babies?" she demanded of one mostly-youthful audience at the University of California at Irvine, shortly before the 1984 elections. Serious, young heads shook quietly. Well then, she continued, "What are you going to do in November?!?!" After a pause, she provided her own answer: "In the next two weeks . . . you put on your running shoes, you stop everything you're doing. You want to grow up and have babies? You're more concerned about your exams? . . . Walk your feet off in the next two weeks. Get out the vote!" She provided a telephone number where they might volunteer; a rustle of papers and pens followed.

But Helen Caldicott has still grander dreams for women: Their role, she said, "is key." They should be running for office, they should be filling half the seats in Congress. The Los Angeles Times' Mehren quoted Caldicott: "[On the speaking circuit] when I give a talk about nuclear war, you can see the women sitting there, and you can see how they feel inadequate. And as they hear how threatened their children are, they rise up in their chairs and assume tremendous power . . . The women have a global perspective.

They understand it intuitively . . . . We've got to take over. Because the men, they're going to blow up the world."

Helen built a Freudian pun into the title of another book, one challenging men's role in the arms buildup. Its title: "Missile Envy: The Arms Race and Nuclear War." In it she suggested that the "hideous weapons of killing and mass genocide may be a symptom of several male emotions: inadequate sexuality and a need to continually prove their virility plus a primitive fascination with killing."

Yet, many men were drawn by Helen's message—including her own husband. For him, he admitted, it was not a gut issue at the beginning. But it became one . . . and Helen began describing the two of them as a team. Bill started representing WAND before some mostly-male audiences. And in 1984—three years after Helen—he, too, left both Harvard and Childrens Hospital to work full-time with his wife and WAND.

For him, the nudge had come through the "Global 2000 Report," a Carter-administration survey that looked toward the turn of the century. Basically, said Bill, it suggested that "we're in deep trouble in a lot of areas . . . The population bomb can do us in, or the damage we're doing the environment, or the underground water, etc . . . and the nuclear arms race."

"I was baffled why we turned our backs on that report," Bill recalled. He finally decided that one of those issues—the nuclear arms race—was so frightening that Americans "turned their backs on the whole lot." Suddenly, medicine—even the distinguished brand he was practicing—didn't seem so important. "What was going on in the world," he reasoned, "wasn't discovering cures for new diseases or something; we were actually deciding whether we wanted to become extinct or not . . . It became very painful to me to go on doing work which didn't sort of add up." What did matter was getting people to face up to their future.

His style before audiences was low-key. While Helen was challenging women to feel white-hot fury, Bill was encouraging men to join the world's soothing caretakers. "I tell men that we have to be nurturers all the time . . . at work . . . in the way we drive our cars, in the way we make our business decisions, in the way we treat our farmland. We just have to be nurturers, because this planet now is so stressed that we're going to have to look after it with just tremendous tender care if our children and our grandchildren are going to have a future."

The response, he found, was good. "It's very close to something very profound for them. The men in an audience will sit very, very still when I talk about men and work and fulfillment and pain, and about my own thing. It's like their eyes turn around and look right back into their heads. And their wives sit very, very still, and they're almost not going to move, because they want their husbands to hear it so badly."

With both Caldicotts in full-time activism, they sold their large Boston home and moved to a modest-sized white, wooden home—one built in the 1740s, before the American revolution—in the quaint resort town of Annisquam. Their back windows looked out on a tranquil scene: a stretch of grass sloping down to a picturesque river, complete with wooden bridge.

That's where I visited them. Helen—with whom I'd spoken earlier, during a California speaking tour—was inside, being interviewed by a film crew. Bill and I talked outside, sitting on lawn chairs.

There was a lot on his mind that day. He and Helen and WAND had been doing some heavy thinking, trying to figure out why—after so many years, so much work, so many good reasons—the anti-nuclear movement still hadn't turned the nation around. One conclusion, Bill reported, was that "we've been extraordinarily unsophisticated in the way we've gone about it."

So, WAND was entering a new era. It would be a change in approach for the movement; it would mean using the latest techniques—sophisticated, issue-driven polling, with campaigns based on the results; it would mean doing a better job with media, so those opposing nuclear weapons got their fair share of coverage. "We're going to change the political climate in Washington if it's successful," Bill asserted.

But—for the time being, at least—it soon turned out that Helen and Bill Caldicott might not be among those leading in that change. On May 15, 1986, a smiling, arms-around-each-others'-waists picture of Helen and Bill Caldicott appeared in the Los Angeles Times. Beverly Beyette's story began:

> Dr. Helen Caldicott, 47, the mother of the nuclear freeze movement, is dropping out. After 16 years—a personal campaign that began in 1971 with a successful protest against France's atomic tests in the South Pacific—she is, she says, "a little bonkers."

In a later phone conversation, Bill said that they would both be leaving the country in October. They'd spend some time in India, and then it would be on to Australia. Home. "Our children are all living in Australia, and they want us back there," Bill said. "We feel we have a role to play there; we've done, for a while, what we can do here."

They would be leaving with a sense of hope, he suggested. "We feel the big American ship of state is starting to turn back to a more sane position." And more, "Every generation living on the planet now has this issue deeply etched in its soul." Would that be enough? Would there be time for the world to confront the issue before blowing itself up? "Yes," he answered thoughtfully, "enough for us to do something about it."

One of the first signs of WAND's new direction was a booklet, "Turnabout," published in August 1986. It reported results of an opinion survey based on "interviews with more than 1,000 Americans, candid talks with 100 key press figures, frank exchanges with 35 members of Congress and key Hill staffers, and analysis of more than 100 grassroots organizations."

Some of the conclusions were pretty well known ahead of time: A majority of Americans think we're spending too much on nuclear weapons; even more think a comprehensive test ban would reduce the risk of war; nearly as many oppose a "Star Wars" system designed to protect only U.S. missiles.

But some of the results may have been less expected. For instance, "Turnabout" reported, there has been an important evolution in what politically-oriented groups need from participants:

> For leaders of the grassroots movements of the 1960s, such as the peace movement and the civil rights movement, political organizing was a matter of stoking the passions of thousands of activists and marshaling them into powerful mass demonstrations.
>
> Now in the 1980s, the key to political organizing is motivating grassroots activists to execute a simple financial transaction—writing a small but substantial check.

"Too many progressive grassroots organizations are wedded to old-fashioned notions about citizen participation," "Turnabout" argued. The reality is something different: "Americans are less able to work on volunteer activities and are more inclined to express their civic, religious, or political activism by simply writing a check . . . . Indeed, writing a check today is as fundamental a form of civic participation as helping new neighbors build a home or plant crops was in the frontier days." Besides, added the booklet, "the trend toward new technology and professional services in politics has placed an added emphasis on fundraising, while simultaneously decreasing the demand for volunteer activities."

No, that does not mean that "fundraising will replace volunteerism/activism," explained Diane D. Aronson, WAND executive director and "Turnabout" editor, in a follow-up letter; it does mean that "a greater amount of energy and focus needs to be placed on fundraising within the peace movement to establish an appropriate stable base."

Even so, such a suggestion discomforts many peace and justice workers, who prefer to work on a people-to-people basis; they distrust deeds that are "bought" by a hefty check. Others, however, including Irvine's Larry Agran, support WAND's position; they've seen goals and projects crippled by limited budgets.

While progressive groups have been slow to pick up on the change, there has been no such hesitancy on the other side of the fence, "Turnabout" observed: "The Republican/conservative coalition recognized this trend early and capitalized on it quickly . . . . . They have built their current financial advantage not by soliciting large contributions from the rich, but by recruiting hundreds of thousands of small donors across America." It was a message the progressive groups had better take to heart, "Turnabout" warned.

Another suggestion, based on discussion with senators and representatives, had more to do with style. Some of those congressmen, "Turnabout" reported, suggested that apocalyptic visions were not effective. Instead of emphasizing the "imminent threat of nuclear war," the movement should concentrate on issues the public already supports, like the need to trim military spending and the deficit.

All in all, the proposals in "Turnabout" were tough and pragmatic. Some challenged basic tenets of the peace and justice movement—including some of the tactics employed by Helen Caldicott, herself. Yet, WAND viewed them as opportunity. "Movement leaders are already forging ahead with new ideas and new strategies suggested by these findings," wrote Aronson in the introduction to "Turnabout." Implementing such techniques and incorporating a well-financed, sophisticated, hard-nosed approach to politics, WAND concluded, is what it will take to fulfill WAND's and the Caldicotts' vision: "to change the political climate in Washington." And, to save the world.

III

CONCERN FOR CHILDREN

Helen Caldicott touched a sensitive human nerve when she tied the nuclear threat to hopes for children, warning that the actions . . . or lack of action . . . by today's adults might mean there was no tomorrow for children.

Such concern is a thread that reaches among a great number of peace and justice workers—one that encourages many Americans who might otherwise shun activism to sign on, once they sense it is their own children who are at risk.

In North Carolina, one busy professional mother took what she had learned about the nuclear threat to her mothers' support group—and the whole group adopted her cause. In New York, an issues-oriented acting troupe added a children's show to their repertoire. In Portland, a teenager decided it was time for young people to take some responsibility for their own generation—and did so. As counterpoint to all of these, educators are now putting together programs aimed at giving youngsters information and possible solutions, not just fear.

"I don't know if we're going to make it," Caldicott had said at the conclusion of her her talk in Irvine, Calif. "But you know what? If you start working on it, you feel fantastic. It relieves your anxiety; you feel joyous."

"And even if we fail, as the bombs start dropping I can turn to my children and I can say, 'I tried.'"

12. EARACHES AND NUCLEAR BOMBS
Edi Irons, Charlotte, N.C.

> *The nuclear peril makes all of us, whether we*
> *happen to have children of our own or not, the*
> *parents of all future generations.*
> —*Jonathan Schell, "The Fate of the Earth"*

Four years ago, Edi Irons was rocking her son Ned in the family's Charlotte, N.C., home. Ned was just 6 months old and he was suffering from a bad ear infection. Irons would try putting him in his crib, but he would howl with pain; the only way he could sleep, it seemed, was with his head on his mother's shoulder. So, Irons spent long hours in the rocking chair, nestling her son. As Ned slept, she would reach over with her free arm to pick up a magazine. One of those magazines would make major changes in Edi Irons' life.

She recalled that incident for me one Sunday evening. I had rung the Irons doorbell just as supper was ending for Edi, a clinical psychologist; her husband Bruce, an elementary school principal, and their two children: Ned, now 4 1/2, bright and friendly, and Lissa, 7 1/2, outgoing and precocious. Irons stacked dishes in the sink, made coffee and then headed for the living room with a steaming cup in her hand as she told the story.

The magazine she had picked up was her husband's Scientific American. Flipping the pages, she had come upon a particular article: "It told how—if the Russians wanted to be effective—what they would do is, they would hit the nuclear power plants." The idea was that they wouldn't even have to worry about spraying bombs over the whole United States; just blowing up the power plants would do the job quite efficiently.

Well, recalls Irons, "as a mother, somehow or other, rocking a baby suffering with an ear infection and reading about the destruction of the earth was this insane juxtaposition. That I could be trying to protect him from the pain of lying down . . . while reading that! It just boggled my mind."

"I went bananas," said Irons. "I absolutely freaked out. I woke my husband up in the middle of the night. He said, 'Oh, babe, I was hoping you wouldn't see that. I meant to hide that article from you. I knew you'd get upset.' "

When Edi Irons gets upset, she acts. She is a high-energy woman, the kind who naturally does two things at once. Sparks fly almost visibly as she talks.

Irons has never hesitated much at putting her ideas into action— and this was not the first time weaponry had upset her. While getting her English degree between 1962 and 1966 at William Smith College in Geneva, N.Y., she had worked hard for that era's presidential candidate Eugene McCarthy; she had been involved in anti-Vietnam demonstrations. "It was easy to be an activist in the '60s," she said, reminiscing. "It was very easy to march through Harvard Square, because everybody was marching through Harvard Square." While earning her doctorate in pyschology and counseling at the University of Massachusetts, she had taken a strong stand against placing anti-ballistic missiles in Massachusetts.

But now she had other pressing responsibilities. She was a clinical psychologist in private practice, as well as the mother of Ned and Lissa, and the wife of an equally-busy husband. The couple had typical young professional responsibilities of meeting house payments and balancing time for both children and careers. And there was no nationwide anti-Vietnam issue to focus the efforts of activists.

"This was the first time, I think, that anything hit me on such a personal, gripping level, and there was nobody else to talk to about it," Irons said. "All of a sudden, it hit me that I had to do something." But what? "I would go to dinner parties with friends," she recalled. "We have very bright, sophisticated, decent friends. We were at a New Year's Eve party with the psychiatrist I work with, a friend who's a cardiologist and his wife . . . some other friends: she's a court counselor, he's a judge; another friend: she's in advertising, he's a lawyer."

"I started talking about this issue. And I started getting teased, and I got furious. The two physicians started teasing me about, 'Oh, it's very intuitive; you just kind of know. Well, what about the window of vulnerability? . . . ' "

Irons decided she needed answers and set out to find them. She still had friends in Cambridge and was familiar with resources there, so she flew back to Massachusetts. She came home loaded down with books and resource lists. Soon she began sharing her information with a mothers support group to which she belonged. "We would basically get together and gripe about toilet training problems, feeding problems," she said. "You know, the real things that mothers need help with." So Irons took her fears about nuclear disaster to the other mothers. And, she recalls, she received "a lot of very warm support from these friends."

The women in the group shared many interests, she said: "They're all Lamaze, La Leche mothers; they're all professional; they're all concerned about civil rights. We were all of a type, I suppose. But none of them had gotten as panicky about this issue as I had." That changed as the other mothers shared Irons' information: "Finally, we decided that they were as scared as I was."

So they all went to work on a plan. They called friends and colleagues, and they pulled together enough money to take out an ad in the Charlotte newspaper on Mothers Day. "It said," recalled Irons, " 'All we want for Mothers Day is a safe world for our children and all children.' "

A nice, simple action. But the result, she said, her voice still quieting with wonder, was "spontaneous combustion." "We got hundreds of phone calls. I mean, people were sending us money.

We must have collected $2,000 beyond the cost of the ad. It was just mind-boggling." So . . . "all of a sudden, we were a group!"

It was one turn of events they had not anticipated. The support group was made up of "six or eight of us who had our babies around the same time," Irons said. They tried to rise to the task. But, "We just found we were going nuts. We were meeting to send out our mailings, and all of us were kind of bleary-eyed. We all had jobs, careers: One of us was a lawyer, I was a counselor; there were two school counselors; there was an editor of a book company, a teacher . . . one woman was working on her doctorate and working at a bank. And everybody had at least two—two of them three— pre-schoolers. So we were just bonkers."

As if that weren't enough, Irons had a dream one night: "It was about putting together a road company to go around the United States to educate people on this issue, a kind of guerrilla theater . . . I saw this very vivid image, like circus cars, like the kids' Fisher-Price circus train."

"Bruce was really being very supportive," she added, "and he said, 'Well, babe, that's a great idea. Talk to someone about it.'" And she did.

Irons had one name she had noticed in a magazine article: It was Dr. Helen Caldicott. Without even knowing of WAND, Irons called Caldicott's pediatric practice and was referred to the WAND office in Boston.

She introduced herself a bit tentatively: "This is going to sound weird, but I have this idea about a roadshow . . . I had this crazy dream . . . ." The voice at the other end of the line, belonging to staff member Phyllis Greenleaf, registered amazement: "I did, too!" It turned out that WAND already had scheduled an initial meeting of actors and artists to talk about putting the show together. Irons was invited to attend. "It was," she says now, "a bizarre coincidence."

So Irons once more got on a plane and headed for Massachusetts. She met once with the roadshow planning group, gathered more material to take home, and left, not at all sure the roadshow would ever materialize.

By then the Charlotte group that evolved as result of the ad had a name: Mothers United to Save Infants and Children. "MUSIC," said Irons, with an apologetic grin. "It borders on the cute." MUSIC was managing to put on workshops and coffees. They affiliated with WAND and worked closely with the Charlotte chapter of SANE. Finally, they decided to do something big . . . and what better, thought Irons, than to bring in that roadshow—if it even existed. So once again, Irons was on the phone to Boston. Yes, the show was up and going; it was being put on by a professional group called the Underground Railway Theater. Yes, they could come to Charlotte.

They did. They tailored their presentation to the local audience, and they were a huge success. So successful, in fact, that MUSIC found itself with $6,000 over costs. This time they spent most of the money by bringing the Underground Railway back to tape the show for TV and for distribution to churches, schools and other organizations, and by giving the group seed money for an educational tour through the South.

But the busy members of MUSIC were still struggling with the impossibility of doing everything. Eventually, they joined forces with the local chapter of the Bilateral Freeze Committee, anticipating that such a move would free MUSIC members from basic, time-consuming, group management duties and allow them to concentrate on outreach. But then—as happens with many activist groups—the freeze committee sputtered out . . . individual MUSIC members started turning toward the upcoming election campaigns . . . and the group drifted out of action.

Irons was one of those who jumped with both feet into the elections. Her candidate was her next door neighbor, a Democrat and a Congressional candidate, who "has chosen all of his life to be deeply involved in working for causes of peace and justice." When the ballots were tallied, he lost—by 132 votes. "When he lost," said Irons, "we were all just miserable, really miserable." But finally, she said, "one of my friends called about a month ago and said, 'Well, are we going to stay miserable forever or are we going to start to do something?' "

"I said, 'I dunno, I'm thinking of staying miserable forever,' " recalled Irons, laughing. " 'What are you thinking of?' "

What's evolved, she said, is a new plan. This time members will form a "project team"—a group of half a dozen women, mostly different from the last time, but again all busy professionals—who will "offer ourselves as a project group to any organization that wants us, because we can go in and put on a spurt of energy . . . . We can put together a program . . . pull together ideas for educational events; we'll do workshops; we'll do teas. But we won't do organizational maintenance." Their first event will be helping PSR put on a big Charlotte appearance by that group's president, Dr. Sidney Alexander.

Getting active again, said Irons, is her best antidote to a depression that still threatens her. An advantage of the new plan is that it will require less time away from her children. "One of the things that happened in the year that I was involved with the anti-nuclear work before the election began is that my little one would go through these terrible upsets when I would leave the house at night. I was away from home a lot during the day anyway. The irony of going out to save the world while leaving him hysterical hit me at some point. I decided that I really want to limit [my activities], that my first priority is the children's emotional and psycholgical and overall health right now."

There was another incident, as well. This one involved Lissa, who was 5 at the time. Even then she sparked with the same high-voltage as her mother. "She taught herself to read when she was 5, so you can't hide a lot from her," said Irons. "She picks up the paper every morning and reads it."

Back then, Irons was helping with the effort to get the city council and county commission to sign nuclear freeze petitions. "The night we went before the city council, I came home," said Irons. "Lissa was waiting up in her bed. It must have been midnight when I walked in. And she said, 'Mom, Mom, did we win?' I said, 'We did! We got it through the city council.' And she started dancing around in her bed. 'Oh, there's not going to be a war, there's not going to be a war. We got it through the city council.' "

"It was very touching," said Irons.

That incident also showed a couple of other things: How much children can be aware, and how parents can deal with that. When the children get concerned, said Irons, she and her husband comfort them by saying, "You don't have to worry about that; that's for the grownups of the world to worry about." It seems to work for the youngsters; Lissa was able to go to sleep that night, knowing her mother was taking responsibility.

But it does not always work so well for the parents. "I mean, the Pershings are in," said Irons. "There are some things that should never have happened that have happened—that move us very close to Armageddon. That's a terrifying thing to me. I would kill anybody who tried to kill my babies, pacifist that I am. The idea that my children could be hurt by this just terrifies me. And I feel like, somehow or other, the whole thing is out of control, and this great charade is being perpetrated on the American people."

Edi Irons, a trained counselor and a loving, concerned parent, does feel good about her ability to protect her children from psychological damage, to help them believe their world "is a pretty safe and secure world, in which mommies and daddies do solve the problems."

"But," she added quietly, "I'm not sure I can protect them from nuclear war. And that terrifies me."

13. A HOPI TALE OF WISDOM
Wes Sanders, Cambridge, Mass.

> *There is a new reality—that man is a part of the
> cosmos and that, just as the individual cell needs
> the organism of which it is a part, mankind
> needs—and therefore cannot destroy—his world.
> Wisdom is becoming the new criterion of fitness.*
> —*Jonas Salk, M.D.*

It's Friday afternoon at Conant Elementary School in Acton,
Mass., northwest of Boston. Third, fifth and sixth graders are
noisily tumbling into the auditorium for a treat: an early end to
afternoon classes, and a chance to watch a live show about Hopi
Indians, "The Vision of Dreaming Branch." The stage already is
set up: an artfully-constructed series of boxy wooden frames covered
with heavy, unbleached cloth, suggesting the high mesas of Arizona
and New Mexico—just enough like the real thing to engage a young
imagination.

This, it turns out, is the Underground Railway Theater—the group
that was fulfilling that dream shared by Edi Irons and WAND's
Phyllis Greanleaf. "The Anything Can Happen Roadshow," billed
as "a musical comic satire on the arms race," is now offered
audiences across the country during Underground Railway Theater
tours. It is one of nine shows in the group's repertoire—which also
includes "Dreaming Branch," a suspenseful, yet gentle tale especially for children.

This particular Friday there is no curtain on the stage as the per-
formance begins. Two men stand there, waiting quietly as the
students assemble. Both are dressed in costumes of unbleached

cotton: loose pullover shirts with rope belts, unfitted pants. Wes Sanders, wearing moccasins, stands in front of the set. John Lewandowski seats himself at left, surrounded by enough musical instruments to make up his own ensemble—which is essentially what he is. There's a harmonium, a guitar, two recorders, an autoharp, a gourd harp, and a number of percussion instruments, all of which he will use to provide background for the show. And the two men, along with a series of puppets, make up the entire cast for the day.

Sanders starts the program casually, conversationally, and the noisy youngsters quiet immediately. They, perhaps best of any audience, recognize quickly the ways of an expert storyteller.

"Do you see this?" Sanders asks, reaching for a brightly-painted object perched atop one of the "mesas." "Can you tell what it is?"

"It's a smurf!" wisecracks one of the youngsters, drawing giggles from the others.

"I'll give you a hint," says Sanders, and with his right hand, he draws the round-faced object up, past his horizontal left hand.

"It's the sun," says a girl.

"The sun kachina!" pronounces Sanders . . . and the story begins. It is a tale weaving fact and fantasy, history and prophesy, as Sanders, the only actor, draws the youngsters with him, switching roles from story teller to the puppet heroine Dreaming Branch and to a whole range of other puppet characters: There's Spider Grandmother, the cackling, but eminently wise embodiment of Dreaming Branch's own heritage; there's a slangy snake, who turns into a dog, a black bear and a straw horse; there's a huge, fuzzy, yellow spider; there's an eagle, strong enough to carry Dreaming Branch through the skies.

In the middle of the show, the children gasp appreciatively as Sanders, on a darkened, lightning-lit stage, suddenly appears from a tepee that has magically risen mid-stage; Sanders is in flowing costume, with a giant mask that covers his whole head. He has become the basso profundo Indian kachina of the fourth world,

Wes Sanders

The show at Conant Elementary School

who holds the tiny, frightened Dreaming Branch and gives her the charge to set out on a long journey, taking the message to all Hopis that they must not only treasure peace, but also stop those who would harm the world. Otherwise, he prophesies, the world will end as the angry sun kachina "will suddenly strike in all his fury, with fire and wind such as never seen," after which the evil men will "set off another fire storm, this time covering all the earth . . . and the earth will become a burning grave." If Dreaming Branch succeeds, he prophesies, "the time will come when people of peace will be not only Hopi, not only brown and white, but all colors and all languages."

The show ends too soon, but with enthusiastic applause. Then hands shoot up.

"Did the story really happen?"

Part of it, reply Sanders and Lewandowski. There was, indeed, an ancient Indian prophesy about the end of the world. The Indians did recognize a kachina of the fourth world. Several of the incidents referred to did happen. But Dreaming Branch is a fantasy.

"How did the tepee rise like that?"

"There is a third pole you didn't see," says Lewandowski, demonstrating how it works.

"How could you play two recorders at once," asks one of the girls, recalling several moments during the play when many youngsters were more entranced with the musician than the story line, as Lewandowski produced ancient-sounding, reedy harmonies with two recorders in his mouth.

"Just stick them both in and hope," he answers, laughing.

The question and answer time is important, Lewandowski and Sanders believe; their show is as much about education as about story-telling. Sanders and Lewandowski are two members of the small professional acting team that makes up the Underground Railway Theater, headquartered in Cambridge, Mass. The other permanent members are Debra Wise, an actress, and Rosemarie Straijer, business manager and singer. "Dreaming Branch" is the major children's show of the troupe. Other shows are fashioned for family or adult audiences. All, like "Dreaming Branch," offer entertainment laced with messages, for the Underground Railway Theater is more than an eminently talented theater company; it is also a collective of strongly committed activists.

"One of the main things that art does . . . that we try to do with our art . . . is to make people feel empowered," said Sanders. "It's a big word these days, but it's a good word. It means that if you feel like you can change something, then you can."

The nuclear arms race is one of the things the Underground Railway troupe would like to change. Ditto, alcoholism; ditto, problems surrounding the abortion issue. They've done a show about the start of the labor movement; they're working toward a show on Central America. Although everything on their schedule is entertaining—their "Anything Can Happen Roadshow," for instance, has its roots squarely back in vaudeville—there is not a single piece of pure entertainment. Personally, said Sanders, "I wouldn't be able to be just an entertainer. I couldn't live with that."

There is one other aspect to their shows: All are innovative, artistically avant-garde. "Aesthetically, our stock in trade is a kind of series of ongoing experiments in the relationship between puppets, actors, masks and music; that's our panoply," said Sanders.

Some of their shows require full symphony orchestra; one, a chamber group. Thus, when Lewandowski—an able puppeteer as well as musician—takes the role of the soldier in "A Soldier's Tale," the soldier appears in the form of a 4½-foot high wagon puppet. The music, Stravinsky's "Firebird Suite," is provided by Collage, a group of Boston Symphony players, "young Turks who like to play new and difficult music," said Sanders. As in other group works based on existing plots, the story line in "The Soldier's Tale" has been revised, this one incorporating the Underground Railway's concern about past and future wars. Some of the scripts are originals by members of the troupe; Sanders researched and wrote "Dreaming Branch."

Underground Railway Theater was founded in 1974, while Sanders was teaching and directing the theater at Oberlin College in Ohio. Oberlin, he explained, "was the end of the Midwestern branch of the [abolitionists'] underground railroad. We named the company for the underground railroad because we are, in our own humble way, continuing some of the ideals of that institution."

Sanders, now 43, taught at Oberlin from 1967 to 1978, a period during which he finally fused politics and art, he said. But he had started in that direction earlier, while studying for his Ph.D. in drama at Northwestern University. During that period, he began getting stage roles in Chicago, fairly often teaming with an actress/activist who introduced him to her world of political action. In 1963, he said, "I started doing marches and started getting a little bit of consciousness." When opposition to the Vietnam War developed, Sanders began to do anti-war street theater.

His political awareness also got a boost in the classroom. "I specialized in modern drama when I was taking my dissertation work," he said, "so I ended up reading a lot of pretty interesting people, like Ibsen, Shaw and Brecht . . . very political playwrights."

And, in fact, Germany's Bertolt Brecht, author of plays like "Mother Courage," "The Good Woman of Setzuan" and "Caucasian Chalk Circle," became an inspiration for Sanders on at least two levels: Brecht offered an artistic model, because he is "the person, both as a director and as a playwright, who has best managed to do theatrical art that is both politically effective and artistically marvelous," said Sanders. And, he provided a cultural model, because he worked in a cooperative environment: "He wrote 'The Three Penny Opera' . . . in his apartment with all kinds of people knocking around, boxers and stuff. He would throw out lines and say, 'What would go in here well?' 'Whatdaya think about this?' and people would throw in a little line or a word."

That, said Sanders, was the example for Underground Railway's choice of organization—as a collective. Now he believes that "the reason our work is as good as it is, is because it's collective, because three heads do it whenever possible, and even more, sometimes."

"Everybody in our company," he added, "regardless of seniority, is paid exactly the same amount. Decisions are made collectively by consensus." As a result, "there are none of the ego trips" . . . no temptations to join commercial ventures, even though each member has been offered lucrative opportunities. "We've made the choice," said Sanders, "and every day we know that the choice costs us something, but that it allows us to be what we really want to be. I think that's as important, actually, as the art, itself."

A significant part of what's important about it, of course, is the chance to offer audiences a new way of thinking about things. The troupe's calendar is full, and there is seldom a problem with the political content of their shows. Sanders has found that "if you are entertaining, if you're funny, if you're moving, if the art is good, people don't mind if you're political. The only time they start minding is when it's not good, or when you're banging them over the head with something." The Underground Railway avoids "banging over the head." Their forte, which Sanders again credits to the inspiration of Brecht, is "dialectical" theater: presenting artistically-packaged ideas that challenge the audience's old notions of how things work.

Often that means that different levels of "message" get through to different members of the audience. "Dreaming Branch," for instance, contains a clear anti-nuclear message, yet many of the Conant School youngsters probably failed to pick it up, said Sanders. "Few kids below the sixth grade get that." But they do pick up on the conflict between the values of the Hopi and those who endanger the world, and they sense the dignity of the Indians. They recognize that some stereotypes don't always work, as they see a large, deep-voiced man tenderly play the part of a little girl, and as some of the scary or ugly characters turn out to be "good," while some physically attractive characters are obviously "bad." And, perhaps, they sense that their efforts—like Dreaming Branch's—can make a difference.

Introducing "Dreaming Branch," Sanders tells the youngsters that his sun kachina was made by a native American, and that it serves as a rattle in the Hopi beandance ceremony—"a ceremony about growing: sprouts into beans, cubs into bears, girls and boys into women and men." And, he tells the youngsters, "John and I are inviting you into a kind of ceremony as well. It's not a bean dance ceremony, obviously, because we're not Hopi Indians. But it is a kind of ceremony to help prevent the end of the world."

14. THE YOUNG SHOW THE WAY
Jill Freidberg, Portland, Ore.

> *In a democratic society, we expect young people to be thinking for themselves—developing choices—in matters that powerfully affect their lives.*
> —*Psychiatrist John E. Mack, Harvard University*

Portland's Catlin Gabel is a small, private school, inobtrusively nestled among trees and rolling hills. Standards are high for lower, middle and upper school students. All are expected to share in the school's high aspirations: to "develop [each student's] fullest powers as an individual and as a group member," as Founder Ruth Catlin wrote in 1928.

If she were there today, Catlin would offer a satisfied nod toward senior Jill Freidberg, who entered the school as a second grader and now is among 200 or so students in the upper school. Next year she'll be going to college—she's applied at the University of California at Santa Cruz, Occidental, Vassar and Tufts—to study marine biology.

Whichever school wins her will get a prime product of Catlin Gabel: Freidberg, a lanky 18, is both her own person and a catalyst for others. While adults wonder how to help young people face the nuclear threat, Freidberg has shown that some of those same young people already have their own clear vision.

Back in the eighth grade, Freidberg approached teacher Steve Saslow following a social sciences unit on Russia. The class, she recalled, "would get in these big talks about relations between the Soviet Union and the United States, and I started getting really worried because I didn't understand anything about it."

"I went to Steve Saslow and asked, 'Is there something that can be done, because nobody in the middle school, I think, understands; I think a lot of people are scared.'" Soon Freidberg and a friend and Saslow worked up a special three-day nuclear curriculum for the middle and upper schools: "classes and writing groups, just about their opinions and about peace and nuclear war," said Freidberg. In addition, there were movies and a panel discussion.

The following year, a visit to the school by Dr. Victor Sidel, one of the founders of Physicians for Social Responsibility, inspired another move. Freidberg—by then an upper school freshman—was one of several students who "decided maybe to start just a group at Catlin of students who were interested in doing something for the peace movement." Her sister Susanne, a junior, took part, too.

The first three months, Freidberg said, were spent "just trying to define what we wanted to do." Their goal, they decided, would be "to educate other people our age on what they could do." Eventually, students from 8 to 10 Portland schools got involved in the group, which named itself Student Alliance for Nuclear Awareness (SANA). They held monthly meetings, started a newsletter, did some fundraising, and—Freidberg, at least—got arrested.

That arrest took place on tax day, April 15, 1984. SANA had spawned a sub-group, No Minor Cause ("kind of a pun, you know"), for students interested in doing civil disobedience. Freidberg was among them. They decided on three tax-day protests, starting at a southeast Portland factory that was making parts for Trident missiles.

"Nobody in Portland knew that there was this factory across the river that was making parts for missiles," said Freidberg. "We figured that if we went and blockaded it, it would make the news. It did; it made the front page."

About 200 Portlanders from different groups participated, said Freidberg. Some young members of her group spent the night at the Freidberg home; then Jill's parents drove them to the factory area, getting them there at 4 a.m. "They didn't drop us off at the

Jill Freidberg

factory, they dropped us off across the bridge," said Freidberg. "We wanted to walk a ways together and talk about it." (Yes, Freidberg agreed, smiling, she knows her parents are unusual, but both are involved in the peace movement, themselves. Her father, Stan, is a doctor and a member of PSR; both he and her mother, Colleen, an artist, are active in Beyond War.)

"So," said Freidberg, "we all went down and piled up around the doors." Eventually, riot police and horses were brought in, and "it was real scary," said Freidberg. "They train the horses to step on people," she explained, "not forcibly, but just to put their hooves on people. Then [the police] would grab whatever was there and just throw it." Nobody was seriously hurt, said Freidberg, but she did get bumped around: "I got a bruise on the back of my head, because they grabbed my feet and yanked."

"But they didn't want to arrest us," she added. "They would move us out of the door, then a couple of people would get in, and then we would all pile back up in front of the door again and they'd pick us up and throw us out again." The demonstrators stayed at the plant until closing.

Then they moved downtown to the Reagan-Bush campaign office. This time the young people took the lead, about 20 of them cramming inside the small office, demanding to talk to Reagan on the phone. But now the authorities became more serious: "They blocked off the street and brought in three paddy wagons and threw us in." Freidberg and the others under 18—and that included most of the young demonstrators—wound up at a juvenile detention center. "They let me out like four hours later," she said. "They handed me a bus ticket and said, 'There's the door.'" After all that, Freidberg kept going—'to the post office, where people were turning in their tax forms, and we had this big rally."

The day, of course, brought instant fame back on campus: "They said, 'We saw you getting dragged by the police on TV, it was great!'" Freidberg recalled with a laugh. And, she added, "It is exciting to say, oh, you know, I went out and got arrested." But even more, "it felt really good to be there with 200 people who were all just really intent on doing this."

That sophomore year also had other, less confrontive satisfactions. She and another girl, a senior, organized an all-city dance . . . signed up three local bands . . . rounded up a bunch of door prizes . . . and made $1,000 on $4-per-person tickets. The money went to Peter Watkins, a professional filmmaker planning to produce "The Global Anti-Nuclear War Movie," which the students felt was worth supporting. The next fall, SANA won a Tom McCall Great Kids Award (named after the late Oregon governor).

But the pace slowed down during Freidberg's junior year. There were growing-up problems with parents . . . a good friend committed suicide . . . "everything kind of went bad." And, of course, older members of the original SANA group were leaving high school. Her sister Susanne had left for Yale to study anthropology. Freidberg still worked some with the group, still went out on Hiroshima Day to paint shadows on the pavement; but the activity level was dropping. And fall this year has been taken up mostly with typical senior problems, like filling out college applications.

That does not mean she has dropped the peace movement, said Freidberg. "I don't know how much I can do here now at Catlin and in Portland, since it seems to kind of have tapered off. I'd like to try and get it going again. But I'd definitely like to get involved in some kind of peace work at college."

"Then sometimes I think, I don't know, I'll just kind of take backstage and do volunteer work and put in my little part," she said. She looks forward to other things as well—things as diverse as poetry writing and, perhaps, politics. At 18, it is hard to know exactly what the future holds.

Yet, Freidberg already has some definite ideas about the nuclear confrontation and what it has done to the world and its peoples. She's thought, for instance, about the nuclear nightmares that some children now report. Such dreams happen most, she thinks, between fifth and ninth grades. Those are the years when young people first become aware of the problem, but don't understand it, she believes. "I think once kids get a little older, either they understand it or they just get to the point where there are so many other things on their minds that they kind of deny it . . . say it doesn't concern me now. They just kind of get over the fear and say, 'Forget it, I can't think about it.'"

"Several of my friends and I, we all read 'On the Beach' in the eighth grade," she said. "We all had 'On the Beach' nightmares. We all had dreams that they had dropped the bomb and we all had to take little cyanide pills, and so we did." There have been other dreams, she added—"one where I was with my whole school and we were up in Seattle near Puget Sound, where they have the base up there. We were all on boats, and they told us that there was going to be a bomb dropped, and that the best thing to do was to jump into the water, because it would be boiling and that would be the quickest way to die. So it did, and we all jumped into the water." Freidberg laughed nervously. "I don't know, I guess we all died."

Yet, Freidberg is optimistic. She sees no imminent danger of nuclear war. "Not right now, I don't," she said. "What I really think is, I don't think that either side is going to say, 'I can't deal with this policy, I can't deal with this situation, it's time to bomb them.'" Should there be a nuclear exchange, she added, "I think it will either be in the hands of a less-developed country, or an accident."

But ending the problem will be a lengthy process, she believes: "To resolve something like this will take generations of time. I think [it will require] sort of the Beyond War attitude, where a different attitude about it has to start being taught. I don't think one day we can just say, OK, let's get rid of all the bombs. Because as soon as any really sticky situation comes up, we can just build them again."

In the meantime, Freidberg sees some steps families can take: "I think it [would help] if today's parents of small children would teach their kids more peaceful attitudes . . . if we got [rid of] the stuff that is on Saturday morning cartoons and after-school TV, where people are blowing each other away every five minutes, and [took] the GI Joe commando laser guns off the shelves in toy stores. Things like that. That's a first step at teaching today's kids that they don't have to go out and blow each other away to solve the problem."

Still part kid, herself, Freidberg has some advice for other young people. "Even though we have this great student group, I see so much . . . [people saying] forget it, who cares. Any time I hear anybody saying something like that, I get so frustrated. I just wish I could make people realize that if there's something they don't like, that they can't sit around and wait for it to change . . . and then, when it doesn't change, get upset about it."

"I'm so sick of hearing people . . . when there happens to be a discussion going on, like in a class, about war or anything like that, all of a sudden they say, 'Oh, my God, that's so terrible; something has to be done.' Then they just forget about it. I just wish there were some way I could say, 'Well, if something has to be done, then do it, because "somebody" isn't going to do it for you!'"

15. TALKING TOUGH STUFF WITH STUDENTS
Merrell Frankel, Los Angeles

We have lovingly fed our children from babyhood with stories that have a happy ending, and it is too painful to discuss with them the very real prospect of their annihilation.
—*Barbara Tizard, University of London Institute of Education*

Merrell Frankel is talking about inner peace with 30-plus seventh grade students at Los Angeles' Berendo Junior High School. She's about to ask them to draw a picture and write a short story describing a personal moment of peace. But first she tells about one of her own, one that goes like this:

"I have two kids living with me. I get up at 5 in the morning and go outside. I sit on my porch, and no one's yelling, 'Mommy, where's my sneaker?' and 'Are there Cheerios for breakfast?' I have nothing I have to do. The phone's not ringing, and I just sit there. The sky's changing colors. Maybe the moon's just fading. The morning star is out. And that's my moment of peace."

In Frankel's classroom, that's the introduction to the new nuclear issues curriculum adopted by the giant Los Angeles Unified School District. By the time Frankel's students move on to 8th grade, they will know about Trident missiles and nuclear bomb damage and Soviet-American differences and INF treaties, as well as about the benefits nuclear technology can offer. They will also know that if there is to be peace in this world, it will likely be up to them.

Berendo Junior High School has been Merrell Frankel's chosen

Merrell Frankel

assignment for the past eight years. She is the kind of teacher parents pray for: quick to smile, quick to praise, able to inspire and able to discipline—all without students quite realizing that they are getting some of the best teaching in the Los Angeles Unified School District. Frankel is that jewel among teachers, one who has taught at private schools, taught at the college level, taught in magnet schools for the best and brightest . . . and who has chosen now to teach at Berendo, a school where English is a second language for 85% of the students, where 99% of the families live below the poverty line, and where many students are refugees from war-torn countries.

But, Frankel proves year after year, these are students who learn. And before this year is up, hers will be tearing stories out of newspapers, trying to dialogue with their parents, and—some of them, at least—writing congressmen and others, telling them that the kids in this world need to be heard.

"The important thing is, our kids don't know they live in the nuclear age," said Frankel. "And for the last 20 years, people that were educated were not taught they live in a nuclear age, and what the issues were around them, and what the possibilities are, and what the prospects are." Los Angeles city schools and Frankel are attempting to change that.

A year and a half ago, Frankel was asked to serve as one of four writers of the nuclear issues curriculum. School board member Jackie Goldberg had battled for months to get such a program introduced, and finally won. The team chosen to develop the curriculum included an elementary and secondary teacher for social science and for science. Frankel represented secondary social science. And in that way, she became the first Los Angeles teacher to introduce the secondary nuclear issues curriculum—at least the social studies part—as she tested her lesson plans last year at Berendo.

Yes, she knows that some experts say adults have no right to push such a heavy load on youngsters. But, she discovered, "the amazing thing is that I never felt I was pushing it on them." Instead, they were eager to know.

That was exactly what the youngsters, themselves, said last year when CNN visited the classroom. Frankel was teaching a lesson on poetry at the time, and she let the cameraman and reporter roam by themselves. Later, she watched the tape. "The reporter kept saying, 'Doesn't this scare you?' And they kept saying, 'No. We need to know this, and other kids need to know.' 'What scares me is, the other kids aren't learning this.' 'What scares me is, my parents don't know.'"

Frankel's own experience as a teacher backs up that last comment. "I don't think adults talk to kids about nuclear issues," she said, "and I think that scares kids more than anything else." Yet, it's tough on the parents, as well, she realizes. They have their own fears, and they don't know how to talk about such frightening situations with their children. And there's one other touchy problem, because—especially as the class progresses—"the kids know a lot more than the parents do."

Those youngsters, themselves, begin with more fear than knowledge, said Frankel. After that initial discussion about "peace," Frankel asks what the word "nuclear" means. Almost all of the response—"99% of it"—is negative. They know almost nothing about the positive potential—in nuclear medicine, for instance. Almost all think in terms of "war and the bomb and what the bomb could do." Yet, their knowledge about what the bomb really could do is "far off from reality."

"They go to extremes," Frankel has found. "Either the whole world is going to blow up, or very small, localized areas." So, the curriculum attempts to set them straight.

As far as the bomb is concerned, Frankel brings the lesson home: She drops a one-megaton bomb on Berendo Junior High School. Using a map of Los Angeles, she draws concentric circles, then tells the students graphically what would occur in the zero- to one-mile range, then up to three miles. It's harsh reality, and it's a tough one for the kids. "I had to keep stopping the lesson, because I could see the shock," Frankel said, recalling the last such presentation. "And as we named streets that they lived on disappearing in the fire storms, tears were in one girl's eyes."

And so, Frankel had moved to the next message, because her goal is to inform and empower, not to frighten. "I said, 'You know, this is really scary stuff, but at the same time, it's been around for 40 years, and I'm still here, and your parents are here. And we've survived. What I'm really letting you know is that you're inheriting a world that has this in it. You're going to have to learn that it's part of the world, and learn as much as you can about it, because that's what it's all about. You can't pretend it's not there. But you have to know that I'm still here, and it's been around since I was a kid. And that's the important thing. Let's take a deep breath and figure out what we're going to do, and let's learn as much as we can.' "

At this point, those earlier lessons—when the class talked about peace and listened to each other's fears—paid off. Students had already gotten to know and accept each other; if some youngsters were afraid, "it was OK, because they had friends in the class." Even she, herself, was sometimes moved to tears, Frankel admitted.

Yet, said Frankel, it was not a depressing lesson. She'd even talked with the mother of the girl who had cried. Were there any nightmares? Had the girl been upset? "No," the mother said. "In fact, she's reading the paper and cutting it up like mad, doing twice as much work for your class." And the girl, herself? She'd said, "It's something we need to know."

The thing that makes it all come together, Frankel believes, is that last step: stressing the positive—the fact that there are, indeed, benefits from nuclear technology, that we can survive, and that when it comes to the problems, there are ways that all of us, including kids, can change things.

It's that step that gives the youngsters hope—not just about the nuclear issue, but about themselves. And that's the basic idea about the whole nuclear curriculum, said Frankel. It's not just to take an issue and look into it in depth, although that's part of it. It's also to teach children skills and belief in their own abilities. The result is "student empowerment," Frankel said, as they learn that "they're capable, they're gaining knowledge, they know how to go about it."

Frankel admits that she, herself, had a lot to learn before she set to work on the curriculum. She'd been involved in the anti-war and civil rights movements during the 1960s, but had mostly dropped out of political or organizational work after coming to California a decade ago.

She and the elementary teacher working with her on the social studies curriculum realized that what they had at the beginning, as they began researching their topic, was "emotions and feelings." They set out to get knowledge.

"I wrote to the defense department," Frankel recalled. "I interviewed people who worked at weapons plants, I spoke with [nuclear physicist Edward] Teller and numerous other people, I spoke to people at the Union of Concerned Scientists, I spoke to other teachers, I read curriculums from across the country, I must have had 11 cartons of books dealing with the subject at my house, I ran a computer search to see what other resources were available in putting together lessons or resources for students and teachers to read, I previewed I don't know how many videotapes people had put together, I read novels written for young readers about the day after the bomb, I previewed interviews with Soviet students on these issues. Anything that came out in the media, I tried to become at least somewhat familiar with. I stole the best of everything."

Frankel already had experience writing curriculum: Earlier, she had written the seventh grade social studies program for the entire city. So, when it came time to put all her new-found nuclear issues knowledge into a formal format, she knew what was needed. Segments on nuclear issues would be fitted into existing classes at the various grades, matching learning objectives at each level. In the seventh grade, for instance, the subject would slip into "current events" during social science. Meanwhile, that information would be coordinated with the seventh grade science program, where students would learn related lessons about technology.

It would be challenging to present the social studies segments, Frankel and her collaborator knew. While the science teachers could offer technical information, the social scientists would face the "gut issues." That meant controversy. And that's touchy in the public schools.

Finally, said Frankel, the two teachers realized their best tactic would be to continue doing what good teachers have always done: to "teach skills . . . tools that will enable the kids to go out and survive in a world." In a social science class, that would mean "critical thinking . . . understanding outlines . . . looking at accuracy . . . looking at cause and effect . . . looking at behavior, seeing relationships." And that's how they did it, wrapping the nuclear information into skills lessons appropriate for each grade. Children would not be told what to think; they would be encouraged "to gather information, collect information and analyze information." They would draw their own conclusions.

Teachers are comfortable with that approach, said Frankel. And her own classes already have proved it works.

Frankel has a favorite story, suggesting just how well the system does work. It happened last year, when a delegation of Soviet women visited Berendo. They had specifically asked to observe a peace class. So, with 36 students already crowded into Frankel's bungalow classroom, 40 visitors pushed in among them—the Soviets, their interpreters, school district officials and the press.

The lesson that day was identifying world problems and listing them in order of importance. The youngsters had made such a list several days earlier, before starting their study of nuclear issues, but "peace" had wound up at the bottom of the pile, and many youngsters wanted a new vote. This time "peace" headed the list.

"Then," Frankel said, "they had to sit down and formulate ways of working toward this. If this is an issue, how are we going to go about solving it?"

"They worked in small groups. Then they read to the Soviet women what their groups had decided . . . They came up with marvelous things, on typical seventh grade developmental levels. Things like, we should have a children's congress, where kids get together from all over; we should learn more about the Soviets."

The youngsters stayed after class to exchange questions with the Soviets. The students included "Vietnamese refugees who've fled from Soviet troops," said Frankel, "and who had very negative feelings."

"Suddenly, they were confronted with these magnificent women who were smiling and understanding and who desperately wanted friendship." At one point, a Soviet woman turned to a Vietnamese youngster and asked, "What do you think of us?" Frankel recalled his hesitant answer:

"He said, 'I was so scared of you before. Russian has always been a dirty word. But I learned something. I learned that you are very beautiful, and that I'm very glad you're here, and that we should be . . . '" and he stuttered and stuttered, and finally said, ' . . . comrades.'"

"It was," Frankel said, her own voice quiet, "a marvelous moment."

How much of a role should schools play in dealing with children's fears . . . or in preparing them to help solve the problem?

"Preventing nuclear war is the greatest ethical priority of our age," wrote Eric Markusen, of the University of Minnesota and Southwest State University, and John B. Harris, University of Minnesota, in the August 1984 Harvard Educational Review, an issue of the magazine dedicated to nuclear concerns. "Unless the educational institutions of democratic society provide citizens with opportunities to learn about the facts and issues of nuclear war, the society will be severely handicapped in its struggle for survival."

Yet, schools—especially at the elementary and secondary level—often are hesitant to introduce classwork on nuclear subjects. There is fear that such classes will be seen as political, even leftist. Teachers doubt their own ability to present such information. And educators wonder if such classes would help the children rather than simply scare them.

What about those fears?

It turns out that even the experts disagree on how much the threat of nuclear devastation affects the average American child. Psychiatrists John E. Mack and Robert Jay Lifton—the first from Harvard University, the second from Yale—say the effect is dramatic and widespread. "Many young people feel that the situation is now hopeless and that nuclear war will occur before they have a chance to complete their lives," Mack reported in the August 1984 Harvard Educational Review. Lifton cited a similar conclusion during a Boston conference on the nuclear threat, then warned that such young people may decide to live for the moment, turning to promiscuity, drug and alcohol abuse, apathy and irresponsibility.

However, psychiatrist Robert Coles—who, like Mack, teaches at Harvard University—disagreed: Those children most worried about the nuclear threat tend to have parents who have passed on their own concerns, he contended—parents who have the time and money to worry about long-range social issues and who already are involved in opposing the arms race. Poor children, Coles determined, worry about "more immediate threats—the apocalypse of a broken slum world, the holocaust of a dazed, despairing migrant farm community." That report was carried by The New York Times Magazine Dec. 8, 1985, in an adaptation from Coles' "The Moral Life of Children."

Merrell Frankel's experience, perhaps, supported both positions: Before the subject of peace was broached in the classroom, few youngsters rated it a major world problem. But once they had some basic facts, peace quickly climbed to the top of the list and the students became anxious for more knowledge—even became angry that adults had failed to share such important information.

Was that dumping adult responsibility onto innocent children? She didn't think so; she strongly believes kids have both the need and right to know information that sets the agenda for the world they're growing into. If adults haven't done so well at solving the problem so far, how will kids do better if they have to take over the world without the basic know-how?

What about that charge that such classes are political, even leftist? Drawing pictures, writing letters, and talking to parents and friends can, of course, be defined as a mild form of political activism. And, for some, any variety of activism is "leftist," even though programs such as Los Angeles' are carefully crafted to present both pros and cons. Frankel would define the whole issue differently, arguing that what she is doing is giving students the basic tools of citizenship.

When you get right down to it, the basic question behind all of this may not really have much to do with kids, anyway. The real question? How willing are adults to address these issues.

That has been the conclusion of one Los Angeles area psychotherapist who has made a specialty of dealing with the nuclear issue. Her name is Lynn Greenberg, and she is founder of the Thursday Night Group (TNG), which attempts to "help adults and children address the emotions that get in the way of people being able to learn about and respond to the nuclear challenge today."

"Children today live in a double jeopardy," said Greenberg, who participated in development of the Los Angeles curriculum. "One is that they truly believe they may not live out their lifetime. And second, they believe the adults in the world don't care." But adults have their own pair of problems: "They feel very often overwhelmed by it. So they don't want the kids to bring up questions, because it just creates problems for themselves."

"Second, as parents we're used to protecting our children. When

I talk to my children about crossing a street . . . taking candy from
strangers . . . I'm able to teach them all these preventive things
designed to protect them. When you deal with the nuclear issue,
you can't do that. You can't say, 'It'll be all right, dear.' . . . That
makes parents feel even more impotent."

So TNG put together a program of workshops, handbooks and
videotapes for adults—especially teachers, but parents and
therapists, as well. The idea was to help them—and children—
deal with the fear and then get on to the problem. Central to their
concept is an acronym, SAFE, that works this way:

S: Share feelings
A: Accept them
F: Fact find, form an opinion, formulate a plan
E: Encourage

As far as formulating a plan, said Greenberg, the steps chosen
should be "small, short-term and measurable." The final step,
encourage, means to join forces with others. "Alone, it's too overwhelming," Greenberg explained. "You need the support system
to encourage you to continue sharing your feelings and accepting
them and functioning."

This, of course, was exactly the concept followed by Merrell
Frankel in her classroom. It is "very urgent" to deal with children
in this way, and to give them a sense of empowerment, said
Greenberg. "We're creating tomorrow's citizens!"

Besides, she has this "what if" kind of dream of her own: "I
still think the world's going to have peace when a couple of the
world's leaders' kids walk in, sit down and say, 'OK, Dad,' or, 'OK,
Grandpa, sit down, let's talk.'"

IV

ON THE CAMPUS

During the Vietnam era, it was college students who seemed to be leading the drive toward peace. Young people ditched class to take part in demonstrations and sit-ins. They embroidered peace signs on clothes, painted them on cars—and sometimes on faces. They turned political, demanding that the war end.

There may not have been any "typical" campus, but one that graphically told the story of that era was the University of Wisconsin at Madison. The surrounding community—till then a peaceful college town—held its collective breath as draft cards were burned, Students for a Democratic Society set up shop, and radical politics exploded.

At one point, city police—called to quell a demonstration against Dow Chemical—moved on campus with batons swinging, unintentionally spawning a full-on riot. Later, National Guard troops moved into the city. Finally, in the early '70s, one angry activist threw a bomb into an army-sponsored research center, blowing up the building and killing a graduate student.

With that seemingly senseless killing—tied to the fact that the Vietnam War was winding down—the steam seemed to go out of the movement, and Madison began to settle back into its previous serenity.

Today, the campus at Madison is still calm; students here—as at most schools today—are more into careers than politics; big business looks good again. Across the country, some activists shake their heads, not quite understanding why the primary push toward peace and justice goals seems to have moved off campus.

Yet, students have shown some of the old activism in protests against South African apartheid and other special issues. And there is growing enthusiam on another front, as well: the classroom. Increasing numbers of students are studying peace, arms and disarmament, or similar topics in academic settings.

Some of those programs are small and innovative. Orange, Calif.'s Chapman College, for instance, required all 400 of its fall 1987 freshmen to attend a one-semester, three-days-a-week seminar on war and peace. The idea wasn't just to talk about war and peace, said director Marilyn Harran; it was to get students to dig into a major contemporary problem and to sharpen their critical thinking.

Programs on some campuses—especially at the larger universities—are large and formal. Some offer degrees, including doctorates. Others, working on a smaller scale, incorporate their concerns into existing curriculums or offer special seminars.

The University of Wisconsin at Madison now has a Center for International Cooperation and Security Studies, according to Peter Dorner, dean of International Studies and Programs. The center issues a newsletter, "Perspectives on War and Peace," offers a lecture series and encourages introduction of peace studies into course work. In the summer of 1987, it held an institute on regulating conflicts and on the prospects of nuclear war.

A number of the larger, more formal campus programs were inspired by a sequence begun by Stanford University in 1971. Theirs was one of the first academic attempts to deal with the nuclear threat. One objective of that program today is a very special one: to train those who one day will actually be helping to decide this country's nuclear policy. That is a role already held by one of the program's co-directors, Dr. Sidney Drell.

16. SO TOMORROW'S DECISION-MAKERS MAY KNOW
Sidney D. Drell, Stanford, Calif.

> *I know of no safe repository of the ultimate power of society but the people. And if we think them not enlightened enough, the remedy is not to take the power from them, but to inform them by education.*
> —*Thomas Jefferson, 1820*

The year was 1960. Russia had recently launched Sputnik. In the United States, government officials quickly sensed the new challenge . . . and recalled how a team of some of the nation's brightest young scientists had captured global scientific leadership during World War II. Maybe such a team could do it again. The result was the Jason Group, and one of those invited to participate was a professor named Sidney D. Drell.

Today Drell, a physicist, serves as co-director of Stanford University's Center for International Security and Arms Control and as deputy director and executive head of theoretical physics at the Stanford Linear Accelerator Center. A quarter century ago, when the call came to join the Jason Group, he had only recently moved to Stanford after several years of teaching particle physics at MIT.

Drell saw the Jason Group as an opportunity—that "there were important technical studies to be made which could contribute to improving the chances for a peaceful world." And the problems brought before the group did include major ones: how to verify treaties without on-site inspections, for instance; how to deal with both offensive and defensive weapons.

From Jason Group, Drell moved to the President's Science

Advisory Committee, on which he would serve under both Johnson and Nixon. He's been adviser to the Arms Control and Disarmament Agency, the National Security Council, the Department of Defense and "so forth." It's been a lengthy career, mixing academia and the world of high-level decision making. For most of three decades, it has involved national security advising; it has led to an intimate knowledge of both pros and cons of nuclear weaponry. And it has turned Drell into something of a scientist/philosopher.

In his book, "Facing the Threat of Nuclear Weapons," Drell wrote that for the scientist, such "weapons of absolute destruction" present a new dilemma. The scientist "is lured from his laboratory into the outer world by the attraction of power and influence, and sometimes by challenging technical opportunities," Drell observed, but may find that, "like Faust, he has sold his soul to the devil." Never before have scientists dealt with "weapons whose use could mean the end of civilization as we know it—if not of mankind itself. And never before has the gulf been so great between the scientific arguments—even the very language of science—and the political leaders whose decisions will shape the future."

Students who will someday be the nation's scientists and decision-makers are among those Drell hopes to reach through the Stanford program. One "distinguishing aspect" of the program, says a Center brochure, "is the high priority which Stanford has given to attracting, motivating, and training the next generation of arms control and international security specialists." It seems to be working: "I can't go to Washington now to testify in Congress or visit a legislator, almost without fail, without running into a graduate of this course who's working on the problem," said Drell.

But he's also pleased that the program's introductory course is one of the university's most popular among the general university population—that it's been chosen as a "must" course by the student paper. He would like to see all students become "informed, responsible citizens when it comes to voting, thinking and acting in this area." All colleges and universities should offer such programs, he believes.

At Stanford, with an abundance of both military and anti-nuclear proponents available locally, plus the clout to attract top talent from other areas, the program offers a wide range of viewpoints. Participants one recent year included a former deputy director of the United States Arms Control and Disarmament Agency; a researcher from the Institute of International Studies, Beijing; the executive director of the Research Institute for Peace and Security, Tokyo; the president emeritus of the Massachusetts Institute of Technology; a former director of the Livermore National Laboratory; a former deputy director of the Central Intelligence Agency, and a long list of others. Both government experts and peace activists get invited to appear. The goal here is to help students make up their own minds, not do the job for them.

As far as his own role, Drell sees himself as a physicist, bringing the scientist's logical mind to problems. His conclusions often differ with those of the government. Drell, for instance, opposes the Strategic Defense Initiative. "Much of the criticism some of us have right now of Star Wars is that we think that it's technical fantasy to [expect to] achieve an 'astrodome,' or a totally-protective umbrella against weapons that are so destructive as nuclear weapons," he explained. "I think this goal of Star Wars technically cannot be achieved." More than that, he believes it actually encourages escalation of the arms race, as the Soviets counter the anticipated new American weaponry. "For Star Wars to lead to any prospects of a safer world," he added, "it would have to be coupled to restraints on offensive nuclear weapons."

As Drell sees it, a better plan would be the controlled decrease in nuclear weaponry. It could be done fairly, he believes. His own idea is to simply "add up the number of existing warheads on each side and choose some number lower than the present level, and let each side decide which ones to keep and which ones to destroy."

Arms control negotiations could determine more specific limitations on future weapons, he added. Government officials have called his plan unworkable; Drell doesn't buy their arguments.

Actually, he said, "we could get rid of nine-tenths of what we have, and we'd have more than enough. I can't see any possible rationale that more than 1,000 nuclear warheads [are needed] on each side. [Yet,] in our strategic forces, we have roughly 10,000, and overall—including our battlefield weapons and short-range weapons—we have more than 25,000. I think that's insane."

"We have more than 50,000 nuclear weapons of mass destruction in the world, most of them in the possession of the United States and the Soviet Union. To my mind, the initial most pressing problem for the next decade or two ahead is to try and improve the stability in strategic relations between the United States and the Soviet Union, to make sure these terrible weapons aren't used."

In the long run, said Drell, "I want to get rid of the weapons, because history has shown that eventually, indeed it is true, we do use every weapon we have." He recalled that in 1139 Pope Innocent II forbade use of the crossbow, declaring it "hateful to God and unfit for Christians." Before long, however, the church decided the crossbow could be used against Moslems . . . and it was soon being used, as well, by Christian against Christian.

However, the day when all nuclear weapons will be banished is probably far in the future, Drell said, musingly. By then, "the world will be very different, politically." Sitting before a wall of shelves filled with books—plus a small, stand-up cutout of Albert Einstein cavorting on his bicycle—Drell continued to mix philosophy with politics: By the time we get rid of nuclear weapons, "in our evolution we will have caught up with the nuclear revolution, which has changed the scale of destructive energy in our explosions by factors of a million. We will learn to effectively resolve our disputes and our differences by different means than the ones which we use now—essentially by confrontation and usually some form of combat."

Yet, he added, "it's beyond my vision to see that coming. It's going to be . . . a fundamental change in human nature." And in the meantime, "we've got to make deterrence work, because we have these weapons now, and we have this danger. I think that avoiding nuclear holocaust is one of the most important, if not THE most important, challenges we face."

"It's perilous policy to live constantly under a nuclear sword of Damocles, or as nuclear hostages facing one another. We have to do better."

17. RECOGNIZING THAT THE EMPEROR HAS NO CLOTHES
Dan Hirsch, Santa Cruz, Calif.

> *We have been called a people of plenty . . . Yet the truth of our condition is our poverty. We are finally defenseless on this earth. Our material belongings have not brought us happiness. Our military defenses will not avert nuclear destruction . . . It would be well for us to rejoin the human race, to accept our essential poverty as a gift, and to share our material wealth with those in need.*
> —*"Habits of the Heart,"* Bellah, Madsen, Sullivan, Swidler and Tipton

Daniel Hirsch—former faculty member at UCLA, now director of the Adlai Stevenson Program on Nuclear Policy at the University of California at Santa Cruz—thinks there are some major things wrong with education today:

"I believe that from birth we are taught to pass over our own will, our powers of volition, to authority. I think the large measure of what goes on in schools is the inculcation of obedience to authority: to sit in a chair, at a desk, below an adult, and have the adult tell you what the truth is." Even civics classes that outline individual and civil rights "tell you this is the best of all possible worlds, our government is great, and [you should] let the government do what it will."

The problem with that, he said, is that "when you are taught to pass over your own judgment to authority, you are then incapable of saying that the emperor has no clothes and to take action yourself."

Today's students, he has found, "have never been taught, anywhere, that they can write a piece of legislation, that they can visit a congressperson and push them to take a particular action. They don't know they can do a press conference, they can call up a reporter and suggest a story, that they can write an opinion piece. The basic actions of being a citizen, the powers that we have to demonstrate the theories of nonviolent action and so forth, are just not accessible to them."

"What has always stunned me," he added, "is that the people in many other countries are being tortured and killed for trying to exercise elementary rights that we have in this country and don't use."

So, in his teaching, Hirsch aims to change that. His goal is to turn out individuals who are willing and able to take a position and to do something about it.

With his specialty, the nuclear threat, he introduces both facts and tactics. Facts cover topics such as nuclear weapons and human rights; tactics include Gandhian nonviolence, lobbying—and such specialized skills as "how to write testimony, respond to environmental impact statements and propose rule makings by agencies." That's how education ought to work, he believes: helping people build their beliefs on knowledge, and then put those beliefs into action.

It is a program that fits the image of UC Santa Cruz—a campus that from its first day, in 1965, drew young people who were politically involved, those committed to "social awareness." In the early years, ideas and ideals were most important; money and power were incidental—even shunned. Politicized youth of the '60s and '70s turned Santa Cruz into a wash of long hair, tie-dyes and backpacks.

That scene, of course, has changed with the times. Students have become more conservative, and the university has moved in that direction, as well. The San Jose Mercury News a couple of years ago ran a story headlined, "UCSC losing its touchie-feelie, hippie-veggie image." It quoted one of the deans as saying that, like everywhere else, the trend at UCSC is toward offering a "college education that will lead to a career."

Hirsch's goal is to reawaken the students. It is something he does as much by personal example as classroom lecture, and during the past year he had been involved in a couple of dramatic incidents that showed just how much impact one determined individual can have.

In one of those cases, Hirsch and two other men had appeared before the Nuclear Regulatory Commission (NRC) and brought off an amazing success. It evolved from their argument that all weapons grade nuclear materials should be removed from U.S.-supplied reactors here and abroad.

"[We] were able to somehow get the commission to reverse its position and to unanimously order all weapons grade nuclear materials, over a period of time, to be removed," Hirsch said. "A major concern brought before the NRC," he added, "[was] the risk that [such uranium could] be stolen from relatively unprotected settings and made into a nuclear weapon by a terrorist or a currently non-nuclear nation." The NRC decision drew national media attention.

A parallel case—one in which Hirsch had been involved for five years—wound up with another major victory about the same time. In that instance, the NRC was asked to force UCLA to either shut down or increase safety at its small, campus reactor. Hirsch had first learned of that reactor's problems while teaching there, when one of his students told him radioactive argon gas was leaking in the math building.

Hirsch became a major spokesperson in the attempt to clean up that situation. "I was in the public press every week or two, on television saying that the engineering department was running a very dangerous reactor, and that it should be shut down or fixed." UCLA didn't like it very much at the time, he admitted, but they were unable to fire him.

UCLA had finally removed the uranium just a few weeks before we talked, after announcing earlier that it would close the reactor. "As I understand it," Hirsch said, "we were the first interveners to ever succeed in shutting down an operating reactor."

But when it comes to example, Hirsch does even more—extending commitment into his personal life style. The idea here, he said, is to attempt to live in a way that will solve problems instead of cause them. He and the woman who has been his partner for the last five years live on a ranch, where they can produce most of their own food. And, "in exchange for reduced rent, we clean out stables and milk goats and feed various animals." "So," he added with a grin, "I get to shovel the real kind of manure, instead of the more urban variety that I do the rest of the day."

"It's close to my principals," said Hirsch, "to grow a fair amount of one's own food, to do some manual work instead of making someone else do that for you."

That lifestyle is in line with something called the Shakertown Pledge, which Hirsch adopted a decade or so ago, agreeing "to try to reduce consumption and to try to transfer wealth to the poor of the world." War, he had decided, is "in large measure related to the inequalities in the world."

"The Shakertown Pledge was a Gandhian attempt, basically, to not preach about what's wrong—that poverty's so bad—but to somehow share one's life with the poor in some fashion and to try to transfer the excess to those who need." It offers one form of the "simple" lifestyle citizens of the United States and other nations will have to adopt, Hirsch believes, if the world is to be saved.

In a sense, Hirsch's current role as teacher and example. for today's students brings his life full circle, for his activism has its roots in his own college days. Hirsch entered Harvard University in 1968, the year both Dr. Martin Luther King Jr. and Robert Kennedy were assassinated. He watched as Harvard students joined the general campus rebellions that year by occupying University Hall, then—after baton-wielding police moved in—declaring a school strike.

Hirsch was not among those who occupied the building; as he saw it, the demonstration was promoted by a small group who wanted to "create an incident" and did not represent the will of the student body. But Hirsch did make a move of his own—helping set up a "free university," a kind of alternative education program that blossomed on numerous campuses during that period.

Then, in his junior year, Hirsch helped found a group—one that still is active—called Bridge the Gap, encouraging other students "to get off the campuses and into the communities." The idea was to "bridge the generational gap and the town-gown gap on the issue of war and similar issues."

By the time the young Californian was ready to graduate, he had decided on a career that didn't appear on any Harvard University job choice list: social change activist.

He put that decision into effect as the United States pulled out of Vietnam. His goal at that time was to end Congressional funding of the fighting that continued in Vietnam after U.S. troops left. That soon took him a step further, as he helped write and promote human rights legislation to cut appropriations for the Vietnamese police and prison system—funding that inadvertently supported "the tiger cages and similar major human rights violations in prisons." After much maneuvering, the proposal was written into law.

That success and others that followed have added up to an admirable pattern of accomplishment, although they still left Hirsch with one of the major problems facing many within today's peace and justice movement: the hard truth that even successful activism seldom pays the bills. So, like many others, Hirsch has held related, part-time jobs. Following college, he first worked for the UCLA Religious Conference, then became area coordinator for Amnesty International, then moved into teaching.

Education, for him, has become an essential tool to encourage the world to face its future. "Somehow," he said, "our priorities have to change, so survival of the species becomes as important to us as some of our creature comforts."

Hirsch admits that's asking a lot—maybe more than is possible for 20th century man. "That's why I think there's a high chance we will die," he said, enunciating his words slowly, with sadness. The death he envisions would likely be world wide . . . and nuclear.

In Hirsch's view, poverty and inequality and children dying in Ethiopia and the nuclear arms race are all tied up into one dangerous package: "I think it's clear that nuclear weapons are merely a symptom of a whole series of other things that are wrong with the way we behave . . . a manifestation of a kind of mass neurosis. But it's a symptom that can kill you. So you have to do something about the symptom AND its cause."

He worries that Americans fail to take action out of ignorance or fear: "I find that people care about these issues deeply. Many care so much, for instance, that they're willing to do civil disobedience and get arrested. But they're terrified of going to talk to their own congressperson, because they feel they don't know enough; they feel immobile."

If people cannot be changed, and if they cannot "mobilize and really force governments to eliminate those weapons," said Hirsch, then ". . . I don't see my students having the natural life that they are entitled to."

"I think," he added, "we are essentially dancing around a set mousetrap . . . and there's only so long you can dance around it without tripping it off."

18. TAKING PERSONAL RESPONSIBILITY
Jeff Myers, Madison, Wis

> *Knowledge is power, and knowledge entails respon-*
> *sibility. Preventing nuclear war is the greatest*
> *ethical priority of our age . . . We must assume*
> *the responsibility to make great changes in our*
> *nation and our world, even though it will require*
> *us to change our lives.*
> *—Eric Markusen, University of Minnesota and*
> *Southwestern State University, and John B. Harris,*
> *University of Minnesota, August 1984*

Today at the University of Wisconsin at Madison there is a jammed-up corner of office space that recalls the high-charged, political days in the '60s. A poster on the wall announces a long-ago el Cordobes bullfight; another features a stylized American flag—some of its stars replaced by swastikas. Tacked up next to the posters are a variety of activist newsletters.

This space happens to be in the University's academic computing center; it belongs to a former student who now works there. His name is Jeff Myers, and even personally—except for the short hair—Myers might have appeared at home two decades earlier. He has metal-rimmed glasses, wears a black T-shirt and a pillowy, beige jacket, and carries a blue student book bag. He's starting a beard.

But when Myers talks about his activism, it's with shy enthusiasm rather than radical fervor. The picture you get is of a young man carrying a heavy load of ideals and not yet quite sure how to fit them into a not-so-idealistic society.

So far in this life, he has done many of the things that make parents proud, earning an undergraduate degree in mathematics

Jeff Myers

and computer science from Marietta College in southeastern Ohio, then a master's in computer science at Madison in 1983. Now 26, he works at the university, half-time as a consultant, half in minicomputer maintenance.

But Myers also is into causing change. And earlier this fall, he admits, he did it in a way that caused his parents—like those a decade or two earlier—to feel concern for his well-being.

Myers chose to protest the United States' intervention in Central America, and to do it by getting involved there, himself. Going as a computer consultant, he paid his own fare, packed his bag and left in early September for two weeks of work in Nicaragua. He went as part of tecNICA, a Berkeley-based group that funnels technical expertise and supplies to that country to help offset U.S. aid to the contras. Myers' work was in Managua, and it was aimed at helping the economy, not the war effort. He spent a short time at the Ministry of Finance, then moved to the Central Bank, then to a pharmaceutical company, COFARMA.

It was at COFARMA that Myers found his biggest challenge. The company, he said, serves as the nation's medical wholesale house, selling to hospitals and smaller wholesalers. In this role, it keeps the data base for the whole country's supply of small medical equipment. When Myers arrived, he learned that the computer that kept the data base had died—"they had been running for several months using their old inventory printouts." The firm had acquired a small Kaypro-II and an Epson printer as replacements, and Myers went to work with "three fairly experienced BASIC programmers" to get the new system into operation. Although the Nicaraguans weren't familiar with the Kaypro, they were quick learners, said Myers. "It really felt like all the training that I have gone through amounted to something down there."

As far as the danger for a gringo in Nicaragua, Myers said, his parents could have spared themselves the worry. "I never felt threatened in Managua at all, and I walked around on my own; I pointedly wanted to do that." He got lost one night, but met a local graduate student along the way and wound up spending the evening talking with the student and his roommates.

The Nicaragua trip, it seemed, had been a natural step in the educational process Myers had set for himself. His interest in the bigger world out there had begun back at Marietta College, he said, when he took a couple of political theory classes on Marxism and the history of authoritarian governments. The switch to a big state university brought additional viewpoints. A close friend in his first-year dorm was a Puerto Rican, who encouraged Myers to add some sociology classes to his tech-oriented computer science diet. He almost wound up with a second specialty in sociology.

While working for his master's, Myers slowly edged into activism. He first joined the Teaching Assistants' Association, which was seeking legal collective bargaining status on campus. Next, he helped found the campus chapter of Computer Professionals for Social Responsibility (CPSR). The chapter helped develop a national CPSR report, "Computer Unreliability and Nuclear War." Because CPSR questions computer reliability at the level required for complex, hair-trigger nuclear war decisions, the national group has been actively combating the Strategic Defense Initiative, said Myers.

When Granada was invaded, he joined a guerrilla theater troupe that staged anti-military street dramas. Once he was among activists who occupied an army recruiting center, shutting it down for a day.

"But gradually things sort of fizzled out and we all went our own ways again," said Myers. His own path took him into the community peace network. He volunteered time and expertise by typesetting newsletters and the local peace directory.

Now he's not sure what the future holds. One strong option is law school. "I'm primarily interested in constitutional issues and international law," he said. "Probably what I would do in the long run would be to help non-profit organizations with constitutional issues." And there are other interests he hopes to continue. He's been exploring philosophy, especially the ideas of Zen Buddhism and some of the ways that philosophy merges with the realm of theoretical mathematics and computer science. He likes poetry and writes haiku. He enjoys rock music—"mostly '60s and early '70s stuff'—but also punk, classical and bluegrass.

Whatever happens, for Myers there is a need that what he does makes a difference. He's not quite sure why that is so important to him, although he's done some thinking about it.

"There's no real short answer I can give," he said. "I'm not a religious person. Well, I'm an agnostic, which means that I'm very interested in religion in a number of ways, but I am not committed to any particular way of looking at the world from a religious perspective. I try to be the best person I can be, although I know I have my own faults and restrictions and problems. But just through my own activity, I try to make things better for myself and everybody else. I've always been partly that way, I guess, but it has become more of a conscious thing, more of a realized goal."

V

CARRYING THE MESSAGE INTO THE COMMUNITY

Education, of course, would have limited use to the peace and justice movement if it were restricted to formal academic settings. Jeff Myers knew that when he set off for Nicaragua to share both his computer skills and his concerns about intervention in Central America. Education, in a variety of modes, has become a basic tool for almost all peace and justice operations—another of those threads that reach among participants.

Two stories that follow show how successfully education can be mixed with a healthy dose of innovation to spread the message. One looks in on a California couple who have relocated in Des Moines, Iowa, as educational missionaries, of a sort, for one of the nation's fastest spreading groups, Beyond War. But first, the tale of one activist and one small college—a college that already had put the "closed" sign on its campus when the activist came along.

19. SO THERE MAY BE AN EARTH FOR FUTURE GENERATIONS
Karen Litfin, Los Angeles

Peace is not absence of war; it is a virtue, a state of mind, a disposition for benevolence, confidence, justice.

—*Benedict Spinoza, 1670*

For many years, Immaculate Heart College in Hollywood was one of Los Angeles' true treasures: a Catholic women's institution housed in lovely old Spanish buildings; one that mixed commitments to religion, education, creativity and social consciousness. The 1970s, however, saw the financial situation turn critical; in June 1980, the college held its final commencement and closed.

But Immaculate Heart refused to quietly disappear. Instead, with money left after selling its campus and paying its debts, the college opened a different kind of educational center—one supporting work in the areas of peace, justice and global cooperation. It was exactly the ambiance that suited the young, ambitious peace activist who showed up a couple of years later.

When Karen Litfin appeared at the Immaculate Heart College Center in West Los Angleles, she brought a big dream: She would put on an extensive series of educational programs—lasting over several months and reaching out to audiences through all of California—on "The Fate of the Earth; Human Values in the Nuclear Age." It would bring in big names and controversial ideas, all to draw in new people and to stir up a fine kettle of debate. The basic question would be one that Litfin had been pondering, herself: "[If] we're in this nuclear predicament because we've gone astray with our values somehow."

Even before she presented her idea to Immaculate Heart, Litfin had received prestigious support—a $50,000 grant from the California Council for the Humanities. The grant, however, came with a worrisome catch: She had to get a matching $50,000 from a sponsoring organization, and her sponsoring organization had just backed out. Litfin hoped the center could take their place.

Immaculate Heart did not have $50,000 to give her—but could offer "in kind" services, such as office space and staff help. The Council for the Humanities accepted their package, and Litfin began turning her dream into reality.

She put together an impressive series. Thirty programs were presented over an 18-month period in locations throughout the state; the conclusion was a two-day conference at Loyola Marymount University in Los Angeles. Overall, some 8,000 participants heard several dozen speakers and workshop leaders—people like author-editor Norman Cousins, producer-director Norman Corwin and Los Angeles Times national reporter Robert Scheer. Topics included "Thinking the Unthinkable: Psychological Dimensions of the Nuclear Threat," "The Role of the Media in the Nuclear Age," "Human Values in the Nuclear Age," "The Artist as Peacemaker" and "Nuclear Theology."

Although none of the speakers claimed there were easy solutions, they offered many approaches—from poet Denise Levertov's proposal that "we have an absolute obligation to all be prophets . . . and to go out upon the housetops and speak what we know to our friends and neighbors" to Cousins' admonition that "we have to create those institutions which begin to translate global necessity into global possibility." By the time the series was over, many ideas had been considered, and many people had been touched. The media had paid attention, taking the message beyond the conference, itself. Both Litfin and the Center were pleased.

For Litfin, personally, the end of the series was a roadmark—a time to rethink her own plans. Without much doubt, she would continue as a peace and justice worker. But now, maybe, with some differences.

She'd gotten into activism in the 1970s, as a student at the University of Maryland. Long before anti-apartheid gained the national limelight, she had begun lobbying for divestiture of funds from South Africa. She was involved in women's and civil rights issues, all while managing to earn her degree in political science.

Once she had the degree, Litfin thumbed her way to the West Coast, arriving in California in 1979. She connected with the fledgling Alliance for Survival and became one of its founders.

Now, still not quite 30, Litfin had decided that education was the road she wanted to follow on a more formal basis. She had applied for Ph.D. programs in the areas of political philosophy or international relations at several prestigious schools. "I want to set myself up so I can teach," she said.

Besides, it seemed time to take a break from activism. The months spent pulling together and putting on the conference had given her a great sense of satisfaction . . . but also a feeling of burnout.

"Organizing is much more than a fulltime job," she said. "It becomes your whole life, and you never really stop thinking about it, because you're taking so much responsibility."

But the sorting out of values—and of dangers that threaten the world—would continue. "I don't think the nuclear issue is our only problem at all; I think that it's just our worst problem," Litfin said, a laugh mixed with a sigh. "There are a lot of problems that are running a close second, and at the rate we're going, if we don't destroy ourselves in a nuclear war, we'll probably destroy ourselves some other way: ecologically, or we'll starve ourselves, or we'll give ourselves so much cancer that the species can't survive, or we'll mutate our genes some way, or we'll have a biological war or chemical war . . . there are so many options for our own extinction right now."

How would she change that situation? Litfin's answer—like that of many of today's activists—combined ideals and action.

"To me," she said, "the changes that have to come about have to be on the level of values . . . even though I think that we [also] need to negotiate treaties, and we need to have the United Nations, and need to have all those political institutions. And they have to go in the right direction. But also [we have to go in the right direction] as individuals, in terms of our consumption, in terms of our lifestyle, in terms of our interpersonal relations . . . Nuclear weapons are sort of the tip of the iceberg."

"I guess I see nuclear fission, the splitting of the atom, as sort of the splitting of ourselves. And it's the splitting of our world into different countries that are competing with each other and warring with each other for resources and for power, the splitting of ourselves in terms of denying that we are connected to everybody else on this earth, and that we are, in fact, all in the same boat together."

"You know," she added, "this sounds sort of romantic and idealistic, but I guess I would say that we need to have some kind of respect for the sacredness of life . . . Because there has been a scientific revolution, I think there is some kind of philosophical values revolution that's going to follow. I don't think it's inevitable, but I think if we're going to survive it's got to happen."

20. A WORLD BEYOND WAR
Ed and Barbara Thomas, Des Moines, Iowa

> *The unleashed power of the atom has changed*
> *everything save our modes of thinking and we thus*
> *drift toward unparalleled catastrophe.*
> —*Albert Einstein*

There's a shocking moment for many of those attending their first Beyond War meeting. Typically, the guests will have been welcomed to a neighborhood living room, maybe even offered homemade cookies or cake. It's likely some of the guests already will know each other and their hosts. That friendly welcome, that pleasant ambiance is part of what defines Beyond War.

The cozy mood shatters, however, as one of the evening's speakers—again, probably a neighbor—begins a traditional Beyond War ritual that first asks the audience to look at two objects: a single BB and a metal tub. What follows goes about like this:

"Now," says the speaker, "please close your eyes." The BB is dropped in the tub. It makes a small, brief noise. "That BB," the speaker says, "represents one million tons of explosives."

"Now I'm going to drop BBs to represent all the aerial bombs used by the Allies in World War II." Three BBs rattle along the side and bottom of the tub.

"And now, here is the sound that represents the explosive power in the nuclear arsenals of the United States and the Soviet Union today." Slowly the speaker pours out more BBs—18,000 in all. For those listeners, their eyes still closed, the sound of thousands of small metal pellets bouncing against each other and echoing into the tub seems to last interminably. When the last BB has fallen, the

Ed and Barbara Thomas

speaker waits a few moments to let it all sink in, then adds solemnly, "And we continue to build five more nuclear weapons each day to add to that arsenal."

Long before any nuclear exchange used up the weaponry that already exists, life would have disappeared from the earth, the speaker says. So now it's not enough to simply fight that weaponry. What's needed is nothing less than a "new way of thinking." One that would recognize the interconnection of all humans around the world; one that would reject all violence, whether international or interpersonal; one that would move the world "beyond war."

That scene—now being repeated in living rooms across the country—is just one tool supporting the major tactic chosen by Beyond War in its effort to cause that world change. The tactic? Education.

The ultimate answer—whether or not the world survives—will depend on whether enough of us join that new way of thinking, Beyond War is convinced. It will take just 5% of the population to get the idea on its way, they contend; 20% to make it unstoppable. And education is the way to make it happen.

The Beyond War story began in 1982, in the posh surroundings of Palo Alto, Calif. Those in at the beginning were basically an upscale group of highly motivated, successful individuals bright enough to make things happen. They quickly realized, however, that to pull in the necessary numbers, they would have to reach out to new audiences and new territories.

Barbara Thomas is one of those who recall how that move began. During a January 1984 national staff meeting, she said, the group agreed, "Let's try an experiment to see what would happen if two couples moved to a state for three months." Those couples would be, in a sense, missionaries. They would invite neighbors to their homes to talk about the Beyond War idea, encouraging those neighbors to repeat the process. If it worked, Beyond War would be on its way.

The state they chose was Iowa. They liked the fact that Iowa held the country's first caucuses, making it something of a trend-setter, and that Iowans seemed to be people who valued a good education and were willing to get involved.

A number of couples said they would like to make the three-month move. Barbara and her husband Ed, however, were not among them. Although Ed had sold his CPA firm the previous June and joined the national volunteer staff on a full-time basis, the timing just didn't seem right. Yet, when final decision time arrived and people were asked to stand if they were ready to take on that responsibility, Ed stood up.

That surprised even his wife. "It wasn't just, 'Who can go?' " Barbara said. "It was, 'Who can go in the next 10 days?' Just pick up and leave." Ten days later, the Thomases, along with Tom and Marianne Moutoux, headed for Des Moines, Iowa.

Barbara vividly remembers that trip. "We were in our van, towing the Moutouxs' car on the back," she said. A bone-chilling Iowa winter greeted them. "The temperature was -20 degrees. One gas station attendant looked at the license plates and asked, 'What are you doing in Iowa?' We said, 'We're here to talk about Beyond War.' " The attendant, Barbara recalled with a laugh, suggested that maybe the Californians were not operating on all cylinders if they chose Iowa in frigid mid-winter just to talk.

"But it was a perfect time to go," Barbara would decide, "because farmers don't have much they can do then." That meant people had time to listen, and the two couples found Iowans cooperative and interested. "They have a commitment to stewardship of the planet because of their ties to the land," Barbara said.

Three months later, when it was time for the couples to return home, Beyond War seemed to have caught on and begun growing. That was the go-ahead the parent group had been seeking. In Palo Alto, it was decided that additional families would leave jobs and homes, temporarily moving to other parts of the country to spread the word of Beyond War. All that would be done at their own expense; it would have to be that important to the couples who participated. And that fall, 17 families, including both Thomases and Moutouxs, set off for a year in other parts of the nation. As the Thomases and Moutouxs returned to Iowa, others headed off to Georgia, Colorado, Maine, Massachusetts, New Hampshire, Oregon, Vermont, Washington, Southern California and Wisconsin.

That first full year was just about ending as I talked with the Thomases. Both couples, they said, felt good about their experience. "Between the four of us, we've spoken to over 10,000 people," said Ed. "There are now 80 to 100 people around the state doing Beyond War interest presentations and then having two-meeting orientation sessions." Beyond War, they believed, was firmly implanted in Iowa and across the nation.

But for the Thomases there was even more to it than that. Personally, it seemed to be the culmination of a journey of personal discovery and commitment that had begun in 1970. Ed was an up-and-coming young CPA at the time, and the family—including Debby, 12, and Royce, 8—had just returned from three years in The Hague, Netherlands, where Ed's company, Arthur Anderson & Co., had sent them. "We came back thinking it was going to be a very easy transition . . . we'd kind of slip into an old lifestyle," Ed said.

But unless their friends had traveled abroad, they didn't really care to hear much about what the couple had learned about the rest of the world, the Thomases discovered. Moreover, many of those friends with whom they'd planned to resume the good California life seemed to be divorcing. "My very best friend moved out of his house two weeks after we got home," recalled Ed. "I was in a state of shock." The homecoming was disillusioning.

But Ed did make a new friend—a man working for the firm, who introduced the couple to a group called Creative Initiative. "He got us to go to a discussion group called 'Challenge to Change,'" said Ed. "It was, as I recall, a seven-week course held in someone's home. We discussed a series of things: . . . What is the purpose of life? How is it that human beings should function? What is the highest functioning of a human being? Who am I? Where am I headed? And so forth."

Both Thomases refer to that class as life-changing. Within a couple of years, Barbara gave up tennis and bridge to sign on as a full-time Creative Initiative volunteer. "I got involved with courses for women and children, on parenting and marriage, energy conservation and drug abuse," said Barbara, "and began, I think, a lifetime study of life and people."

In 1981, Creative Initiative decided there was just one overriding issue: the threat of nuclear war and the potential end of all civilization as we know it. And so, the following year, all efforts were turned to founding Beyond War.

Ed and Barbara did not participate in the early formation of Beyond War, because they already were fully commited to another Creative Initiative program. They were living, temporarily, in a Palo Alto house with 12 young women—all 18 and sharing the home for one year to "prepare for the rest of their lives." It was a year of work, study and contemplation between high school and college. Barbara was resident director. When that year ended in June 1982, the Thomases got into the new Beyond War movement, opening their home and inviting friends to introductory sessions.

Along the way, the Thomases decided that if this was a problem involving the whole world, they needed to learn more about the rest of it. "Ed took two months off from his business," said Barbara, "and we took a trip to Japan, India and Nepal."

"I think that trip made us realize how really significant the United States is in what happens on this planet," she said. "This country holds the whole planet in its hands," added Ed.

With those kinds of thoughts, the Thomases began asking whether they could commit the rest of their lives to Beyond War—whether they could live on what Ed could make from the sale of his own business, which he had started in 1977. The Thomases decided to take the gamble. In June 1983, Ed joined Barbara as a full-time

Beyond War national staffperson.

Three months later, Ed was one of a team who made a preliminary trip to Iowa, wondering if it would be possible to seed the movement in another state. They talked with peace groups, church and civic leaders, businessmen and politicans; they left resource material for local groups. In November, they checked back: Sure enough, the material was still in use, the ideas were still being discussed.

That led to the January decision that sent the Thomases and Moutouxs to Iowa for the first on-the-spot experiment, and eventually back for another year.

But now, as the two couples ended that full year, they faced another decision. For even as the success of Beyond War encouraged them, they sensed it would be helpful if they could stay in Iowa to offer leadership for one more year.

The Moutouxs quickly signed on, but that decision was harder for the Thomases. Their gamble that the proceeds from Ed's business would carry them was falling apart. Ed would have to go back to work. So the Thomases, with some sadness, were heading back to California.

Ed had good business connections there. Their own condo was waiting them. Their friends and colleagues would welcome them back.

But, the Thomases had decided, that wasn't the way it was going to work. Instead, they would put their home up as a long-term rental. "It's large and very nice," admitted Barbara, "and I have a little bit of trouble detaching; it's a big step." Ed already had begun hunting for a job, but not in Palo Alto.

The Thomases would be moving. Permanently, this time. From now on, they would be Beyond War workers Ed and Barbara Thomas of Des Moines, Iowa.

There are other Beyond War stories comparable to that of the Thomases. In Decatur, Ga., I talked with David and Louise Smith.

Nine years earlier, David had been 37 years old and a successful commercial real estate developer and salesman when he, too, had sold his business, committing himself full time to Creative Initiative and then Beyond War. As the Thomases moved to Iowa for their first full year, the Smiths left for Georgia.

"We have tremendous privilege," David Smith told me. "We have time, we have money, we have knowledge, and there is a need for some people to invest themselves, because there are a lot of people who can't." Beyond War claims 400 full-time volunteers among its 8,000 workers.

The Smiths, who had almost finished their first year in Georgia as we talked, were planning to sign on for another in the Atlanta area. "The biggest drawing power," said Louise, "has been the fact that we picked ourselves up and moved here." That one fact, she has found, tells people "this is serious."

Along the way, David Smith also became something of an international Beyond War ambassador, appearing on some of the sophisticated national and international television shows produced by the Palo Alto headquarters. Those shows included a first-time-ever satellite "space bridge" with communication among seven countries on five continents for its 1985 International Beyond War Award. Part of the previous year's show had been beamed from the Soviet Union. The 1986 awards honored the Contadora Group, those Latin American presidents attempting to bring peace to their part of the world, and technology took another jump as all four Contadora leaders were "on line" simultaneously.

Those shows also represented an expansion of tactics. Beyond War's early game plan had brought some criticism: It was too elitist, too much talk and too little action; its long-range goals might be noble, but short-range actions by angry governments could blow the world apart while Beyond War was still hosting gatherings over coffee and crumpets in neighborhood livingrooms.

Beyond War has not given up those livingroom meetings, and education still ranks as a major objective, but it has added new techniques. One fall 1987 campaign saw Californians writing personal letters to voters in New Hampshire, urging them to use their early primaries to ask tough questions of presidential candidates who would be touring there.

Then, an October 1987 Beyond War television production, "down-linked" via satellite to more than 400 sites in 38 states, called on viewers to talk with neighbors and confront political candidates. Dialogue, the show suggested, should consider how to support the peace process in Central America, and how to encourage better relations between the United States and Soviet Union. Beyond War leaders already had visited the Soviet Union, Nicaragua and Costa Rica, and had conferred with many politicians and candidates within our own country, to gather facts and encourage discussion.

"Some other groups emphasize the problem," Louise had told me. "Our emphasis is on the solution: changing thinking . . . actually developing the adequate response to the reality." As the Smiths defined it, that process would be challenging. It involves, Louise said, "a quantum change . . . because of the introduction of the atomic weapons." What's needed now, the Smiths contend, is an equal change in humans . . . what might even be called an evolutionary leap.

Violence is more than engaging in war, Louise said. It's also failing to confront problems of world hunger, overpopulation and diminishing resources; it's turning anger on your husband or wife or children.

The effort will require "nothing less than actually changing our basic attitudes about how we relate to one another and to the whole planet," David said. It will mean a worldwide effort, pulling together all nations and races and religions, added Louise.

"I think it's a very precarious and serious time; I'm not unrealistic about that," Louise said. "I think we're pushed up against the wall. But I think it's the opportunity for the human race to make a change—a profound change, in how to relate."

VI

THE SPIRITUAL CONNECTION

While I was in Iowa, Barbara and Ed Thomas had talked about how their kind of dedication develops.

Ed told how it happened for him: "I'm totally doing what I'm doing from a spiritual base. You don't up and do what we've done for just a cause. Personally, I have a very eclectic religious sense; it's not tied to a particular denomination. But it doesn't take that much thought to see that this beautiful system has a direction to it."

And that led to another thought: "You know, the peace movement is actually a spiritual movement . . . and if the churches had been doing their job, there wouldn't be a need for a peace movement."

It's true that many churches and church members approach peace activism with all the enthusiasm of a timid swimmer edging a toe into chilly water. Yet, a growing number have moved strongly into activism. The traditional peace churches are among these, of course—the Mennonites, Brethren and Quakers. But Catholics, Presbyterians, Unitarians, Methodists, Lutherans, Baptists and other churches and synagogues and their members have swelled the ranks. In fact, without a lot of recognition outside of those who participate, the spiritual connection has become a basic thread woven through the peace and justice movement—a thread that sometimes calls people to dramatic confrontation with society.

21. THE BATTLE TO SAVE THE EARTH
Joseph R. Hacala, S.J., Washington, D.C.

*A purely political definition does not adequately
identify the threat posed by modern warfare.
Today, the stakes involved in the nuclear issue
make it a moral issue of compelling urgency. The
church must be involved . . . . Silence in this
instance would be a betrayal of its mission.*
                                  —*Joseph Cardinal Bernardin*

Joe Hacala, now 40, still smiles when he recalls the four years immediately after high school—especially his Thursday "escapes" from the Jesuit seminary in Pennsylvania where he was studying. The seminary expected its young students to concentrate on "a very monastic training . . . pretty much a life of prayer and solitude and study of the classics, of languages and philosophy, and the beginnings of some scripture and theology," Hacala recalled. But the young man had additional ideas.

Hacala, however, wasn't up to standard student mischief on those Thursdays. His adventures took him into the disadvantaged areas of nearby Reading, where he made visits with a caseworker friend. "I tried to really discover [how it was with] some of the poor there. I used to . . . visit some people and just listen to what some of their struggles and problems were."

"I think at that point I could see that . . . somehow God's creation . . . was being betrayed or desecrated," he said, "and that somehow [the people], as part of that creation of God, could have some say in changing that, and in bringing forth life where there was really death and destruction."

That became the young man's vision and helped launch him on the double career as Jesuit and social activist that he still follows today. Now it is as Father Joseph R. Hacala, S.J., director of the National Office of Jesuit Social Ministries in Washington, D.C. Since those schoolboy years, he has expanded his range of community activism—organizing poor tenants, joining Martin Luther King's crusade, picketing for Caesar Chavez, opposing Vietnam, and fighting strip mining in Virginia. His current focus is the one he now believes the most important of all: trying to bring peace to the world.

Along the way, Hacala earned his undergraduate degree in sociology at Loyola University in Chicago, while studying problems in the city around him: "the powerlessness of people that I saw in the slums of Chicago . . . their struggles with things as small as not having control over garbage collection . . . to the lack of control over the political structure in Chicago at that time." He began working with a number of community action projects and helped organize tenants in urban housing projects.

As he moved on to graduate work at the Universities of Illinois and Chicago, he became a tenant union organizer on the south side of Chicago, working with Al Raby, who was then Martin Luther King Jr.'s housing director.

Upon graduation in 1970, Hacala moved to Philadelphia with a teaching assignment at a central-city Jesuit high school. Then, in 1972, he left for Canada and three years of theology studies prior to his ordination.

While in Canada, Hacala heard people complain about the United States—for instance, about economic policies that hurt Canada and about refugee limitations that forced many refugees to turn to Canada. Along the way, he became aware "that our nation, being about 6% of the world's population, was consuming approximately 40% of the world's natural resources."

"I became upset, almost angry with the fact that I was an American."

It was about then that Caesar Chavez was waging one of his campaigns to unionize farmworkers in the United States. As a result, grapes and lettuce—non-union produce that couldn't be sold in the United States—were being dumped on Canadian markets. Hacala joined Canadian picketers to protest. For the young man, grapes and lettuce came to represent a picture of American business run amuck. It seemed, said Hacala, "we had lost any sense of cooperation, any sense of stewardship, any sense of trust—in God and in one another, and in, really, God's creation in the world."

Vietnam appeared to be part of the same cloth, a tool to promote American interests—specifically, the interests of the military-industrial complex. "I think this was the beginning of my sense of the role of corporate America in the warmaking machine." Following his ordination in 1975, Hacala decided to put that growing, focusing fervor into action.

The church of that day was supportive. Catholics had been encouraged to get involved in social justice issues following Vatican II. Then, the year before Hacala was ordained, his own order "called us, as Jesuits, to really integrate faith and justice . . . to be involved in the transformation of society, of overcoming the injustices of the world, to be deeply involved in the issues of justice and peace." Shortly after that, the 25 Catholic bishops of Appalachia—the area where Hacala had grown up—issued a pastoral letter charging, Hacala reported, "that Appalachia was really a colony of the multinational corporations of the world, who controlled the land, the resources, the coal, the natural gas . . . and thereby, people's lives."

With that inspiration, Hacala moved back to Appalachia. His goal was to block strip mining and other land abuse. He saw the mining as a "desecration of God's creation, the violation of his land entrusted to us in Genesis."

"For a short-term gain, the timber, the land, the earth, the sustenance out of which we receive our food, the beauty of that land was being pushed over the mountainside, was being washed away."

By now a seasoned community organizer, Hacala drew local and regional residents into the battle against strip mining. The effort succeeded "beyond any expectations." A special success was in Lincoln County, W.Va., where strip mining had been proposed on seven rolling hills. Hacala and two other Jesuits, working out of a simple mountain home, helped organize residents and got the state of West Virginia to rule that there would be no strip mining in that county.

"To this day, seven years later, that ruling, based largely on the expressed wishes of the people, still stands intact," Hacala said proudly. The Jesuit still gets pleasure out of driving along the top of a nearby ridge, pulling off the road and looking at the hills that were preserved. "I have a sense that I'd like to be buried among those mountains," he added quietly.

But Hacala—still youthful-looking today, wearing a woolly, crew neck sweater, corduroy slacks and sports oxfords—anticipates much more work before that time. In his current post, he's let go of some of the earlier projects. For him now, there is only one long-term goal: peace. "I have come to want to commit myself totally . . . to peacemaking as a way of life." Peace, he believes, means more than doing away with war and violence; it also means replacing them with social justice . . . "belief in God's creation . . . faith in the brotherhood and sisterhood of all peoples working together to call forth life, freedom and love."

He admits to a special urgency because of the nuclear buildup. He sees his current role with Jesuit Social Ministries as that of a "facilitator," pulling other Jesuits and lay colleagues throughout the country into the peacemaking role. "I feel," he said, "like so many people, that we could face—because of the greed and stupidity of so many of our world leaders—the ultimate destruction of our world."

Yet, he said, "If people really believe, as I do, that peace and justice are possible, then it can come to be. For I've seen it happen in many small ways; I see it happening in the peace movement, for instance. It is my deep-seated belief that there will one day be a peaceful and just world. And it is life-giving to be a part of that struggle, of that dream."

22. CHURCHES, NETWORKING AND POLITICS
Richard Healey, Washington, D.C.

*People are always expecting to get peace in
heaven; but you know whatever peace they get
there will be ready-made. Whatever making of
peace THEY can be blest for must be on the earth
here.*

—*John Ruskin*

There are many sides to Richard Healey: He earned his Ph.D.
in mathematics with a specialty in statistics, but works as a political
activist. He considers himself a Social Democrat, while espous-
ing a return to the politics of the nation's founders. His background
is Jewish, yet he works and finds hope in a mostly Christian movement. His goal: to help churches and related groups around the
nation work together toward peace, and to make sure their efforts
have political impact.

Politics are nothing new for Healey; back in the 1960s, he was
part of the counterculture movement. Today, however, he fades easily
into the Washington, D.C., scene, where his job as director of the
Coalition for a New Foreign and Military Policy frequently requires
quick trips to Capitol Hill. Healey is slim, with neatly-trimmed,
slightly receding light brown hair; he wears casual, but correct
clothes; and he has a wide grin that often lights up his face.

But Healey has never backed off from the moral/ethical battleline
that he believes was drawn in the '60s. Back then, he marched
against Vietnam, argued against development of nuclear weaponry,
joined Students for a Democratic Society (SDS) and worked for
the Peace and Freedom Party. Today, SDS has faded from the scene

and the Peace and Freedom Party seldom generates headlines. Healey, however, still fights—now against nuclear weapons and for human rights—as director of the Coalition.

His tactics involve a good deal of education: keeping 56 member organizations informed about what's happening and what can be done about actions in Congress in the areas of disarmament, human rights and the military budget. Specific concerns include missile development and funding, especially the MX and Trident II, and U.S. involvement in Central America.

A majority of coalition members are church-related, with representation among major denominations: "Washington office of the American Baptist Churches, the Episcopal Church, the Presbyterian Church, the National United Methodist Church . . . ," said Healey, reading from his letterhead.

His work with those churches has convinced Healey that one of the major stories of the '80s is taking place right before his eyes— even if the media and much of the American public don't seem to realize it. As Healey sees it, the struggles of the '60s didn't just end or evaporate—they evolved into a strong base of concern and activism that is now centered in the nation's churches. The '60s, he said, "had lots of crazy, fringey elements, it's true. But it was a moral upsurge, a revulsion against racism, against a horrible war. People were grappling with it, trying to figure what to do. A lot of them took it as Christians and thought about it." They were, said Healey, "concerned, moral people, [who] went slowly and carefully; they didn't want to be marginalized."

But, Healey believes, within the past five years that concern has begun to take shape. "One of the most exciting things is that a lot of these denominations are setting up national networks to deal with policy issues, to deal with Congress," he said. "The United Church of Christ has over 200 congressional district coordinators for peace!"

Meanwhile, the media concentrate on "the Jerry Falwells and the far right . . . because they're loud and noisy," said Healey.

Richard Healey

"They're ignoring a growing movement at the base, within the Catholic and the Protestant communities, of millions of people who are good Christians, who are moral Americans, who are concerned, who are involved, and who are appalled at the direction of United States foreign policy, as well as domestic."

These are people who tend to "think in terms of witness," said Healey. "They don't think in terms of congressional lobbying; they don't feel even that comfortable with the political process; they suspect it." But they also have realized that Falwell and others like him have been able to affect policy, said Healey, and "increasingly over the last five years they've seen that they have to not just bear witness in the religious sense, but bear witness politically, have an impact. I think these people are the hope of the United States."

Healey views such community group action as a return to early American values. "I feel it was a formative part of America, that the notion of what this country was about was these kinds of voluntary associations, working together: the activist community."

Healey had recently visited Monticello and read some of Thomas Jefferson's writings. "What an extraordinary man! His notion of the republic was of everyone being a citizen, and what he meant by citizen, was active. He had a notion of dividing the country into wards of 100 people each, forming communities which would come together to discuss issues of their day and have a voice in them." That kind of involvement is rare today, Healey said: "We've given it away to the professionals, the politicians." But now, he believes, citizens are taking it back, in groups like those forming in the nation's churches.

Richard Healey might appear an unusual shepherd for such a movement, since he shares neither Christianity nor a traditional political point of view. But his politics are not as off-center as they may sound, he suggested. The Democratic Socialists of America, he said, are "affiliated with the Socialists International, with the Willy Brandts (former chancellor of West Germany), the British

Labor Party types." Its roots go back to the Norman Thomas, Eugene Debs socialists, many of whose social platforms wound up as part of the New Deal and in later reform legislation.

As a child, Healey grew up among more radical politics: His mother was Dorothy Healey, then chairman of the Southern California Communist Party. She also served on the party's national executive committee for some years. His stepfather was editor of People's World, the Communist newspaper, and both mother and stepfather spent time in jail because of their politics; his father, stepmother, grandmother and grandfather all were Communists. Healey appears at ease with that background—no embarrassment, no apologies; if anything, a quiet pride. "The best thing about my upbringing was that it convinced me it's worthwhile to be involved in public politics and the public debates of this time," he said. "That's exciting."

However, Healey emphasizes, the Communist days are long gone. Even Dorothy Healey has left the party; she now lives with her son and his family in the nation's capital. She has her own radio show and participates in many projects with her son.

As for Healey, himself, "I am equally opposed to Soviet [and American] weapons and see them as equally dangerous. There is no excuse for what [the Soviets] are doing, either with their SS22s or their new mobile SS24s and 25s." The Coalition has called on both the Soviet Union and the United States to begin getting rid of their most destabilizing weapons; it has condemned the Soviet invasion and occupation of Afghanistan. "We don't think there are any clean hands," said Healey, "or any good bombs."

Healey, the activist, is also Healey, the scholar: He earned his bachelor's degree in 1965 from Reed College in Portland, Ore.; his master's and Ph.D. (the latter in 1972) from UCLA, all in mathematics with a specialization in statistics. He also holds a master's degree in public health, earned at Harvard University, which he entered in 1979. He has taught at California State University at Hayward, the University of Chicago and Loyola University of Chicago. Healey also worked for the Massachusetts Department of Public Health, doing community statistical studies aimed at pinpointing why certain people were showing high degrees of cancer or birth defects.

Throughout this period, however, Healey managed to continue what he calls his "second life in politics." Born in 1943, Healey first got involved in high school, when he helped pass petitions to stop nuclear testing and joined the early marches. At Reed College he joined the Student Peace Union and at UCLA he got involved in SDS. When the latter group broke up, he helped found the New American Movement, which promoted democratic socialism and feminism, and he worked on energy and labor issues. Along the way, he spent time in the South, involved in anti-war and civil rights issues.

He was working in the Public Health job when the Washington, D.C., post opened up. For Healey, it was a natural: "After a year and a half of Ronald Reagan in office, I was getting more and more upset about foreign policy and the dangers of nuclear war." He applied for the post, and got it in 1982.

Once on the job, Healey saw counteracting the Reagan charisma as a major task. He worried that while the activists could win "bits and pieces of battles," Reagan was "winning a larger political fight of definition"—convincing politicians and voters that "we need new missiles, that somehow the Russians got ahead of us."

With such simplistic argument, said Healey, it's hard to convince people, including politicians, that the Russians are not ahead . . . and that new weapons could bring more danger than security, because they would almost surely cause the Russians to expand their own arms development.

But Healey admits he enjoys the battle. Discussion usually spills over into family dinnertime conversations, he said, pulling in comment from his wife, who works on many of the same issues as a staff member at the national office for the League of Women Voters, and from his mother.

His two sons are still too young to have much concern for politics, but both already have participated, said Healey. Benjamin, now 3, attended—well, slept through—his first demonstration at just 3 weeks, snoozing in a Snuggly inside his father's parka. Both Benjamin and Joshua, now just under 10 months, were with their parents at a recent South Africa demonstration—one where Healey got arrested, an action he takes calmy. He's "never tried to count" the number of arrests in his long activist history, he admits, grinning; arrest is just one of the tactics he's comfortable using to get government attention.

When government acts without public backing—proposing to escalate involvement in Central America even though "78% of the American people oppose it," for instance, or ordering more MX missiles even though public opinion is "split" on the issue—citizens must reclaim those rights enunciated by the founding fathers, said Healey.

He thinks it's starting to happen, especially among those church groups he works with. "We have a long way to go, but at least I think we're beginning to see a direction."

When the media talk about the growth of political activism within the church, the subjects of their stories these days may be, as Healey suggested, mostly the Pat Robertsons and Jerry Fallwells on the ideological right. But with less noise—and surely less ballyhoo from the media—the mainline churches also have strengthened their hand.

A major move came in the early '80s, when the Catholic bishops issued their pastoral letter denouncing nuclear war and weaponry. The letter "reflect[s] the enormous changes that are sweeping through the Catholic Church in America," commented Time magazine in a Nov. 29, 1982, cover story. Previously, Time observed, "as a group, American bishops were almost jingoistic in their endorsements of U.S. foreign policy."

A message even stronger in some ways was issued in 1986 by the United Methodist bishops. Where the Catholics had conditionally accepted nuclear deterrence, the Methodists rejected it as "a position that cannot receive the church's blessing." Regarding the Strategic Defense Initiative, the Methodists said, "We state our complete lack of confidence in 'proposed defenses' against nuclear attack and are convinced that the enormous cost of developing such defenses is one more witness to the obvious fact that the arms race is a social justice issue, not only a war and peace issue."

In addition, of course, many individual church members and leaders have taken their own stands. Sometimes that involvement is as low-key as talking with friends or sending notes to legislators. Other times, however, the activism becomes confrontive. Jim Wallis, editor of Sojourner's magazine, recalled one such incident in an article written for the July 1984 Progressive magazine. In May 1983, Wallis wrote, he was among some 3,000 clergy and lay leaders who gathered in Washington, D.C., to protest the nuclear arms race. Wallis and 241 others went a step further—they entered the Capitol and "turned the Rotunda into a sanctuary filled with gospel songs and prayers, while—within earshot—Congress debated funding for the MX missile."

"We were dragged away by the police for praying for peace, in what was the largest mass arrest in Washington since the Vietnam war," said Wallis. The event topped the evening's NBC "Nightly News"; Bob Abernathy reported, "The protestors are Christians . . . convinced [that] legal protests against the arms race are no longer enough, that there must also be nonviolent civil disobedience like that of the civil rights movement 20 years ago, and that the church should lead it."

Time magazine's story noted that even while the Catholic bishops were "weighing their words" before issuing their pastoral letter, a number of priests, nuns and lay people were putting their beliefs into action: Nine Catholic protesters were sentenced for trying to damage a nuclear submarine in Groton, Conn.; two nuns were convicted of forging government passes to enter the Rocky Flats plant; a Cheyenne, Wyo., sister was coordinating a coalition opposing deployment of MX missiles; Jesuit Father Daniel Berrigan was facing a 5- to 10-year sentence for damaging warhead cones in Pennsylvania.

"Indeed," wrote Jim Wallis, "something is stirring in America's churches . . . . Call it renewal, revival, or conversion, the gospel is coming alive in new and unexpected ways."

Larry Peacock, who shares the ministry of Malibu (Calif.) United Methodist Church with his wife, Anne Broyles, is one of those who have been been both participants and observers in the continuing give and take between activism and religion. He was involved in discussions about stopping anti-ballistic missiles as far back as his high school days in the mid-'60s. During the Vietnam era, he joined campus sit-ins and participated in Washington, D.C., marches and demonstrations. While in seminary, he learned of Third World hunger and "began doing fasting, became a vegetarian and led hunger workshops." Now, however, in his church work, he said, "I'm probably focusing more on spiritual development, the life of prayer."

But Peacock thinks the two go hand in hand. That "strand of concern" has always been there. "Sunday school training can result in radical politics," he pointed out. "Whenever you begin talking about God's love for all of the people . . . it doesn't take much of a step to say, 'Well, not all persons are experiencing God's love. Why not?' " And that can lead to activism.

Beyond that, said Peacock, many of those already in the peace and justice movement are realizing they need both the resources and spiritual support of the church. "I think," he said, "for the movement to sustain the ongoing, longterm commitment to peace and justice which is required, it will require that spiritual sustenance . . . . It's not a short battle."

An update on Richard Healey arrived in the mail some time after our talk. He had moved on to a new job—one that might give him a chance to do something about public and media awareness of what was happening in the peace movement. His new title: executive director of Nuclear Times magazine.

Again, the job would involve networking. This time, he would be working with eight supporting peace groups who hoped to turn the magazine into a strong voice for political and social change. He would also be "setting up some kind of meetings between activists and academics to share ideas, strategies and anything else we can come up with."

"I hope it will lead to better communication, more ideas, and more cooperative projects," he said.

23. SANCTUARY FOR THOSE IN NEED
Renny Golden, Chicago

If our aim is to save humanity, we must respect the humanity of every person. For who would be the enemy?

—*Jonathan Schell*

In the spring of 1983, two American women found themselves traveling through Mexico on a mission that involved breaking the law, evading the police, harboring law-breakers . . . and, they hoped, saving lives.

One was Renny Golden, now 48, slim and fair-skinned, with graying hair; the other was Robin Semer, younger, with curly dark hair and an olive complexion. They had gone deep into Southern Mexico, where they met Sanctuary leader Jim Corbett of Tucson. The three planned to gather up a dozen Guatemalan refugees, then break into two teams and bring them into the United States. Corbett, with experience behind him, would take some into Arizona; the women, new to the task, would take the rest into Texas. The women's plan was to cross the river between the two nations on a rubber raft, then put the refugees on the "underground railroad," safely headed north.

Golden and Semer knew their trip could be dangerous . . . that it was not truly prudent for two North American women to play games with both the Mexican and American legal system. But they were willing to take their chances. Both were strong supporters of Sanctuary, the North American movement that operates almost entirely through churches and synagogues, and which has brought thousands of Central Americans into the United States.

In Mexico, the three North Americans were dealing with a sensitive situation. The refugees they sought were being sheltered by the Mexican clandestine church, said Golden. "People who harbor refugees in Mexico risk much more than we do," she added. "We can just go to prison; they can get disappeared." Still, a priest near the Guatemalan border was willing to hide refugees on their way north.

Soon after the visitors arrived, decisions were made about which refugees would travel with Corbett, which with Golden and Semer. The priest had a suggestion for the two women: Travel on the Virgin of Guadalupe pilgrimage train, he counseled. With such a train, "no hay problemas, there's no problem, they won't catch you." So that's what they decided to do.

But, said Golden, "They caught us." The two women and their charges were taken to la Migra, the immigration office. "We spent two days at the migra station, trying to get them out," said Golden. "We said we wouldn't leave these young men, because Jim Corbett had said, 'The world abandons them; we won't.'"

But eventually, sadly, they did. The Mexican authorities warned them, Golden recalled, "'If you continue this, you'll be accused,' which meant we'd have to go up before the Mexican court system." In distress, the women had called the Mexican priest. But he had said he could not help, that "we cannot save a few when we have to save thousands." By then the women realized they were no longer helping the men—"that we were jeopardizing them more." The men's future already was chancey. They could be deported back across the Guatemalan border.

To Golden and Semer, that seemed to be a sad, frustrating conclusion to the story. But a month later they heard there had been a happy ending after all: The young men had been picked up by another Corbett team, and this time, successfully spirited across the border.

For Renny Golden, her confrontation with authority spotlighted an intriguing split in the life she now leads. For, in spite of that

Renny Golden

incident, Golden earns her living very much on the side of law and order: She teaches in a criminal justice program at Chicago's Northeastern University. Meanwhile, she puts her off-hours energy into a group called the Chicago Religious Task Force on Central America—a group she helped found, and one that coordinates the "underground railroad" that now brings Central American refugees into the northern United States as part of the Sanctuary movement.

But there is still more to the story, for Golden is a former Dominican nun, with a long history of activism.

While still a nun, she had taught at an inner-city, black area of Detroit between 1960 and 1967, years that saw American society trying to deal with the challenge of civil rights. They were frustrating years for the young woman.

"I felt the question of justice for poor blacks was not being addressed . . . at least, I wasn't allowed to address it in a way that made sense to me," she said, speaking quietly, but tapping her finger to emphasize important words. Teaching sisters, for instance, were not allowed to travel freely in the city: "I couldn't go and visit families; I had to have a companion if I even went to the store."

Golden was in Detroit when the black riots exploded. "It was evident to me that I was going to have to make more than a superficial response."

She took dramatic action—leaving the order, moving to Chicago, and signing on with an alternative high school for black and hispanic youngsters. There she was free to get involved and to try new ideas with the students.

But she also wanted to help area adults. "Probably 40% of them were on welfare, some were in factory jobs; most of them didn't have high school diplomas." So Golden drew on the ideas of Paolo Freire, a Brazilian educator who had taught illiterate peasants to read in 12 weeks by relating the reading to their own lives and needs. Looking at her own students' needs, Golden put together a program that would teach reading, offer diplomas and "empower" the participants. The program for blacks lasted seven years, said

Golden, and when it ended 1,500 people a year were participating. The Hispanic program, a much smaller one, continues today.

During those years, Golden also reached out to the anti-Vietnam struggle. She recalls joining a mid-'60s crowd that gathered at the White House, when "we thought that if we lit enough candles and prayed and were willing to be arrested and were willing to go to jail, we would say to the nation, 'Listen to your children. Can you not see the errors of this war?' " She was with protestors outside the Democratic convention in 1968 in Chicago: "I was gassed with everybody else . . . and watched with great shock as the police beat people up . . . beat heads open."

Golden stayed with the Chicago program for 10 years, but eventually sensed the start of burnout. She decided to enroll at Chicago Theological Seminary as an attempt "to understand what, in faith terms, this journey had been for 10 years in the black community." That move led to further politicization, for while earning her doctorate in theology, she also was introduced to Latin American liberation theology, which supports the church's social/political involvement in its community, and to feminist theology. "Both of these were very intriguing to me and were to have a tremendous effect on my life," she said.

Upon graduation, Golden was invited to spend a year as teacher/researcher in a women's religious studies program at Harvard University Divinity School, and that led to more social involvement. The course she taught—again based on the work of Friere—joined literacy and political education.

When inmates of nearby Walpole Prison heard about it, they asked that she and a group of other educators and organizers introduce those ideas through Walpole's Prison Education Program. So, "while I was at Harvard for part of the week, I also went out to Walpole, which is a maximum security prison, and for eight hours a day, we would sit down with the men and create a program and a political process." It was an educational process for her, as well, she said: "I learned a tremendous amount—about the marginated, about crime, and about justice denied—from the clients of the criminal justice system."

That apparently was enough to bring an offer from Northeastern University in Chicago to join the staff of their criminal justice program. And that is how she has paid the bills for the last eight years. "I'm an associate professor and I teach theory," Golden said.

One day, after her return to Chicago, she had joined a group of Catholic women outside the Salvadoran consulate there. Four nuns had just been murdered in El Salvador. The women who had gathered were repeating "sort of a litany of the saints and martyrs," recalled Golden. "I remember turning to people next to me and saying, 'You know, I think this is where we quote Mother Jones: "Pray for the dead, but fight like hell for the living." These women died for something; we have to take up their task, not do a litany.' "

The result was formation of the Chicago Religious Task Force on Central America, the group that has supported Sanctuary's underground railroad for the past three years. Today the task force's coalition of socially-concerned religious groups includes Clergy and Laity Concerned, the National Assembly of Women Religious, the National Coalition of American Nuns, the American Friends Service Committee, the Eight State Center for Peace and Justice, and the Presbyterian Task Force on Latin America, plus the 12 Chicago Sanctuary churches. For Golden, the group is a logical follow-through to that commitment to Central America dating back to her seminary days and that class on liberation theology. Through the class she had become active in a program called Theology in the Americas, bringing together Latin and North American theologians; that group had encouraged her belief in an activist church.

As Golden sees it now, the success of Sanctuary, which calls on participants to risk arrest for the sake of their moral beliefs, signals nothing less than a rebirth of the church as a voice of social conscience. When churches or synagogues agree to harbor a refugee, as 220 in the country already have done (a larger number participate as supporters), "that means those congregations are willing to face—if the Immigration and Naturalization Service were to break into the sanctuary—a prison term of five years and a $2,000 fine for each refugee harbored," said Golden. Yet, some 70,000 United States citizens are active in transporting, housing and feeding the refugees, she estimated.

"I think it's very difficult for middle-class churches, which is what the Sanctuary movement is. It is a profound conversion experience. The strength of the Sanctuary movement is that it's the first time the anglo church . . . has had to choose sides . . . has had to risk and to place itself on the side of the poor and the oppressed . . . and has discovered in the process of walking with these refugees, standing by their side, that it IS the church."

That new political awareness has challenging implications, Golden believes. Walking with the refugees has meant recognizing that "we have to stop the source of the exodus, which is our own government's interference and intervention in Central America," she said. It has meant "not to simply say, 'I will feed the hungry, clothe the naked and shelter the homeless,' but 'I will face WHY they are hungry, homeless and naked . . . and act against that.'"

It hasn't been an easy development, said Golden: "People, all of us, went toward Sanctuary kicking all the way, because we didn't want to have to face the odds, didn't want to confront this Goliath." But with the refugees in their midst, she said, the Americans are finding it impossible to close their eyes. "The Central Americans have not allowed the church of the north to remain comfortable any more," Golden added. "These prophets have come into our midst and told of their suffering; now we can never not know the human cost of these wars."

Golden now terms Sanctuary "part of a struggle against militarism." The Vietnam War she once demonstrated against may have ended, she will tell you, but the same problems of militarism and intervention are continuing in Central America, and militarism won't end until the problems that cause it are solved. "Issues of militarism are linked to the issues of justice denied," she said, punctuating the statement with firm taps on the table. "If we can't talk about peace AND justice, we really won't be able to overcome."

Renny Golden freely admits that in spite of any turn toward "resistance" among American churches, not all Catholics applaud her challenging brand of activism. She recalls the time she and other demonstrators raised protest banners while Notre Dame University was awarding an honorary degree to El Salvador's President Duarte, and how "14,000 people there were hostile to everything we were standing for." Yet, a growing number of Americans are finding that their religious faith inspires the kinds of activism that others may reject or for which they simply are not ready.

"For the third time in as many centuries, some religious historians argue, America is undergoing a profound religious revival," Michael Ferber wrote in The Nation (July 6, 1985). And activism is part of it: " 'Resistance' is now commonplace in the rhetoric of many quite respectable church representatives." That resistance may be the result, Ferber proposed, of some tough questions church members are asking themselves: "What is the good society? Are there means to get there that do not pervert the ends? What are we called on to do? What sacrifice is right, and how do we summon the courage to make it?"

Ferber cited the Sanctuary movement as "the most spectacular example of religious opposition to U.S. foreign policy," pointing out that as of June 1985 "more than 1,300 local congregations— Catholic, Protestant and Jewish—had declared their support for sanctuaries of conscience," even though a number of leaders already had been indicted.

24. A WOMAN WHO CHANGED THE LAW
Barbara Elfbrandt, Tucson, Ariz.

> *What is the use of postmarking our mail with exhortations to "pray for peace" and then spending billions of dollars on atomic submarines, thermonuclear weapons, and ballistic missiles?*
> —Thomas Merton

In 1966, Barbara Elfbrandt made headlines.

The soft-spoken high school teacher from Tucson had taught without pay for the preceding five years rather than sign the loyalty oath passed by the state in 1961. But now she was vindicated: Her case had gone all the way to the Supreme Court, and the court had determined that Arizona's oath—requiring the signer to declare that he or she did not belong to the Communist Party or any successor or subordinate organization—was unconstitutional. The state law was struck down.

It was a wonderful victory—one that was political, philosophical and financial—for Elfbrandt and her husband. He, too, had taught most of those years without pay, although his name did not appear in the suit. "The year the case came up, he was taking a leave of absence," explained Elfbrandt. "But when he went back to teaching, he didn't sign either." For both, it had taken a special brand of courage.

The Elfbrandts were Quakers, not Communists, but they believed the oath was setting "a very dangerous precedent." Part of that related to Quaker (Religious Society of Friends) history. "It comes out of their experience in England 300 years ago," Elfbrandt explained. "When religious people or any British citizens were asked to sign oaths—for example, that they were not Catholic—Friends didn't sign. They felt, 'OK, I'm not a Catholic, but you have a right to be a Catholic. And if I sign that now, next week they'll be back with one that says I'm not a Friend.' "

Her refusal to sign the school oath was tied to the civil rights movement. The time period was "right after the McCarthy era," said Elfbrandt. She had found people who supported the oath "demonstrating in front of the state legislature and passing out little flyers that said the organizations they had in mind . . . that were probably Communist dominated . . . [included] the National Association for the Advancement of Colored People, American Civil Liberties Union, Student Nonviolent Coordinating Committee and Congress of Racial Equality." What groups would get added to the list next? Besides, most states had struck down such loyalty oaths several years earlier.

Financially, the Supreme Court decision meant the end to five years of unbelievable money-stretching by the Elfbrandts, who had survived only through determination buoyed by creative tactics. "We had a strong, but small, support committee," said Elfbrandt. "We did things as practical as having people invite us permanently out to dinner a specific day every week. Our landlady was wealthy and excused the rent for a few years. There were a lot of projects to raise money; we were in constant fund-raising."

"We actually borrowed from people, saying that if they would give us money on a contingency basis—that we might win—we'd pay them back [when we did]." When the case was closed and the couple got their back pay for those years, said Elfbrandt, "that was exciting. It was really fun to be able to pay people back."

Yet, said Elfbrandt, the satisfaction was much more than monetary: "The kinds of things you learn from an experience like this are invaluable, and one is that money is not the important thing; it's the emotional support. That's what makes you able to continue doing something that seems like you're swimming against the stream."

And that is exactly what she has done. She first went back to school, herself, to become an attorney, which allowed her to get involved in Vietnam era draft and veterans rights problems, and finally took on the job as administrator of the American Friends Service Committee office in Tucson, the job she still holds. She has never stopped pushing and prodding her community and state to do what she has seen as morally and ethically right, although now she does it alone, since her husband died not many months after the AFSC office opened in January 1981.

As AFSC administrator, Elfbrandt has developed a peace studies program for inmates, staff and administrators at the prisons; she also has put together a program for teachers, "Children's Creative Response to Conflict." She has encouraged the University of Arizona to begin a conflict studies program.

There is more: Elfbrandt and AFSC have worked toward peace conversion plans for local industry; they have organized a committee specializing in Central American affairs—a committee that supported growth of the Sanctuary movement in Tucson. Elfbrandt still works with local lawyers, trying to make sure that activists and young men who refuse to register for the draft have legal help available.

Part of her goal, she said, is to make sure Tucson remembers its own involvement in war preparedness. "Southern Arizona has a lot of military industries and bases here . . . including Davis Monthan Air Force Base," she said. "Until recently, we had the Titan missiles that surrounded Tucson. Now that the Titans have been replaced with Cruise missiles, ground-to-air missile personnel train at Davis Monthan. There's Fort Huachuca, of course, and there's Hughes Aircraft right here in Tucson that produces missiles, too. and I haven't even mentioned the new Silicon Valley-type industries moving in."

Elfbrandt, who works with only one paid staff member, a part-time secretary, is responsible for the entire state, not just Tucson. AFSC duties also require occasional travel to California or Philadelphia. She even fit in a trip to the Soviet Union in 1984 as part of a three-week United States-Soviet friendship project.

"That gives you some idea of why we're really busy around here," said Elfbrandt, "but it's fun; I like it. It's one of the best jobs I've ever had."

"It didn't make much difference what I was doing—teaching school or practicing law—I always seemed to end up doing community organizing," she added, laughing. "I decided I might as well get paid for what I liked to do."

A quarter of a centry earlier, when Elfbrandt first moved into the peace movement, she had helped put together a peace walk supporting the nuclear test ban treaty. "I guess even then I began to see that the resources that we needed to have in our society for the problems of poverty and social change were going into the arms race," said Elfbrandt.

"I still have that concern. With the vast resources of a society like ours, we really have no excuse for people living on the street and standing in soup lines. It's absurd . . . I would say obscene . . . where we spend our money. I think we can judge the values of a society by where it spends its money, and by that test we are a militaristic society. I would like to help change that."

———

As in Tucson, AFSC has become a major pulse point for peace workers in many communities across the nation. Quakers, themselves, play a peace and justice movement role that exceeds their representation among American religions. Yet, one of their major objectives has been to facilitate participation by those who may not share their particular form of worship. A catalyst toward that goal is AFSC, which typically operates as a networking and outreach agency within any area it serves.

While the committee carries the Quaker name, it is not an all-Quaker organization. Elfbrandt reported that "about 78% of AFSC staff and committee members are not Friends; our executive secretary in this region is not a Friend." While Elfbrandt, herself, is Quaker, she considers that coincidental.

25. NEW UNDERSTANDING, NEW DIRECTIONS
Tom Rauch, Denver, Colo.

> *If nuclear war should occur, it will come about*
> *not because it was inevitable but because not*
> *enough people took the trouble to avert it.*
> —*Norman Cousins, 1981*

U.S. 40 leading to Denver from Salt Lake City is considered the scenic route. If your goal is speed, you take Interstate 80 to the north, or 70 to the south. But there was no particular rush the day I made that drive, so I turned onto 40. It was a stunningly beautiful fall drive, starting between canyon walls covered with pine, aspen and cottonwood; autumn leaves were delicate pinky-orange and yellow pastels. Further on, shrubs replaced the trees, and colors turned to the deep shades of the tundra.

The year's big tourist season already was over for Dinosaur National Monument, located at the side of this highway. Yet, a few travelers were inspecting the dinosaur excavation display—a slanting wall of rock with bones left where they were found, still held by the rock and only partially exposed to sight. It was an incredible look at earth history.

Further east in the park were Indian petroglyphs. No protective fence guarded them, merely a sign pleading with visitors: "Nine centuries ago native Americans pecked symbols on these mineral stained rocks. Today, fingerprints and bullet holes mar the ancient works. America's heritage deserves better. Will you help?" On the road back to the dinosaur exhibit, an even more urgent question was posed on another sign. Standing before a dramatic vista of sand

and rock, it carried this message:

> Rocks in the rugged landscape ahead were formed during a chapter of geologic time—the age of reptiles. The fossil record reveals that life flourished during those 140 million years. Natural change is slow but effective.
>
> Man has been here almost no time at all. Yet he is rapidly making the world less fit for life—including his own. Will the human story amount to even a page in time in the history book of the earth?

That final question confronting visitors to Dinosaur National Monument was one Denver's Tom Rauch could have adopted as his own. He has dedicated his life to encouraging a positive response.

Rauch—slim, gray-haired, smiling—had been working in the garden just before opening the door to the modest home he shares with his wife, Maureen Hendricks; he was still in casual clothes as he settled into a comfortable chair in the small living room.

His job these days is director of the Rocky Flats/Disarmament Project, part of the American Friends Service Committee program in Denver. In spite of that title, however, Rauch does not really work much with Rocky Flats any more; his two main projects now are promoting better understanding of the Soviet Union and fighting Star Wars. His wife is a clinical psychologist in private practice; her special interest focuses on sexism and its damaging effects on women. She is away this day at a conference.

It's a pretty good life, a satisfying one, said Rauch, although for both him and his wife life has turned upside down from the dreams they set out to fulfill in their youth.

Both had entered Catholic religious orders: Hendricks, the Daughters of Wisdom, where she became a nurse-nun; Rauch, the Jesuits, where he served as a college teacher and then a parish priest. Both are now excommunicated—essentially a result of marrying without Vatican permission after leaving their respective orders. They still worship as Catholics, but with a small, unsanctioned

Tom Rauch

group of friends who meet in each others' homes. They call it a feminist worship group, said Rauch, because "women are fully involved in the worship leadership, as well as men."

Earlier, Hendricks had joined the Daughters of Wisdom as a young woman, said Rauch, "because in confession one day she had talked to a priest about something, and he had said, 'I think you have a vocation and should do something about it.' She kind of took that as the voice of God speaking to her." But it never did feel right, and after 15 difficult years, she left. Hendricks then completed her bachelor's degree in nursing and looked around for a graduate program. In 1970, she received a scholarship to study community health nursing at the University of Colorado. She packed a U-Haul and drove to Denver.

Rauch's seminary years began in 1951, and brought some early seeds of activism. "I was one of a group that was fortunate to go to Washington, D.C., for the great civil rights march of '63, when Martin Luther King Jr. gave his 'I have a dream' speech," he recalled. "It was a marvelous experience, at the end of a very hot day. They'd had talks and music from noon until 5, and it was just too much. I was tired, and I think most of the crowd was pretty tired. King gave the final talk and it lifted everyone up. I can still remember the exhilaration and inspiration."

About that time, Rauch also read a pamphlet by Dan Berrigan, "talking about his transformation in the Jesuits . . . [how he'd come to see] that the Christian faith should impel people to take responsibility for the world."

But the event that finally bumped Rauch into activism, he believes, took place two years after his June 1964 ordination, at the start of a teaching assignment at Denver's Regis College. During a pre-term gathering for freshmen, a young man began questioning him about Vietnam. At that time, recalled Rauch, "I said, 'Well, I haven't really thought a lot about it. I think we're probably there helping that government against communism.'" But the student persisted, and soon the priest was reading literature arguing that

United States involvement in Vietnam was wrong.

As Rauch began to oppose the Vietnam action and learn about the peace and justice community, he found his work in the Jesuits more and more constraining. He tried moving from academia to parish work, but nowhere did he find the freedom to do what he had come to believe was most important—to dedicate his life to peace. In 1971 he took a year's leave and headed back to Denver; in 1972 he left the Jesuits.

By a felicitous twist of fate, when Rauch returned to Denver he also returned to an alternative Catholic worship community he had helped form before leaving town. There he met a new member, Hendricks. They were married almost a year later.

In the years that followed, both grew into new careers. Hendricks, entered the University of Northern Colorado in Greeley, where she earned her doctorate in clinical psychology and family health maintenance. Her dissertation, aptly, was a study of the marriages and subsequent lives of former Roman Catholic priests and their spouses. She found that about half of those priests had—like her own husband—married former nuns.

Rauch, meanwhile, found a job with Clergy and Laity Concerned (CALC) . . . then, in 1975, began an eight-year stint with a Franciscan campus ministry . . . and finally, in 1983, signed on with the Rocky Flats project.

Rauch had first connected with AFSC as a volunteer in 1966. Then, he recalled, AFSC had been "busy with draft counseling and educational programs about Vietnam." But over the years, its role had changed. By the mid-'70s, AFSC had begun looking at the Rocky Flats weapons plant—the same one Marge Roberts was still opposing a decade later. The plant had been opened in the early '50s by Dow Chemical, which operated it until 1975. In the early '70s, the county health director had done a study showing that "an extremely large amount of plutonium contamination had escaped from the plant," said Rauch. "It was quite likely some of it had come as far as Denver." The Rocky Flats Action Group was set up in 1974.

In those earlier days, AFSC put on rallies that drew thousands of protesters, did door-to-door canvassing, and sponsored educational programs. After Rockwell took over, they approached the company and the government, seeking good data on exactly what was going on at the plant. There were a couple of years, Rauch said, when the federal government actually required anyone buying a home within a 10-mile radius of the Rocky Flats facility to sign an affadavit saying they knew about the plutonium contamination and would evacuate if there were an accident at the plant. Houses still sold, said Rauch, because "realtors, I think, pretty much pooh-poohed it and probably told people that some radicals forced this through."

Today, however, the major AFSC interest has moved on. For one thing, Rauch said, "I have to admit, as critical as I am of the place out there, that I think Rockwell has done a better job of caring for the safety and health of people than Dow did." Really forcing the plant to move or to close—the early goal of AFSC—would require convincing the federal government that the plant is a hazard; activists are sure that is true, but their data was disputed by the government. Even before Rauch signed on, AFSC had begun reaching out to other areas—helping the nuclear freeze campaign, organizing peace conferences and doing community educational work.

So, Rauch's work has evolved, as well—now including a major concern about Star Wars. "As you may know, Colorado Springs is very rapidly becoming the center for the U.S. militarization of space," he said. "The unified military space command is located there; they're building a facility which will eventually control all of the military shuttle flights and all the military satellites. If Star Wars is developed, I think it's very likely that Colorado Springs will be the center of much of that."

As Rauch had told me, it was satisfying work, though frustrating, as well. Sometimes, even when priorities are carefully set—as they are these days at AFSC—it's tough to see results.

"I get tired sometimes, I feel there's a lot of hassle," said Rauch. "This year, especially, I've felt very hopeless much of the time over our ability to effect any change in national policy. I operate with not a great deal of hope . . . but kind of feeling that at least it's important to do something with my life that's making a different statement. There are a lot of people all around the country doing things like this. Maybe something will happen, some person or some event will bring all of this together. That's kind of what happened to the civil rights movement. Somehow events happened at a certain time that brought a lot of people together, and it touched the conscience of some of the white community. Maybe that's what's going to happen with the peace movement."

26. NO LONGER A TRAITOR
Esther Webb, Greenbelt, Md.

> *Many will tell you with mockery and ridicule that*
> *the abolition of war can be only a dream . . : .*
> *But we must go on or we will go under . . . . We*
> *must have sufficient imagination and courage to*
> *translate the universal wish for peace—which is*
> *rapidly becoming a universal necessity—into*
> *actuality.*
>
> —Gen. Douglas MacArthur, 1961

Soon after Esther Webb became a pacifist, she found that much of American society had another word for her: Traitor.

It was the tumultuous period of American entry into World War II. "Loyalty" was suddenly defined as support for the war effort; those who didn't were suspect. It was as simple as that.

For a young woman recently out of college, seeking her first full-time job in the nation's capital and struggling to promote peace in a world caught up in global war, that was an uneasy time.

"It was a very popular war," said Webb, now 67. "Anybody who was a pacifist or for peace then was really [considered] sort of a weirdo. It was really a very lonely thing."

Four decades later, I found Webb at the small home she and her husband share in Greenbelt, Md., just outside Washington, D.C. When I arrived, the sleeves of her red turtleneck were pushed up and she was energetically mopping the kitchen floor. She turned the mop over to her husband, and we settled down to talk in her tiny office. Webb's gray hair was cut in a severe Dutch bob; beneath the bangs, she wore brown-rimmed glasses. Sometimes the eyes

Esther Webb

behind those glasses looked pensively out the window as she talked.

Webb had embraced pacifism while attending Antioch College in Yellow Springs, Ohio. Before enrolling there, she had wanted to study medicine, but her parents objected: Didn't she realize that women doctors became old maids and never had children? So Webb dutifully cast about for a new goal and wound up majoring in social science, entering a work-study project at an Ohio Farm Bureau cooperative . . . and becoming interested in peace. While at Antioch, she joined the Religious Society of Friends.

The only thing she really knew about Quakers then, she said, was that "they were a peace church and against war . . . . I felt at that time that peace was going to be THE most important issue of that time, and I wanted to be part of it." By joining, she said, "I felt there was sort of a commitment to peace that I had made."

Following graduation, Webb headed for Washington, D.C. It was 1943 and a frenetic time in the capital—a time of "very rapid military buildup, just as there is right now," she said. Yet, it was still during the lingering days of the depression, and young women—even bright, well-trained young women—were not prized by employers. "When a woman with a college degree came to town looking for a job, they asked, 'What do you know how to do?' " said Webb. "By that they meant, 'Do you know how to type? Do you know how to take shorthand? Or do you know how to run an office machine?' "

Webb got a temporary job with the federal government running a calculating machine and considered herself lucky. She ran through a series of clerical positions as the nation's war fever heated up, but never landed a permanent spot.

Before Pearl Harbor, there were "enormous demonstrations in the District of Columbia to keep us out of the war," said Webb. She participated in most of them. But then the Japanese attacked in Hawaii . . . the nation went to war . . . and Webb found that many of the groups she was involved with were suddenly out of business and their members were considered suspect. Webb discovered that her name had been "flagged" by the Civil Service Commission—"unsuitable" for federal employment. She no longer could hope for work with the government, which had been her major employer.

At a Quaker meeting about that time, Webb met a young biologist—her future husband, John Webb. He was seeking conscientious objector status and had joined the Quakers, but did not have the history of membership that the draft board required. By the time the couple married, said Webb, the FBI had a file "that thick"—Webb held her thumb and forefinger a good distance apart—on John, and "he was expecting to go to jail." But he never did; he kept fighting for his CO status through the lengthy appeals procedure and finally succeeded with a decision by the appeals court.

The young couple settled into Washington for the duration. Esther found work as a high school biology teacher. After the war ended, the couple moved to Hawaii for four years when John was offered a post with the government's plant quarantine service. Esther began raising a family, which grew to include four children.

By the time the youngest was ready for school, the couple had returned to the nation's capital and Esther was anxious to go back to work. She began teaching and later served as a counselor in the District of Columbia Schools, where she continued until retirement at 60.

"I always specifically asked to work in a poorer neighborhood," she said, "because I felt you can do more good there." Most of the schools in which she worked were 100% black.

The couple had purchased their home in nearby Greenbelt, Md., an idealistic New Deal "garden city"—a model town built by workers and for workers through the Works Progress Administration (WPA) during the tough depression days. By the time the Webbs settled in, the government—which originally owned the project—had sold out to the residents, and Greenbelt had become the nation's "largest housing cooperative." Now land and structures, including the supermarket and gas station, are jointly owned by the residents, Esther

Webb said with pride.

The couple still lives there in the same compact unit in which they raised their youngsters. Greenbelt is showing its age now, but for the Webbs it's home, it's theirs, and it's cooperative, all of which are important. After all, Esther Webb had been involved in the cooperative movement during college. What's more, her father had developed a string of co-op credit unions throughout the South; and now her husband, retired from the Fish and Wildlife Service, devotes most of his concern to the cooperatives.

But Esther Webb's major interest remains her peace work. During the early '60s, when Esther was juggling child rearing and teaching, she "didn't really take a very active role," she said. Yet she did find time for some activities, mostly with the Women Strike for Peace, one of the first post-war peace groups. Her activities broadened as the children grew older.

Recalling those days, Esther now admits she gets a bit mixed up over dates, especially when trying to pinpoint just what happened during which war—"there were so many of them"—but she recalls specific incidents vividly:

—There was the time she was helping hand out literature against the draft at D.C. high schools. "Newspaper reporters were there, and the principal got all uptight and kicked us off school property," recalled Webb, by now able to grin at the memory. "Then students decided to have a little fun, so they took our literature and made a bonfire." The reporters turned their cameras on the bonfire—but also on Webb. "That evening I was sure my principal was going to kick me out of the school, because they interviewed me and had me on full evening TV, what I thought about the war and everything." But it turned out all right, she said, laughing: "Fortunately we had a PTA meeting that night, so the principal didn't see it."

—There was the day she testified against the draft before a congressional committee. One of the congressmen at the hearing read a letter from a serviceman, asking what the legislator thought about people—"traitors"—who would hand out peace literature like the flyer he enclosed. When the congressman held up the flyer, it was the one Webb had been distributing at the high schools, "and there I was, sitting right there!" She didn't tell the congressman about her role in handing out the leaflet. "I must admit, I didn't have the courage to, because I knew what was coming. But I wrote a letter to the committee later saying we had been responsible for it."

—There was the fight she led to oust the Cadet Corps, which offered military-type training, from the district schools. It was a long battle, but the corps eventually left.

During those same years, Webb helped organize a Greenbelt Committee for Peace in Vietnam. She did it soon after the United States got involved, she said, before national sentiment had turned against the war. And she joined the board of the Washington Peace Center.

Recalling those years elicits a sigh from Webb. They were difficult. But she was not about to quit. And after retirement, she just added more activities.

One of the stories Webb most enjoys telling is how she tried to get arrested demonstrating against nuclear weapons. "I figure that once you retire and you get your pension check every month, it really doesn't matter whether you go to jail; more older people should go to jail," she said, pleased to realize that her story held a bit of shock value. "So, I thought it was about time for me."

Webb joined other volunteers at a government building they had targeted. They placed themselves in front of the doors as employees tried to move in and out during the lunch hour. But the police declined to arrest them. Closing time arrived, and the demonstrators lay down in front of the doors; employees carefully stepped among the bodies.

The demonstrators were frustrated: "The head of our group was pleading with the police, 'You're supposed to arrest us!'" Webb recalled, laughing. "But the policeman said, 'I'm the one who decides whom I arrest.'" It turned out, Webb said, that the police

had orders not to arrest anyone, so the demonstrators went home—
and the day's headlines were stolen by a large group of New York
City demonstrators arrested on Wall Street.

Less dramatically, Webb pulled together a local Gray Panthers
group, hoping to get more elders involved in peace; she helped
organize the local drive calling for a nuclear freeze; she got involved
in a local Rainbow Coalition; she found time to serve on the SANE
phone bank, alerting groups around the nation to needed peace
efforts.

"I plan to keep working for peace till the day I die, even if I
go blind and lose my hearing," she said, ending with another laugh,
knowing she was being a bit outrageous again. "I can still lick
envelopes."

Now, after more than four decades of peace work and a lot of
pain and frustration, Esther Webb feels hopeful. "In the old days,
in World War II, the only people who worked for peace were
pacifists," she said. "But now, just plain ordinary people are coming
to meetings and saying, 'What can I do?'" There's a larger number
now, a broader base, she said. Peace has become a popular issue.

For a long-time worker who recalls those lonely days many years
ago, she admitted, it's nice to talk about peace, to find that "people
respect you" . . . and to know that Esther Webb is no longer considered a traitor.

VII

TAKING CHANCES

For some activists, taking chances is just part of the lifestyle they choose. Marge Roberts was one, with her bodyguarding stint in Nicaragua. Renny Golden was another, with her attempt to bring refugees across the border. Perhaps all those who risk arrest must be included among the chance-takers—and these number among the thousands in the United States.

Among such activists, perhaps the best known are those who have participated in a number of incidents known as the Plowshares Actions. These are individuals who take the Biblical words of Isaiah, prophesying a future when swords will be beaten into plowshares, as a call to action—a call to physically challenge the war machine. That may mean breaking into military production facilities to damage or deface the weaponry being produced.

While observers may brand their acts violent and radical, the activists argue back: Not only are such acts nonviolent, since they cause no personal injury, but they are in response to the higher call from God. Mostly the Plowshares Actions have been carried out by a small number of people acting together. One, however, was the work of a single man.

27. SYMBOLICALLY DISMANTLING THE WAR MACHINE
Peter DeMott, Baltimore

> *The nations will not study war any more; they will beat their swords into plowshares and their spears into pruning hooks, and one nation shall not raise the sword against another, nor shall they train for war ever again.*
>
> —*Isaiah 2:4*

On Dec. 13, 1980, Peter DeMott—former member of a Jesuit order, former Marine, former truck driver—did the unthinkable.

He had joined a couple of thousand other Americans to view launch ceremonies for a fast-attack submarine at General Dynamics' Electric Boat Division in Groton, Conn. The boat was being christened the Baltimore; DeMott and the friends accompanying him were there as a personal protest to the use of their city's name for such a purpose.

While most other eyes were on the official activities, DeMott looked around. Off to one side he noticed another sub—one of the big ones: a "four-story tall" Trident. It was the kind that one day would be fitted with "two dozen Trident missiles, each of which can have 5 to 17 warheads," DeMott thought to himself; the kind that all by itself would be able to "end all of life forever on this planet."

While those thoughts were running through his mind, DeMott became aware of an empty security van nearby, keys still in the ignition.

"So," as he tells the story today, "I got into the van, rolled up the windows . . . backed up to the sub . . . floored the accelerator and smashed into the rudder, then did it again (clapping one palm against the other), and again (clap), and again . . . " until security guards raced up, pulled DeMott out of the van, got him arrested and sent him off to jail.

That particular action may have been unplanned, but it was not out of character for DeMott: In other actions—these all with other activists—he has poured his own blood on the Pentagon; he's returned to the Groton shipyard with his wife, Ellen Grady, and five other activists to pour more blood, hammer on missile hatches and begin to "disarm" the USS Georgia; he's interrupted talks by Secretary of Defense Caspar Weinberger and Vice President George Bush, shouting his opposition to the arms buildup. Often such incidents have been followed by wrists snapped into handcuffs, appearances before the court, and time in jail.

Some may decry such actions as unnecessary, as illegal or as violent, DeMott said; but as far as he is concerned, there's a better description: "personal obligation." The goal, he said, is to begin the disarmament process, and to avoid repeating that period "when Hitler was making crematoria in Poland, but nobody spoke out."

Today DeMott lives with a group of similarly-committed activists in a home they call Jonah House, a big, Victorian-era row house in a mostly black area of Baltimore. Inside, there's a sense of family: Youngsters scamper through the rooms; a songbook on the well-worn upright piano is opened to "Three Little Kittens"; noises from the kitchen signal meal preparation. Life at Jonah includes regular Sunday liturgies and Wednesday evening Bible studies.

But life at Jonah is not simple tranquility. The youngsters, it turns out, are Frieda, 10; Jerry, 9, and Katie, 3, all children of Philip Berrigan, 50, a former Josephite priest, and his wife, Elizabeth McAlister, 45, a former nun; the parents are the couple who founded Jonah House in 1973. Activism and headlines were nothing new to Berrigan, his brother Dan Berrigan, a Jesuit priest, and McAlister, who all were deeply involved in Vietnam War resistance.

Jonah House, Phil Berrigan and McAlister decided, would be one way of opposing the continuing arms buildup.

This day Elizabeth McAlister would not be home to help dish up the dinner that was being prepared for the Jonah community, including her children: She was serving time for her part in a Thanksgiving Day 1983 break-in at Griffiss Air Force Base, Rome, N.Y. In that incident, the group of seven hammered and poured blood on a B-52 converted to carry cruise missiles. All were sentenced to three years in federal penitentiaries.

Only a few days ago, during Easter week, all current occupants of the house had left, said DeMott, heading for Washington, D.C., to pour more blood and demonstrate at the Pentagon—actions the group schedules three times a year. Adult members within the community draw their own blood at intervals, even when no action is imminent. The blood is frozen until needed. At the latest action, DeMott was not among the three blood-pourers, the only ones who were arrested.

With the exception of DeMott's spur-of-the-moment van attack on a submarine, those actions that may result in arrest are carefully planned, so potential jail time is shared, he said. Half a dozen from Jonah are in jail at the moment; eight adults are left at home, plus the three youngsters.

Berrigan and McAlister schedule carefully so that both will not wind up in jail at the same time, which would deprive the children of both parents, said DeMott. Because Jonah House functions as a community, meaning all members share responsibilities, Elizabeth McAlister "can go to jail with a clear conscience," DeMott added, "knowing that . . . her children will have the nurturing they need." Although not every mother would feel comfortable with that argument, the Berrigan youngsters—including blue-eyed, angel-faced Katie, 3—do appear comfortable connecting with any available adult within the home.

It is, all in all, a lifestyle that would not fit many. But it suits Peter DeMott well . . . and he tried a number of others before settling on this one. DeMott grew up the second of nine kids in a poor family; he had the added problem of severe acne, which led to shyness with other young people. Joining the church seemed the answer to a lot of problems, and DeMott signed on with the Jesuits when he was 17 and just out of high school. His goal was to become a lay worker, not a priest.

But DeMott was unhappy in that life, so in a major about-face, he left the Jesuits and joined the Marines. He was 21. Looking back on that action, he philosophizes: "Well, I was raised on John Wayne . . . and I guess I saw it as part of the ethos, what it meant to be a man in our culture . . . a rite of passage." DeMott wound up in Vietnam as a communications specialist, spending most of his time "in the rear with the beer and the gear." It was not, he added, an especially traumatic or politicizing experience.

Finishing his term with the Marines, DeMott tried college and didn't like it, then took a job driving a truck and didn't care much for that, either. He decided to get back in the military. This time he chose the Army and contracted for training as a linguist. He was sent to the Monterey, Calif., language school to learn Ottoman Turkish, then given extra training in secretarial skills before being sent to Turkey. His fluency in the language made his stay interesting: "I enjoyed Turkey and the Turks very much," he said. But his time on the job was mostly "lots of errand-running."

Next DeMott thought he'd like to learn Russian, so he contracted for another tour of duty, with more studies at Monterey. The Army, however, decided there was no room for him in that program, so DeMott left the service. Then he tried the religious life once again, entering a Catholic diocesan program in St. Paul, Minn.—"this time with a lot more idealism"—but left after a year, again dissatisfied, and renewed the search for a life that fit.

For a while he did odd jobs in St. Paul, which left lots of time for reading and thinking. Along the way, he met some people involved in the Catholic Worker movement, which ministers to the poor and homeless. These were people who were taking responsibility for their world, he decided. Some of those he met had participated in civil disobedience.

Eventually, DeMott joined a Catholic Worker community in Des Moines, Iowa. It was there that he heard about Jonah House's plan to demonstrate at the Pentagon. So in September 1979, DeMott traveled to Washington, D.C., and helped pour blood. He was arrested and spent five months in a federal prison before going home . . . this time to Baltimore and Jonah House.

Since the house basically supports itself through manual labor of its members, DeMott, like other men in the group, now works as a painter. He was just back from the day's work as the interview for this story began, his blue pants splattered with paint.

Asked to describe Jonah, DeMott said it is "a community of non-violent, radically Christian activists, concerned primarily with resistance to the arms race." He bristled slightly at the thought that this interview could wind up—as others have, apparently—portraying the Jonah community as a bunch of violent, fringe crazies. Yes, their actions involve damaging property, trespassing and the like, he said. But no, they're not violent. Actually, he said, it's the opposite: "I'm a nonviolent person. This whole thing is about nonviolence. We've got to learn to live nonviolently or we're all going to kill each other." Yet, he said, it is imperative that individuals begin the process of disarmament. "We say, not only do we have a right to do this, we're obligated to."

With that, DeMott pulled out a nearby Bible and read the passage from Isaiah: "The nations will not study war any more; they will beat their swords into ploughshares . . . ."

"We're trying," said DeMott, "to follow the same life that Christ led." He recalled stories of Jesus speaking out against "the unjust power structure of his day . . . and then paying the penalty for having done so."

"In his case," added DeMott, "it cost him his life."

So, it's not too much to hammer on a few weapons of war and spend some time in jail for something that important, suggested

DeMott. "The Bulletin of the Atomic Scientists says the doomsday clock is at 3 minutes to midnight, that any second, or for all
we know, even as we sit here and speak, nuclear missiles could
be in flight, either to the Soviet Union or from the Soviet Union
to here. It could all end, just like that. For everybody."

———————

Elizabeth McAlister, writing after her 1983 arrest, described the
Plowshares Action in which she participated:

> I was in [jail] because, with six friends, I had entered Grif-
> fiss Air Force Base in Rome, N.Y., in the early hours of
> Thanksgiving morning [1983] and entered what they call
> Building 101. The building housed, among other things, a
> B-52 bomber which they were in the process of outfitting to
> carry a full complement of cruise missiles. We hammered
> on the bomb-bay doors of the B-52; poured our own blood
> on the fuselage of the plane; spray-painted the phrases "320
> Hiroshimas" and "Thou Shalt Not Kill" and "If I Had a Ham-
> mer" on the plane; taped to it photos of our children and
> children with whom we work, as well as a "people's indict-
> ment" of Griffiss Air Force Base that we had drawn up.
> Meanwhile, the other half of our group did similar work in
> a storage area nearby dealing especially with the engines for
> the B-52 and one engine for the Fighter Bomber. They painted
> "Omnicide" and "Stop Cruise" in strategic locations.

After their arrest, the seven were indicted for sabotage, destruction of government property and conspiracy. It could mean,
McAlister realized at the time, as much as 25 years in jail. And
that, she added, "can be frightening, especially when the one facing it has three young children whom she loves deeply."

Just days before the action, McAlister wrote, she and Phil
Berrigan and their children, along with other members of Jonah

community, had watched the TV show, "The Day After," describing the world that might follow a nuclear attack. After the film, parents and children talked about the action McAlister planned four days later.

Even though her children had seen their mother and father and other members of the community arrested in the past, the Griffiss action could mean their mother would be gone for "an indefinite amount of time." McAlister recalled that the two older children, then 9 and 8, "said that they understood, in a new way, why this resistance was so necessary. They were willing to accept the personal sacrifice of my absence as their part in trying to stop a nuclear war from happening, as their part in trying to avoid the suffering that the movie displayed." All in all, concluded McAlister, "It was a moment of extreme closeness for the four of us; a moment of accepting together whatever might come down; and we concluded our conversation with prayer and big, big hugs."

It would be hard, McAlister admitted, to leave 2-year-old Katie, for "watching her grow is watching a miracle unfold; it is hard to think about missing all that."

"And for her part," added McAlister, "I have to agonize over the potential damage to her spirit. At the same time as she is a deterrent to this kind of risk, she is a spur to it." There is a need, McAlister suggested, for any parent "to ask, 'How can I best love my children?' and to answer by working to provide for them and the millions like them a hope for the future." McAlister titled her article, "For Love of the Children."

The booklet, "For Swords Into Plowshares, the Hammer Has to Fall," which included McAlister's recollections, also carried a commentary by Sidney Lens, a labor organizer, writer and peace advocate. Many Americans may agree with the Plowshares goals, he said, yet ask, "Why don't they do it the 'right' way—for instance by running for political office themselves or working for a 'good' presidential candidate committed to 'arms control'? Why don't they try to change things from 'within' the system? Why don't they do something 'practical'?"

His response: "The Plowshare people—and other nonviolent activists—are in fact the most practical of all Americans. They know that change will come not just by electing good people, but by a drastic change in American thinking and in the American conscience . . . . The Plowshares do not necessarily disparage elections. But they know that it is impossible to end the arms race through the ballot box alone . . . . In an age of nuclear madness, theirs is as yet one of the few tiny lights guiding us to sanity."

28. SHARING THE DANGER
Ellie Foster, Santa Cruz, Calif.

> *Courage is the price that life exacts for granting peace.*
>
> —*Amelia Earhart*

The road through Northern California from San Jose to Santa Cruz is a fine one. It leads over gentle, seemingly pristine, forested ridges, then suddenly drops toward sea level, offering dazzling views of a crescent-shaped shoreline, a 1907-vintage casino, and a boardwalk flanked by a roller coaster, an antique merry-go-round and other delights.

There are many old sea-town homes here, wearing the comfortable patina that comes with age and salt air. Some have been artfully embellished—among them, one at 511 Broadway, a Victorian complete with bay windows and decorative wood siding. The exterior has fairly recently been painted blue, with white and dark blue trim. At the top of the white chimney, some fey hand has added a comical happy face; from an upstairs window, someone has hung a multi-colored Japanese paper fish. It is not, perhaps, the setting one would expect for an organization that sponsors one of contemporary activism's more daring programs.

A sign at the lower left corner of the house announces the home's occupants: Santa Cruz Hostel Society, Hit and Run Theatre, and Witness for Peace. It's the last of the three that we're after.

Inside, hard at work, is Ellie Foster. Lunchtime is the only hour Foster has free this February day, so talk takes place over bowls of thick broccoli soup and a shared spinach salad at a nearby vegetarian deli.

Ellie Foster

Foster—now 58, with close-cropped grey hair and an infectious smile—talks eagerly, yet quietly, almost shyly, about herself and Witness for Peace. The group, she explains, takes American citizens to the borders of Nicaragua, where they live, pray and vigil with those natives who often are the victims of attacks by U.S.-sponsored contras. Foster, who previously had been a career adviser and coordinator of peer advising at the University of California at Santa Cruz, serves as coordinator of United States operations.

Witness for Peace was started in the summer of 1983, Foster said. It seems that a group of peace people—"mostly kind of leading church people"—had gone to Nicaragua to see for themselves what was going on. While there, the group did some vigiling along the border where contra guerrillas were known to make raids. They discovered something interesting: As long as the Americans were there, the contras mostly stayed away. So, the group decided, why not have a continuing presence in Nicaragua. And that's when they founded Witness for Peace.

Since then, the group has run two simultaneous witness programs: "a long-term team that stays there six months to a year, and rotating delegations of people who just take two or three weeks off from work." So far, said Foster, "we have about 1,000 returned delegates now from across the states, and we have support groups in all the states and all the major cities."

Sure, it can be dangerous, she said, because the groups tend to spend their time along the borders where attacks take place. But Witness for Peace is not quite so concerned as it once was, because it does seem that the contras bide their time while the Americans are around.

Foster visited Nicaragua once, herself. "It was great. We went into Managua for a couple of days and then went right out to the border villages in the mountains, around the Honduran border. We talked a lot with the people, and then spent time vigiling on the border, because . . . contras with binoculars are very aware of all the movement on the border. We held out a banner there. Just as a way of saying, 'We're here watching,' and as a statement for peace."

There had been a raid in the area shortly before Foster's group arrived, and villagers wondered if the Americans would prefer staying together in a block house within a village. But the group decided unanimously that they would rather spread out with families.

As Foster recalls it, village homes were mostly made with materials like mud and banana leaves. One she stayed in, she said, "was earth on some kind of a wood framework, kind of like mud building blocks, with a dirt floor."

"If they had a cot in the house, they would always give that to us, so we got to sleep on a cot instead of on the floor," she said. "In some places they didn't have one, and then you just slept on a mat on the floor." Foster took along a flannel sheet: "It was so warm . . . that was all you needed." And the visitors "always took a bag of rice and a bag of beans and left them with them, because they were all desperately poor."

Witness for Peace today is one of many groups sending delegations to Nicaragua, said Foster. Witness draws mostly from those with a strong religious foundation, but represents many faiths; some other groups are more politically based.

Even when she was there, evidence of United States' support of the contras was easy to find for visitors who got out in the villages, she added. "We saw equipment that was left from the contras, with 'United States' on it, you know. There were empty boxes of cartridges that said 'U.S.' . . . there were NATO shells there and Israeli equipment."

Usually it's the young and the old who are killed or captured and tortured in the border raids, she said, since most young, able-bodied people are serving with the army. Witness for Peace hopes to let the Nicaraguans know that many Americans oppose such actions, she said, and "that we are speaking for peace."

For the time being, Foster's work has little to do with the anti-nuclear movement, although she thinks all anti-war efforts are knitted into the same cloth. She's been a nuclear power protestor in the past, even spending two weeks in jail after joining a demonstration at the Lawrence Livermore labs.

Her commitment to pacifism developed in the late '40s, she said, while she was working toward a double major in philosophy and psychology at Redlands University, a private, liberal arts college in Southern California. That led to joining the Quakers. After graduation, she married a fellow Quaker. The young couple left for post-war Europe, where they worked with refugees for three years. Then, moving back to Chicago, they co-directed a black tenement project, while living in the tenement area, themselves.

Returning to California, Foster got involved in developing child care centers for the mostly Mexican farm workers and in assisting unions in the Central Valley; that's probably where her current interest in Central America began, she said. Her next job was the one at UC Santa Cruz.

Her husband, Herb Foster, also has continued in peace and social justice work. For some years he helped develop low-cost housing; he now spends much of his time as West Coast representative for a Friends committee on national legislation, watchdogging and lobbying, and serves on the Friends committee on East-West relations.

Meanwhile, Ellie's Witness for Peace office is responsible for overseeing educational work with her group's support communities in the United States—communities that involve many of the former vigilers. An office in North Carolina coordinates the Nicaraguan activities.

Walking back from lunch to the blue house, Ellie Foster thought quietly about the effect of all her effort. "It's sort of miniscule, whatever you do," she said, smiling. "But you feel kind of like an ant: At least you're doing something."

Ellie Foster identified one frustating problem facing Witness for Peace and similar groups: It is difficult to get their story out to the American public. Media tend to adopt the government point of view, she said. "They just kind of automatically talk about the 'totalitarian' regime or the 'communist' regime when they talk about the Sandinistas." Even some media representatives get frustrated, she added: "We talked to a New York Times reporter in Managua, the capital of Nicaragua, and he said he gets so discouraged he doesn't even read his stories after they're printed, because they leave out so much information."

Groups like Witness for Peace are slowly building their own "experiential" base for opinion, she added—involving, at the time we talked, the more than 1,000 Americans who had visited the Central American country through Witness for Peace, with more regularly on their way. That, she believes, is what gives her group a special ability to "speak truth to what we've seen and not be caught into following some party or ideological line."

Witness for Peace did break briefly into the news in late August 1985, she wrote later, "when a group of witnesses navigating down the Rio San Juan were captured and detained 30 hours by contras attacking from Costa Rica."

"The river forms the boundary between Nicaragua and Costa Rica," Foster continued, "and the trip was a nonviolent demonstration of the formal peace existing between Costa Rica and Nicaragua, often subverted by counter-revolutionary forces based in Costa Rica attacking across the border. The Witness for Peace passengers on the boat heard the chants of the Nicaraguan peasants who lined the bank in the night awaiting the passage of the boat: '!Queremos la paz!' (We want peace!)"

VIII

THE LEGACY OF GANDHI AND MARTIN LUTHER KING

Ellie Foster's letter had mentioned the nonviolent nature of the Rio San Juan boat trip along the border between Costa Rica and Nicaragua. Peter DeMott had used the same term to describe his attack on the Trident submarine. Through these incidents and many more, before and after, "nonviolence" has become a fundamental thread within the peace and justice movement.

Nonviolence means that activists disavow violence in their protests and that people are not injured. That is not the same as "passive," for it may encompass vigorous demonstrations, civil disobedience, or damage to property.

Most activists trace their definition of nonviolence back to Mahatma Gandhi and Martin Luther King Jr. Today, the tactics developed by those two leaders and others like them are being taught by teachers across the country. I spoke with a teacher who happens to live in a city far better known for one mythical citizen—J.R.— than for peace activism. Mavis Belisle's home town, of course, is Dallas.

29. TRAINING TO BREAK THE LAW
Mavis Belisle, Dallas, Texas

> *Those who discovered the law of nonviolence in the midst of violence were greater geniuses than Newton.*
>
> —*Mahatma Gandhi*

Mavis Belisle met me this Sunday morning wearing faded jeans with wide, turned-under hems, a cotton gauze blouse and well-worn white sandals. It was an outfit that could have been plucked right out of the '60s, and it was surely no attempt to keep up the styles in her home town, trendy Dallas.

No, Belisle agreed, wearing "in" outfits is not important to her: "I try to dress appropriately. If I'm doing a program, I try to wear nice slacks or a skirt. But I don't think gray flannel suits and silk blouses are important." Happily, the latest look doesn't matter for Belisle's specialty: teaching nonviolent protest techniques.

The skills she offers are those recognized across the nation; today almost all groups planning civil disobedience—moving into offices of legislators, for instance, or jumping fences or sitting on railroad tracks—require that members planning to risk arrest get nonviolence training. In that process, groups reject the old confrontational tactics, the kind that sometimes brought angry battles and human injury. Sometimes anger breaks out anyway, activists admit, but people like Belisle are working hard to prevent it.

Belisle and others like her draw inspiration from both India's Mahatma Gandhi and America's Dr. Martin Luther King Jr. King wrote in a 1963 "Letter from Birmingham Jail" that while those in a nonviolent campign must "present [their] very bodies as a means of laying [their] case before the conscience of the local and national community," they must also be "able to accept blows without retaliating . . . able to endure the ordeal of jail."

Today, Belisle attempts to carry on that ideal. She tells those planning civil disobedience about the history of nonviolence, how it causes social change, how it affects people psychologically as well as physically, and how it could help to change the world. It is, she suggests, an alternative to "the whole cultural acceptance of war and violence as a means of solving problems." It provides, she is convinced, a model for a future world of peace.

Belisle also teaches how to make decisions under pressure; how to organize within small, closely-knit affinity groups; how to keep communications open between demonstrators and law enforcement officers. She trains "peacekeepers" to monitor rallies and marches, and to deal with problems as they arise. She arranges practice demonstrations ahead of time.

Some of Belisle's tactical know-how comes from personal experience. She, herself, has been arrested six times during civil disobedience actions: once at the Pentagon, opposing nuclear weapons; once in New York, during the United Nations special session on disarmament; once in Austin, and three times at Dallas' own Comanche Peak nuclear power site.

Arrest can be a meaningful tactic, one that makes a statement and expresses personal commitment, Belisle believes. But she does not condone excesses of the kind that took place during some Vietnam-era demonstrations, "when people would use the protest action as an excuse to burn cars, break out windows, et cetera."

These days, much of Belisle's work is with the Pledge of Resistance, which opposes United States intervention in Central America. Thousands of the group's members across the country have put themselves on call to do civil disobedience opposing any significant escalation of intervention. Their disobedience is mostly a mild variety, where members crowd into offices of legislators and refuse to leave, hoping to gain the attention and support that eventually will lead to change.

Belisle's own concern about social change reaches back to her junior high school years. That was when Little Rock, Ark., was being torn by the court's desegregation decision, and when Dallas was squirming as blacks began moving across the Trinity River and into an area where the Belisle family lived. As the young girl saw it, both actions were welcome. "It seemed to me—I guess because of my church background—very clear what was right and what was wrong."

Then, as a student at the University of Texas at Austin, Belisle flouted tradition by signing up for the first women's co-op to mix black and white roommates; that seemed right, too. She got involved in the early anti-Vietnam activities. And once she received her degree, with a double major in political science and journalism, she joined the Peace Corps.

Her three Peace Corps years were spent in Belau, part of the Western Carolines in Micronesia, where Belisle taught school and helped develop plans for a tourist industry. While there, Belisle made a discovery that would help set her direction for the years to come: "I can remember pulling a little handmade book off the school library shelf. It was describing sea life in the area, [and] I kept running across the phrase, 'edible except in certain parts of the Marshalls.' I couldn't figure out why it would be OK to eat the red snapper where I was in Belau, but not OK to eat them in the Marshalls."

She soon learned that it was because the Marshalls—also in Micronesia—were where the United States had tested nuclear bombs in the 1950s. The fish there were still "radiation contaminated"— especially those living in lagoons. "A lagoon is a fairly closed biological system," said Belisle, "so instead of going away in shell-fish like clams and so forth, the radiation actually accumulates over time rather than deteriorates."

That introduced Belisle to some of the long-term effects of nuclear weapons. She would learn about the short-term effects when she left the Peace Corps and traveled to Japan, visiting the Hiroshima peace museum, with its graphic depiction of the destruction caused by one World War II atomic bomb. "So when I came back home, I became involved in peace and disarmament issues," said Belisle. "I have been ever since."

For now, she feels content to continue that work in Dallas, in spite of the town's emphasis on values that are not hers. "I really love it here," she said. Whatever else it may be, she believes, Dallas is a city where a woman like Mavis Belisle may be able to make a difference.

Today, the typical student reached by Belisle and other teachers of nonviolence is an otherwise law-abiding, middle class American—often one who claims strong spiritual motivation. These are people who feel their willingness to confront authority and to face arrest makes a powerful, personal statement opposing government policies they believe to be wrong. Mostly, they plan ahead carefully; spur-of-the-moment participation in arrest actions is discouraged by leaders and groups. For these people and these groups, arrest has a new definition: It's an intentional tactic, chosen to make a personal statement, not just the unpleasant consequence of some illegal action.

All of the above suggests some questions: How does the idea of "planned" arrest fit into the American justice system? Doesn't a proliferation of such arrests trivialize them? What does this whole scene say about the media, which tend to report the number of arrests during a demonstration as just one more battle statistic, without mentioning that those being arrested may see the arrests as symbolic rather than punitive? How should the police react? Isn't all of this a publicity ploy and a waste of taxpayers' money?

Answers to those questions, of course, tend to be highly subjective. From the activists' viewpoint, these arrests are not so much a part of the justice system as of a larger protest of government in general.

Interestingly enough, many law enforcement personnel seem to go along—at least part way—with that interpretation; there may be little sense of adversarial confrontation during an arrest action. In fact, many officers introduce their own brand of nonviolence. While the evening news may still show protestors being escorted to paddy wagons, check the nightsticks—they may still be in the belts. The officers may have dealt with the same group often enough to know the leaders on a first-name basis; those leaders probably told the officials ahead of time just what they were planning, including the number who expected arrest. It may play out like a pre-arranged script.

In the typical scenario, demonstrators who do get arrested may be back home by the same evening—though they often have to appear later to answer legal charges. Some activists plan arrests to fit neatly into their schedules: a business meeting here, an arrest action there. Jail sentences, when there are any, tend to be brief. It may appear, in fact, a rather civilized procedure.

So, how about that idea of trivializing the whole thing? Not so, say the activists; such actions may not neatly fit the old definition of arrest built on the notion of cops vs. criminals, but they have their own meaningful significance. And while leaders of demonstrations may worry about getting publicity, one activist added, most participants are not particularly concerned about the media; for them, the value is personal.

That picture seemed to hold true during one arrest action I observed, the 1986 Hiroshima Day protest against nuclear testing held at the Nuclear Test Site north of Las Vegas. Larry Peacock, the long-time activist who now shares with his wife the ministry at Malibu (Calif.) United Methodist Church, had told me before the demonstration, "I think you will be surprised at how spiritual an event it will be." He was right.

An estimated 350 demonstrators participated. Few were full-time peace activists. Many had taken time off from jobs or school; some had traveled most of the way across the country.

They had come to Las Vegas as much as two days early to prepare for the August 6 demonstration. During that time, support groups were formed—each group to accompany one or more would-be arrestees to the line. A sense of community was strengthened through shared meals, meetings, prayers and music; many in the large Los Angeles delegation even spent the night together, laying out their sleeping bags on the grass behind the Catholic Worker house.

The day of the protest, itself, brought both symbolism and ritual. Prior to the actual demonstration on Aug. 6, some 200 persons gathered under the desert sun to celebrate the Eucharist, led by a priest wearing a white cassock. Then, in a less formal ceremony, all demonstrators brought forward slips of paper they had been handed on their way to the site. Each slip carried the names of two past nuclear tests; all were symbolically placed in a small hibachi and then burned. In return, each demonstrator received a small origami peace crane.

As the day's major action began, the demonstrators moved to the stretch of highway designated as the arrest site. Sheriff's officers already were there; they had been present since early morning, before demonstrators began walking the final two miles that brought them to the area. As demonstrators lined up on both sides of the road, those who planned to be arrested—90 in all—placed themselves at the far end. Then, one by one or in small groups, those 90 and their supporters slowly walked to the line where the officers waited them. The deputy who met each one carefully repeated their "rights"; he waited calmly while some spoke of the beliefs that brought them here or dropped to their knees for prayer. In a sense, that officer symbolically accepted the sacrifice of each of those who crossed the line.

Once on the other side, each arrestee held out his or her wrists for a pair of light, plastic handcuffs. And then, for almost all arrestees, the mood changed. They grinned, looked back to the other demonstrators, joked with the officers. It seemed to be a true, joyous event of affirmation.

Yet, say activists, no matter how you cut it, getting arrested is no minor action. Sure, you may be free before the sun sets, but you also may have a record for the rest of your life; even though many law enforcement people are used to handling such situations, demonstrators still may be roughed up and injured; you still may have jail time (those at the Nevada Test Site were told to expect six days).

But it's worth it, they add: Taking such serious action together brings a sense of sharing and hope that's hard to find any other way; jumping that fence or breaching that barrier does bring its own kind of idealistic, psychological high; in facing arrest, you are putting yourself on the line for something that means very much to you . . . and, you hope, to the world.

30. THE DAYS OF TRIBULATION
Glenn Smiley, Glendale, Calif.

> *. . . one day we've got to sit down together at the table of brotherhood.*
> —Martin Luther King Jr., 1967

The time period was a tense one: the height of the civil rights struggle.

The place was Birmingham, Ala.

And the incident that day began simply . . . as Glenn Smiley, a white, Methodist clergyman, his wife Helen and a black clergyman walked together toward the Smileys' car following a Sunday afternoon workshop on nonviolence at the black clergyman's church.

"We walked down about a half block to my car, which was parked in front of a grocery store that was closed up," recalled Smiley. "When we got quite close to the car, five men came up in a taxicab and jumped out of the taxicab and encircled us, with their fists doubled up like this!" Smiley clenched his own fists, remembering the incident. He could smell the liquor on their breath, he said, and "I knew they weren't there to help me with my books."

"I knew that I couldn't run," said Smiley, "because I'm not the running type. Besides, I wouldn't want to run off and leave my wife there. I knew I wasn't going to fall down on my knees and beg for mercy, because that's the worst thing I could have done. So, I said, reaching out with my free hand—the other one being full of books—'Good afternoooon, brethren!' and continued to walk straight toward one of the fellows who had his fist doubled up, smiling as much as I could. He jumped out of the way and let me pass

Glenn Smiley

through, and my wife passed through next, and the black minister followed her.

"There the car was. I opened it up. My wife got in. By then the men were in a half moon around us, but their hands weren't doubled up any more . . . they were just sitting there with their mouths open." At that point, said Smiley, the black minister shook hands with Helen Smiley, something that could have been dangerous during those days in Birmingham . . . "but in that particular circumstance, it was great, because they kept getting surprised.

"Then the minister went back through the circle and went on into his church. I brushed off the windshield and then got into the car and drove away. When I saw, after two or three blocks, that we weren't being followed, I began to think about what could have happened. And then I pulled off to the side of the road and my wife and I shook for about 15 minutes." The memory still carries emotional impact; Glenn Smiley let out a quick laugh, then sighed, "Oh, boy!"

In those days, Smiley was working full time with Martin Luther King Jr.'s civil rights campaign, although his salary was being paid by the Fellowship of Reconciliation (FOR), a group whose basic premise, he said, is "rejection of war." Like other groups, they see social injustice as one of the causes of war . . . and with that premise, they were one of the first to jump into the desegregation battles.

Smiley was in his 40s by then. He'd begun preaching in Southern churches at 16; he'd been given his own church, in Tucson, Ariz., at 19. In the years while war fever was heating up in Europe, he became a pacifist. When the United States got into the war and pacifism became unpopular, with even the churches pulling in behind the war effort, Smiley left the pastorate and accepted his first post with the pacifist FOR, as Pacific Southwest regional secretary.

Almost immediately, he was confronted with a major issue: West Coast Japanese-Americans were being rounded up, losing their homes and possessions, and being sent away to desert internment camps. Smiley was new on the job, and looking back, he says, "I don't feel very good about it; I didn't know what to do." But his small group and a few Quakers were about the only ones doing anything: "We took them sandwiches, we held their hands, we told them of our friendship and our love . . . and they were taken away."

Meanwhile, Smiley had initiated his personal battle with the military draft. First, he refused his exemption as a minister—ministers should be treated like everyone else, he and his wife believed. So, the government sent a classification for a married man with three children . . . and when those exemptions were terminated, they sent a conscientious objector classification.

By then, said Smiley, "I had advanced a bit more in my convictions and took the non-registrant position." The government ignored that and sent him an assignment to a civilian public service camp. Smiley refused to go . . . and "they eventually jerked me up and tried me and sent me away on a three-year sentence." He wound up spending almost 16 months at McNeil Island Federal Prison on Washington's Puget Sound, and quickly found himself in something of a pickle with the prison administration. Because he was a clergyman who rated an automatic exemption . . . because he was older than the typical conscientious objector . . . and because his mail often came from important personages, the administrators thought they smelled "something fishy."

"They figured," said Smiley, "it was a conspiracy . . . that I came to spy on them."

And that is the reason, he believes, why he spent a fair amount of that 16 months in the "mainline" maximum security prison—where his nine cellmates included three multiple-murderers—rather than the minimum security "farm." However, in both locations, Smiley gave his free time to counseling other inmates. In prison, he said, "everybody's in need." When he was at the farm, he recalled, "men would come, sometimes several in a night, almost waiting until the other fellow left. They would ask me to write a letter, or they would cry, or just want someone to sympathize with them."

When the war ended, Smiley was released. He went straight back to work with FOR on the West Coast and quickly got involved in the civil rights movement.

FOR had introduced sit-ins as a technique to fight segregation even during the war years—their first in Chicago in 1942. Working out of his Los Angeles headquarters, Smiley saw a chance to use the technique at one of the city's nicer tearooms, located in the upper-class Bullocks Department Store. Soon racially-mixed groups began going to the tearoom each Saturday, effectively reducing tearoom profits by simply sitting in their chairs from the time the room opened until it closed—never getting served.

Eventually, Smiley told one of FOR's local supporters—"a formidable-looking dowager"—what was happening. She protested that the Bullocks she knew and patronized could never do such a thing. So, one Saturday she invited a black woman psychiatrist to accompany her, and they joined the group at the tearoom.

"She tried to get a waitress," said Smiley, "but no, not as long as the black woman was there." However, the dowager did know Bullocks' president . . . and she did complain. And that is likely one of the reasons, Smiley believes, why the tearoom manager one Saturday—after three months—finally made an announcement: "He said, with a great smile on his face, 'Serve these people!'" And with that, said Smiley, everyone in the tearoom "broke into thunderous applause."

By 1954, Smiley had been named FOR's national field secretary, so the family moved to New York. But in 1956, he got a new assignment: Martin Luther King Jr. had asked FOR for help in the use of nonviolence, and Smiley was told to "give him all the help you can."

It would be three years before Smiley would leave King and return to his fulltime duties at FOR headquarters. Smiley felt an immediate empathy with the black civil rights leader: "I was absolutely engrossed and charmed by this whole thing. I said to myself, 'He may be asking me to come down and teach him nonviolence, but I'm already his disciple.'"

And Smiley did teach the nonviolence he had been studying since the early '40s—not only to King, but to black church leaders throughout the South and to hundreds of black citizens. King was a fast learner, said Smiley. Once, at a convention of the NAACP, King introduced Smiley as his teacher. "I was tremendously complimented," said Smiley.

Those were crazy, frightening, inspiring, active, wonderful years. Smiley was involved in bus boardings, demonstrations, workshops, press conferences and strategy sessions; he preached two or three times every Sunday, and often again on Wednesday, all at black churches; he was personally threatened by the police.

Finally, finances pulled Smiley back to New York: FOR was having its own budget problems; they could no longer support him fulltime in the South. However, for some years, Smiley kept working "on call" for the King campaign—and was actually helping with King's Poor People's Campaign in Washington, D.C., on the day in 1968 that King was shot and killed in Memphis, Tenn.

By then, Smiley had left FOR, where he had risen to the rank of associate general secretary—a job that focused on fundraising. Raising money, said Smiley, was "no problem for me." But the long-time activist twisted uncomfortably in the role. And so, after 25 years with FOR, he resigned, to fulfill a new commitment in Latin America.

Smiley had offered to teach nonviolence to a group of South American trade unions—and that's what he did through mid-1970. Then he got a call to do similar work in the Philippines, and spent a month giving workshops there. On his way home from that stop, while in Tokyo, Smiley suffered a series of small strokes. And so, he said, "I retired for health reasons . . . though now it looks as if I may live forever."

After his health improved, he worked for several years as a family and marriage counselor in the Los Angeles area; he is now retired from that, too, and said that he was serving his final year on FOR's national council. When this interview was held, he was spending a few days in the Catskills, prior to a FOR council meeting in Nyack, N.Y. Then he would return to his home in California.

All in all, he said, life has been pretty good to him: "I think that many things have happened that I don't understand, and I'm awfully glad they happened. But who am I to deserve this? Because, you see, I have been arrested, I've been in jail, I've been thrown in Southern jails, and I've been confronted by a mob and have talked myself out of it. I have never had a hand laid on me. And my wife, who has been with me on several occasions when we've had these experiences, has never had a hand laid on her. There are an awful lot of men much better than I who've been beaten up, their legs broken, and in Martin's case, shot."

"Now, why did that happen to me?" he asked quietly. "I can't claim that God had any special purpose for looking after me."

31. CONTINUING THE STRUGGLE
John Collins, New Rochelle, N.Y.

> *If the human race can't learn to get along with*
> *itself, it will soon exterminate itself.*
> —*Ken Keyes Jr., "The Hundredth Monkey"*

This Friday evening John Collins is running late. He arrives at his New Rochelle home, just outside New York City, with a brown bag of fresh strawberries under an arm, red juice staining the bag's corner. He apologizes for being late—especially because there isn't much time to talk: In an hour of so he must leave to pick up his wife Sheila, who's arriving at Newark Airport. In the meantime, there's dinner to fix and eat.

But Collins is capable host. While I sit at the kitchen counter, he begins talking even as removes his jacket, sorts and cleans the strawberries for shortcake to be eaten later, takes leftovers out of the refrigerator, dumps them into a pan and puts them on the stove to heat.

Life, it seems, is rather like that on a routine basis for Collins, who is co-director of Clergy and Laity Concerned, a religiously-based, ecumenical group with national headquarters on Manhattan Island. In the process of trying to pull together groups and individuals from around the nation to work on peace and social justice issues, there isn't much free time to spread around.

There are many extra activities as well: Collins had been at Columbia University the night before, for instance, joining students protesting the university's investments in South Africa and that country's apartheid. He was leaving on Sunday for Washington, D.C., to join the April Actions for Peace, Jobs and Justice; he planned to join the scheduled civil disobedience on Monday, which would presumably mean getting arrested. However, he was skipping the Saturday march and rally, he said; Saturday was the day to take down storm windows at home . . . those things needed to be done, too.

As far as Clergy and Laity is concerned, Collins said during the dinnertime interview—by now he was cradling a tiny ceramic cup of stove-top espresso coffee in his hand—"we no longer think of ourselves as a peace group. We're a peace and justice network."

And the fundamental problem—the one underlying the nation's and world's ills—is not simply the peace vs. war issue, he would argue during the conversation that was extended to include the ride to Newark Airport. The problem underneath it all, said John Collins, is racism. There will not be peace in the world, he argued, until we learn to deal justly with our own people of color and with the Third World nations around the globe. "Justice," said Collins, "is the way to peace."

Developing that philosophy has been a long process for John Collins. It may have begun in the '30s, he believes, while he was growing up in Chicago. In those years he would often hear his father passionately denounce the lack of justice in Hitler's pre-war Germany. World War II ended while Collins was in high school. The young man signed on with the Navy and served in the Pacific during the Korean War; he went through law school and practiced law for a couple of years. But he found he wanted something more: "a way to become involved in issues I thought were critical in the world."

With that, Collins packed his belongings and headed for New York's Union Theological Seminary. The year was 1957, and Collins was 28 years old. It was a challenging, invigorating time to be at Union, as racial tension erupted, sending the whole nation into a period of moral/ethical crisis. The seminarians spread out through New York, doing field work in the city's churches; they entertained international visitors, including a delegation of Soviet students and a brother of Tibet's Dali Lama; they watched as Martin Luther King Jr. asserted leadership in the civil rights struggle.

During Collins' second year at the seminary, the first black sit-ins were held at a lunch counter in Greensboro, N.C. That summer Collins and three other seminarians went south to work in the black churches. The idea caught on, and each summer after that the number of seminarians grew. Before Collins graduated, the program had been formally organized into the Student International Ministries. "I guess," said Collins, "that was one of the things I'm most proud of in my lifetime."

In 1961, Collins left Union with his first assignment, as minister for a Methodist church in East Harlem. His task was to build a black congregation, which he did.

Meanwhile, the seven years he spent at the church were significant ones for the civil rights struggle: They included the big 1962 March on Washington, the Harlem and East Harlem riots, and major school desegregation battles. At one point, Collins traveled to Jackson, Miss., where he teamed up with a black minister in an attempt to break church color bars; as the two worshiped together in a white Methodist church, both were arrested. Back in East Harlem, Collins organized a youth employment program that would evolve into the Neighborhood Youth Corps; he served on the anti-poverty program board.

East Harlem also was where Collins met his wife, Sheila, when she showed up at his church as a Union Theological Seminary field worker intern. It was where the family established its first home, and where the children were born.

In 1968, Collins accepted a job on the Methodist Church's New York conference staff, with offices in Rye. The job was largely administrative, and it brought advantages of prestige, good pay and security. But by 1977, Collins felt a need to get back into the community.

Although it would mean belt-tightening for his growing family, Collins went to work with the Interfaith Center on Corporate

Responsibility, sponsored by a large number of churches to study church investments. A lot of money was involved, and the churches were determined to put that clout behind their moral positions. Collins' assignment was to fight red-lining, the practice of withholding mortgage money from less desirable neighborhoods. "We tried to get the banks to loan money in the neighborhoods in which they were situated," said Collins.

Then, in 1979, he was invited to apply for his present post as co-director of Clergy and Laity Concerned (CALC), which had begun as part of the anti-Vietnam struggle.

His years in that job, said Collins, have been "pretty amazing." When he thinks back, a number CALC projects spring to mind: in 1982, arranging the first visit of European peace leaders to the United States, which turned out to be "kind of the beginning of the real connection between the European and American peace movements" . . . organizing the United States Friends of Comiso, dedicated to helping the village of Comiso, Italy, oppose deployment of cruise missiles there . . . joining with a couple of other groups to organize the national freeze campaign . . . helping pull together the Witness for Peace program. Collins still serves on the Witness for Peace national steering committee; he also gives time to the Pledge of Resistance.

In the fall of 1984, Collins and his wife were invited to Yugoslavia, to attend an annual conference of socialist and communist nations. The conference topic that year was peace—and the sponsors had been told they could not understand the American peace movement without considering the churches; the couple were invited to tell that story.

Like her husband, Sheila has a history of activism dating back to those Union Seminary days. She has written a book, "A Different Heaven and Earth, a Feminist Perspective on Religion," which became a key text in some women's studies courses; at one point, she jumped into a Mississippi political battle, defending a black mayor whom she felt was being attacked by the white power structure—and lost her own job in that controversial process.

In 1984, both John and Sheila signed on with Jesse Jackson's presidential campaign: John was co-organizer of White Religious Leaders for Jackson; Sheila became national Rainbow coordinator.

"It was really exciting!" said Collins. But it also meant sidetracking some of his "more mundane responsibilities" at CALC. So 1985 saw him returning to administrative basics: "spending about 80% of my time on fundraising." That fundraising, however, often ties directly into Collins' commitment to justice; one proposal, for instance, would support a project opposing apartheid in South Africa.

By the time Collins finished telling his story, it was near the end of a very long day, winding up with the drive to the airport. It was close to midnight before Sheila Collins finally threw in her bag and climbed into the car. She was tired—but the topic that had been under discussion was important to her; she'd just come from Detroit, where she had done interviews for a book she was writing on Jesse Jackson's Rainbow Coalition. So for a few minutes she talked about it. "You've got to understand," she said quietly, the fatigue showing, "that I believe the black movement in this country is the key to any radical transformation."

Finally back in New Rochelle, both Collinses were ready to end the interview . . . and to head into the house for some quiet, catching-up talk, and perhaps for some of the strawberry shortcake John had prepared earlier that busy evening.

IX

THE BUSINESS ANGLE

It is a recurring topic of head-shaking questioning among peace and justice activists and among those who try to understand what's going on: How come, with so much at stake and with so many persons committed to so many good causes, this country has not been moved more dramatically off its course toward war?

There are many answers, of course, and a number already have shown up in previous chapters: Activists go off in so many directions that they may seem ineffective; while activists may be willing to confront the issues, most other people are so overwhelmed by the whole situation that they would rather not get involved; all of us may hate the bomb, but it's all we've got to entrust with our security. And so on.

But there is another big reason . . . one that could be more unswayable than all the others: The fact that war-making is big business in the world today and that the United States is the best there is when it comes to that particular big business. It is ingrained in our economy, it adds the zeroes to paychecks, and it makes many very wealthy and powerful individuals even more wealthy and powerful. It is a house of green-colored dollar signs that could collapse the whole economy if it came tumbling down.

Peace and justice activists often avoid specifics in talking about those issues. The generalities are more comfortable: Once the bomb-making machinery is closed, there will be money for housing and feeding and educating our people; once we quit depending on the bomb, we could relearn dependence on human being working with human being.

It's tougher to talk about what would happen to all those people thrown out of work—not just the big money-makers, but the average guys who live down the block and happen to work at United Technologies. And how about American business? Would it just fold up and die away? Would we become a third-rate economic power?

There are, however, a number of peace and justice people who are tackling those difficult questions. They may not have perfect answers, but they're working on them—some from the angle of business, some from personal ethics.

The following stories tell of a businessman who is proving against all common "wisdom" that he can survive, and survive well, without defense contracts—even in a world of high tech that bows obsequiously before the Pentagon; a sociologist who is trying to convince the American defense industry that "peace conversion" is a viable option; a community organizer who helped stop an expansion by Lockheed; the leader of an ecumenical coalition who is trying to change the nation's image of General Electric; and a pair of Philadelphia septuagenarians who years ago quit paying taxes—all taxes—as their personal protest against the war machine.

32. "NO, THANKS" TO MILITARY CONTRACTS
Theodore Williams, Los Angeles

> *Once this nation was the world's leader in the*
> *innovation of products and processes. Over the*
> *past two decades, however, the U.S. has fallen far*
> *behind other countries in the rate of technological*
> *progress. This is due in large measure to the fact*
> *that the military sector claims 30% to 50% of all*
> *the scientists and engineers in America.*
> —*Harold Willens, "The Trimtab Factor"*

Ted Williams is a man whose career fits easily under the heading of American success story. Yet, he is also an anomaly: a businessman whose financial future is tied to high tech—exactly the area most dependent on government contracts—but one who shuns those very contracts. As Williams sees it, such contracts are not good for his business—or for the nation.

That was the story he had come to tell this evening for members of the Southern California Federation of Scientists (SCFS), who had gathered in front of the fireplace at a home in Anaheim, Calif. And that audience was as much an anomaly as the businessman they had come to hear: As scientists drawn from Jet Propulsion Laboratory, the local aerospace industry and others, all had strong implied interest in defense; yet, their goal was to contain weaponry, not encourage it. The speaker already was a friend of some of those who had come to listen.

Williams began by telling how he started his own business in California in 1950, manufacturing aircraft hydraulic equipment. When computers appeared, he added mechanical components such as tape drives, clutches and guides. Now, he said, "I specialize in the very, very difficult close tolerance components and assemblies."

In 1968, Williams merged his operation with Bell Industries. It was a move that led to near disaster two years later, when the president resigned and left a firm in deep trouble. Bell, which began in electronic components distribution, had diversified too widely, picking up "a carpet company, a furniture company, a boat company, you name it," Williams said. In 1970, Williams recalled, while the company was doing about $50 million a year in sales, it was showing a $1 million annual loss.

When the president resigned, said Williams, "about four or five of us who had our whole lives invested in the stock we had in Bell had to roll up our sleeves and go to work." They managed to turn things around: "Last year our sales were in excess of $300 million and we earned about $11 or $12 million after taxes. We have between 2,000 and 2,500 employees. I think we're about the 75th largest company in California . . . with 50-odd facilities in about 20 states."

And that is in spite of the concentration on non-government contracts. "When I assumed leadership of the company, we had a small amount of military business," said Williams, but the new management decided against expanding that area, choosing to aim for a different market.

That choice seemed to make good business sense: Bell managers had dealt with the military in the past and had found that such work led to "difficulties and red tape and the total loss of control of your own destiny," said Williams. "We decided we wanted to remain in control of our own destiny. We just expanded our efforts in the commercial direction." Today, 80% of their business is in distribution of products that include electronic components, graphic art supplies and building products; 20% is in manufacturing, largely for the electronic marketplace.

The company won't even hire scientists who have been working in defense industries, Williams added. "I don't think I've ever been successful in hiring anybody—and that goes from engineers to machinists—who has worked in a large airframe company or in a large defense establishment." Such people simply can't discard the free-spending ways of their former employers, he explained. And at Bell, "the mentality we require to survive is one that has to be tuned to frugality, and where waste has got to be minimal. We don't have any cost-plus contracts."

But for Williams, there was yet another reason to avoid the defense industry: As a businessman who thinks he's learned a thing or two about the economy in his 30 years dealing with profit and loss statements, Williams is convinced that the nation's emphasis on military buildup is robbing other sectors. Among the points Williams made in his carefully-researched talk:

> It has been proposed that our nation should build 226 MX missilies, which would cost $110 million each. If just one less of these missiles were built . . . we could end poverty for 100,000 female-headed households; if the whole program were scrapped, we would be able to eliminate poverty for all 12 million children below the poverty level . . . .
>
> There are at least 50,000 nuclear warheads, between the U.S. and the Soviet Union . . . the equivalent of 1,600,000 times the power of the bomb that completely devastated Hiroshima in 1945 . . . . If we were to explode one of these warheads each hour, the explosions could go on without cessation for 5.7 years. [This overabundance of weaponry has been put together in] the same world where 5 million children die every year from diseases which could be prevented by immunization.

These are the kinds of thoughts that impel Williams to add extra hours to his working days so he can bring his concerns before groups such as the SCFS. "What I'm doing now," he told the Anaheim gathering, "is an effort to get you all involved in the system. Maybe to write your congressperson, maybe to be sure you vote, maybe to tell other people their vote is important. You know, we've got the greatest democracy in the world. I think we have the best capitalist system in the world. But we're giving it up, because we're not fighting for it, we're not taking an interest, we're not participating—and that's what's going to lose it for us."

33. HOW TO GIVE UP THE BOMB AND ENJOY DOING IT
Michael Closson, Mountain View, Calif.

> *Industrialized countries that devote a smaller portion of their economic output to military purposes have higher productivity and stronger economies.*
> —*Council on Economic Priorities, 1981*

You can call it Santa Clara County . . . or Silicon Valley. Whichever way you put it, this is a special place: a world-class, elite center of high-tech, a magnet for those electronic wizards who turn out state-of-the-art computers and ingenious microchips.

Understandably, Santa Clara County also has attracted major military contractors. Names displayed on buildings dotting the landscape include Westinghouse, GTE, United Technologies, Hewlett Packard, Applied Technology, Ford Aerospace and Litton. Lockheed Missiles and Space Company is the county's largest employer, with some 26,000 employees working on sea-launched ballistic missiles and military satellite controls and electronics.

But Santa Clara County also is home to an organization dedicated to changing much of that. Not the wizardry, but the use to which it is put. The Center for Economic Conversion, located in Mountain View, is a small operation with a big vision: nothing less than turning the country's huge war machine away from military dependence, and redirecting it into projects compatible with peace.

The Center's man in charge of pursuing that objective is Michael Closson. He is a Ph.D. sociologist from Cornell University, a slim man with neatly-cropped red hair and mustache, and round, wire-rimmed glasses. He defines the task ahead in careful terms: "The

Center's major goal," he said, "is to promote viable alternatives to continuing dependence upon military spending for economic prosperity—particularly [by] assisting local companies, and others like them throughout the country, to move out of the defense business and into civilian projects."

This is a process typically called economic—or peace—conversion. It is also a process that suggests major economic questions. What would happen, for instance, to General Dynamics, McDonnell Douglas, United Technologies, and others like them if they were shunted out of defense production? How could we replace the money they pump into the economy? What about the employees?

Closson does not pretend there are easy answers to such questions. But finding those answers is a primary task adopted by the Center: to plan "some sort of smooth transition, because we do have about 3 million people who are directly employed by the defense industry in the United States right now, and probably at least that many who are indirectly impacted."

But Closson does believe there are solutions. In the long run, he is convinced, an economy focused on human needs will be healthier than one heavily dedicated to the military.

"I think there is money to be made doing good," he said. Still, in the short run, "it's going to be hard," he admitted. Closson recognizes the problems: the thousands of people involved, for instance, as well as the "giant, massive infrastructure built up around the military—not just the Department of Defense, because there are all these other sectors of the American government: NASA and the Department of Energy and the Veterans Administration."

Yet, Closson said, it can work. The economy made a similar adjustment after World War II, when industry successfully shifted back to peacetime production, he pointed out, although he expects the process to be harder this time around. Back then, he explained, there was a huge, pent-up demand for consumer products; jobs opened up as wartime "Rosie the riveters" returned to homemaking; and the WWII defense companies had previous experience in civilian production, making it reasonably easy to move back into that area. None of those descriptions apply today.

"In spite of all that, I think the major lesson is that there was a national commitment to moving toward a civilian economy, and it happened," said Closson. "I have incredible faith in the American people. I think we have a wealth of untapped talent, energy, enthusiasm and drive, [and that] a lot of the anomie and isolation and hostility that comes out is because people don't feel much sense of purpose."

Under the current situation, said Closson, the Center is not calling for the United States to simply pull out of the defense business, or for unilateral disarmament: "In the current climate of hostility, unfortunately, there's a need for an adequate defense." But, he added, "I think an adequate defense could be maintained with much less devotion of national talent and treasure than we are currently applying to it. Now over two-thirds of government research and development money is spent on military projects. It's frightening!" And, he added, "it diverts all sorts of resources away from other sectors."

The Center would like to see such money reallocated to "mass transit, alternative energy sources, to infrastructure rebuilding, that sort of thing." These are areas we have not addressed adequately in recent years, Closson said, and the price has been a failure to support the society and to serve human needs.

One major defense firm, McDonnell Douglas in Long Beach, already has been approached with an initial conversion project. "We worked with the union, and we had a lot of talks with management, actually about producing light rail vehicles—modern trolley cars—at the facility," said Closson. It was a good experience, he added, and there seemed to be some sincere interest, although McDonnell Douglas never adopted the plan. "In the end they turned us down, because they had a big new military contract coming in and they didn't want to screw up their chances for that."

The Center staff has taken other tacks as well: At one point, they put out a carefully-researched study on "Creating Solar Jobs," analyzing the chances for moving defense workers to new positions in solar power. They've done outreach work in some other communities and have helped plan peace conversion conferences in Boston and San Diego.

In addition, said Closson, "We do a lot of public education." That involves publishing a newspaper called Plowshare Press, speaking to groups like the Kiwanis and Junior League and anyone else who is interested, and working with labor and peace movements to encourage commitment to economic conversion.

Closson has been part of this effort since becoming director in 1982, succeeding Dave McFadden, who founded the operation six years earlier. Closson arrived with an impressive resume of peace work already behind him. During the Vietnam era at Cornell, he had taught a course on racism and helped start an experimental public school. His interest in education helped win a job as assistant dean at Stanford University, working with alternative undergraduate programs, a post he held from 1972 to 1976. During that period, he said, "I got very interested in work-related issues." The next move was to a nearby Palo Alto group called New Ways to Work, a non-profit organization that counseled individuals about career changes and tried to help organizations improve job conditions.

From there, Closson joined the Center for Economic Conversion. It seemed a natural step: moving from concern for individuals and their jobs to concern for the national work scene. His views fit neatly into the Center's philosophy that economic priorities and the distribution of jobs in the United States need to change if we are going to find lasting peace.

Peace also will require, he said, that this country learn new ways of relating to the rest of the world: "Clearly, the United States, by virtue of our power and wealth, has a role of leadership to play . . . but I think it's a very different role than the current administration conceives of. I think it's much less of a military role and more of a moral leadership that we can assert."

Planning that hoped-for tomorrow should be a joint effort, involving many areas, said Closson: "What we'd ideally like to see is a democratic planning process, where workers, managers, community members and other people who have a national perspective to give them insight sit down and talk about their capabilities in terms of their plants, their facilities, their equipment and their skills—and what's needed out there in the world—to try to identify products and markets that really are profitable and meet human needs."

Yet, said Closson, even success at getting industry turned around would not complete the process of "conversion." The next level would be "revitalizing our economy," which would include getting some of "those so-called sunset industries" back on their feet. "We can't exist totally without a steel industry or without an auto industry," said Closson. "We need to figure out ways to commit resources creatively to revitalize them, and also to have some sort of national plan for how our economy should remain vital."

And a final level of change, the "trickiest one," said Closson, would be a "conversion of values." He believes that "without at least some movement on that last one, we're not going to get the first two, either."

"I'm saying," he added, "we have to start conveying visions: defining the problem in big terms and also talking about visions, solutions that can really move us beyond it."

"We're talking," said Closson with some hesitation, aware that he was showing his own idealism, "about restructuring the world. And I think that's really exciting."

"I think there is this reservoir of commitment and compassion and energy that could be tapped," he said, suggesting the model could be the Peace Corps, as it was introduced a quarter century ago. The result, Closson said, could be a national dedication to peace: not only to converting industry and revitalizing the economy here, but also to working conscientiously with the Soviets to reach valid agreements. "We're so locked into this good guy-bad guy adversarial thing with communism," he added. "We have to somehow break out of that."

With such challenges ahead, Closson calls himself a "hopeful pessimist." His "pessimism" has affected his personal as well as his professional life: "I mean, I don't have children. And there are various reasons why I don't. But one of the reasons is, I'm not sure they would make it through their lives without nuclear holocaust."

But without hope, he said, he would not be dedicating his professional life to peace conversion. His personal vision of that conversion goes even further than the Center's official plan, Closson admitted, again hesitating to push his personal idealism: "I'll just speak for myself. Basically, I don't think there's a chance for peace, either domestically or internationally, without social justice. By that I mean there has to be better treatment of people—socially, and especially economically—in the world. Another way of putting it is, I don't think there is a chance for international peace until the United States stops consuming a third of the world's resources."

"I think," he added thoughtfully, "we're talking about some revolutionary changes in the world. I think that hopefully the revolution can be accomplished nonviolently, because I'm personally a real subscriber to nonviolence, although every day that goes by, where the disparities increase, makes that chance less and less likely."

If the United States were to reach out to the Third World, for instance—"not helping them develop cash crops for export, but helping them develop their own domestic economies into self-sustainable economies"—there would be great economic and political benefits for us as well as them, Closson proposed. Moreover, it would be the ideal way to challenge the Russians: "The Soviets would have a hard time competing with us in that regard."

And, added Closson, "you may laugh at this, but I'd like to see a much more feminized world—in terms of what we typically view as feminine values right now . . . cooperation, nurturing, caring, those sorts of things." As he talked, trash from the previous weekend's Superbowl game was still stacked up at the Stanford University stadium a few miles up the road, waiting to be picked up. That game, he suggested, is "kind of the antithesis of this. Not just the game, but the whole culture surrounding it—this macho, aggressive, pent-up violence, sexist sort of culture that's predominant in our society right now."

Sometimes, with their challenging goals, the Center's workers wonder if they are making a dent in the whole situation, Closson said. But, he added, "you know Gandhi's great quote: 'Almost anything you do will seem insignificant, but it's very important that you do it anyway.' And I think that's true."

The idea of economic conversion appeals to many within the peace and justice movement. A major theorist and spokesman is Dr. Seymour Melman, professor of economics at Columbia University, who sees many of this nation's economic and social problems resulting from 40 years of a military-based economy. It is largely through Melman's efforts that a bill aimed at easing transition to a civilian economy, HR 813, has been introduced in the House of Representatives. It would require that defense contracting firms have plans for their own conversion. In addition, a percentage of each Department of Defense contract would be allocated to conversion, including retraining and relocation of employees.

Yet, that bill has not been passed, and economic conversion remains a controversial idea, often pitting activists against economists. One scuffle was played out in the pages of the Bulletin of the Atomic Scientists. It began when Gordon Adams, director of the Defense Budget Project in Washington, D.C., declared in the February 1986 issue that "economic conversion has come to a dead end." After citing a number of projects—including the

McDonnell Douglas venture—and calling them all failures, he recommended, among other things, that conversion advocates were too narrow in their focus—that they "should deal with local economic diversification and planning for all communities, not just communities that depend upon defense spending." He also suggested that "few of these advocates have credibility or experience as economic planners."

One reponse in the June/July issue came from two writers with carefully footnoted credentials: Lloyd J. Dumas, professor of political economy at the University of Texas at Dallas and author of "The Overburdened Economy" (1986), and Suzanne Gordon, director of the International Economic Conversion Conference and co-editor of "Economic Conversion: Revitalizing America's Economy" (1984). After challenging many of Adams' points—including his contention that military spending is "economically neutral"—they countered that "military spending at high levels for long periods is very much at the heart of what is wrong with the U.S. economy . . . . [It] is not economically neutral; it is, instead, a critical economic disadvantage." And, added Kevin Bean, chairman of the Economic Conversion Task Force of the Connecticut Campaign for a U.S.-U.S.S.R. Nuclear Arms Freeze, conversion does encompass a broader picture. He wrote, "Our present efforts in Connecticut . . . are not to be viewed as an appendage to arms control advocacy, but fundamentally as an expression of immediate concerns for the job security of defense-dependent and other workforces."

Michael Closson in Mountain View already had confronted such concerns. "Many people think of economic conversion as converting Lockheed down here from building a Trident missile to building subways, or something like that," he said. "Well, that's part of it, a really small part." The bigger part is changing the way the whole world works. "What kind of world are we talking about?" he asked. "Are we talking just about an absence of war? I hope it's beyond that."

34. TAKING ON GOLIATH
Peter Klotz-Chamberlin, Santa Cruz, Calif.

> *I refuse to accept the cynical notion that nation after nation must spiral down a militaristic stairway into the hell of nuclear destruction. I believe that unarmed truth and unconditional love will have the final word in reality.*
> —Martin Luther King Jr.

Peter Klotz-Chamberlin, a lanky, sandy-haired 36-year-old, had forgotten our appointment. Two Russian Orthodox churchwomen from the Soviet Union were due shortly, and he was worried about being ready on time. This was an important event for him and for the Resource Center for Nonviolence, where he volunteers.

But with my promise that the interview would be short, Klotz-Chamberlin led the way upstairs and sank into a well-worn upholstered chair, stretching his feet onto the braided rug lying on the wood floor. Books lined the far wall, and a sign announced, "More library through kitchen." This cozy upstairs was an appealing contradiction to the austere downstairs; it was almost as if a pleasant old home had been lifted up and and a functional meeting and office area had been slipped underneath. And, it turned out, that's exactly what the Resource Center had done to gain more space.

The goal at the Center, said Klotz-Chamberlin, is to seek "nonviolent social change," drawing heavily on inspiration from Mahatma Gandhi. They see that change happening on two levels, he added: personal and social. For Klotz-Chamberlin and those with whom he works, that means living with others, as well as joining them for "organized social action and social resistance to injustice and oppression." Some of that resistance has been aimed at business.

The Center, Klotz-Chamberlin said, is not a one-issue operation. "We have been involved in the anti-nuclear power movement, the disarmament movement, the movement against intervention in Central America."

But for Klotz-Chamberlin, personally, the first move into activism took place in Belfast, Ireland. He'd gone there on a six-month leave from studies at the University of California at Santa Cruz, inspired by a class that advocated joining "action and study." In conflict-ridden Belfast, he found himself at a work camp for Catholic children.

"My introduction to community organizing," Klotz-Chamberlin recalled with a laugh, "was helping get wood for them . . . so they could make little swords and go charging across the courtyards, having battles with each other. I would try to encourage them to make more tame things, like boats, but that's pretty hard to do with kids who have that military all around them." That time in Belfast did, however, help Klotz-Chamberlin deal with his own growing concerns about war; he left Ireland as a committed pacifist.

Returning to Santa Cruz, Klotz-Chamberlin completed his degree in politics, then moved to Santa Barbara, Calif., where he helped form a Gandhi study group. That group evolved into the Resource Center in 1976, although Gandhi's ideals continued to offer major inspiration.

Today, the Klotz-Chamberlin family—Peter, Liz (the Chamberlin part of the name), Isaac, 6, and Ruth, 1 1/2—lives as part of a loosely-structured community of some 20 adults and children. The couple own their own home, but share it with two others; child care and a percentage of income are shared among the entire group. Klotz-Chamberlin has organized his working life so there is time for the Center: During one three-year period he was a Center staff member; now he volunteers, while earning his living as an electrical contractor.

On a social action level, Klotz-Chamberlin has gotten involved with a number of causes. He was among founders of the Abalone Alliance, a group opposing the Diablo Canyon nuclear power plant near San Luis Obispo, Calif., and he offered some of the first non-violence training sessions in that city. At one point he joined a blockade of the Diablo Canyon road and wound up spending two months in jail. He helped pull together Santa Cruz's first anti-nuclear group, People for a Nuclear-Free Future; he has supported the Witness for Peace office, located next door. In the early 1970s he became a tax resister, withholding the amount presumably destined for the military. In May 1983, he participated in Fellowship of Reconciliation's first trip to the Soviet Union, then joined a Santa Cruz city committee that is trying to establish a sister-city relationship in that country.

But perhaps his most memorable experience was another one—the time the Center for Nonviolence decided to take on the giant Lockheed Missiles and Space Company. Lockheed, it turns out, has a facility in the hills above Santa Cruz, where it tests and manufactures a component for the Trident missile. The glove in that situation was flung in the mid-70s, when Lockheed applied for county permits to expand the plant. They wanted to build five new buildings; one would house Trident II missile production. Klotz-Chamberlin and other Center workers fought the proposal through planning commission and board of supervisor hearings over a period of some two years.

"We saw the clear parallel between our responsibility as citizens and the responsibility that in many cases was denied by citizens of Germany during the Nazi era," said Klotz-Chamberlin. "Wouldn't nuclear missiles have consequences similar to those of death camps? Wouldn't we ask people in Germany to have said more to their officials about things going on right under their noses? We felt that we needed to do the same."

When the final board of supervisors vote came in at 3-2 in favor of Lockheed, the Center volunteers refused to give up. They next pushed a county ballot initiative that would have required phase-out of local nuclear weapon production. That lost, too, again by a margin of about 3-2. At that point, the workers figured wearily, that was the end of it—they'd lost.

But five years later, the Lockheed matter reappeared. It seemed the company needed a grading permit.

"We sort of shuddered at the thought of having to engage this issue again," said Klotz-Chamberlin. The volunteers asked themselves, "Is there any chance of doing anything? What could stop a grading permit?" They decided to at least attend a hearing . . . and soon returned to the fray.

What brought them back was the discovery of a bureaucratic snafu: The original application had failed to note the size of the Trident missile building, which turned out to be a sprawling 3/4-acre, 32,000-square-foot facility. Joining forces with the Sierra Club, the Center's workers "kept digging."

Finally it came to the last hearing before the board of supervisors. The volunteers knew they had two out of five votes; they pinned their hopes for a win on one man. But that man actually seconded the motion to grant the permit. Then another supervisor—thought to be a solid conservative, though something of an environmentalist—took his turn.

Klotz-Chamberlin recalls it well: "He said something like, 'When it comes down to it, I want to vote to put whatever roadblock I can in the way of those weapons at Lockheed.'"

Klotz-Chamberlin still laughs with glee in telling the tale. All the hard work had paid off. "The whole room just erupted in applause and surprise. We were just amazed. So then we had it, 3-2!"

For Klotz-Chamberlin, obviously, the feeling would long remain: David had taken on Goliath, and once again, the slingshot had won.

35. CHALLENGING THE GE IMAGE
Robert Smith, Media, Penn.

> *The world waits for a great nation that has the*
> *common sense, the imagination, and the faith to*
> *devote to the science and practice of nonviolence*
> *so much as a tenth of the money, brains, skill and*
> *devotion which it now devotes to the madness of*
> *war preparation. What is that nation waiting for*
> *before it undertakes its mission?*
>
> —*A.J. Muste*

Here's a test.

Close your eyes, then pull up a picture for "General Electric." Ready? Did you see lightbulbs? Toasters? Microwave ovens? Maybe even hear that catchy tune telling how GE "brings good things to life"?

Now, meet Pennsylvania's Bob Smith. If he has his way, the next time you hear that tune your brain will change the words to "brings nuclear war to life"; you'll envision submarines spewing destruction across the oceans, and space satellites passing along military signals. That's how it is today with General Electric, argues Smith: Just within the Greater Philadelphia area, GE is producing components for MX missiles, as well as "satellite systems for the command and control of United States nuclear war plans," and is involved in research and development for Trident II's multiple-warhead missile systems. GE is the nation's fourth largest war contractor, he said, and operates as "a little Pentagon—actually a very large Pentagon . . . a superpower."

"GE has an income greater than the country of Brazil," Smith

Robert Smith, Sarah and missile casing

continued. (A Philadelphia Inquirer story the next day reported GE's income from military contracts at $4.5 billion during fiscal 1983.) "Every aspect of the arms race—the preparations for nuclear war, not only technologically, financially, but politically—is represented in General Electric . . . the number one war contractor in the Greater Philadelphia area."

For the past seven years, Smith and his local group of co-workers, calling themselves the Brandywine Peace Community, have made it their goal to change GE's homespun image by holding weekly vigils, monthly religious services, and occasional incidents of civil disobedience, all at one or the other of the firm's two local plants.

"All our actions are rooted in nonviolence, and rooted in the most fundamental belief that joins all religions—that life is more powerful than death, and that hope will triumph," said Smith.

When Brandywiners do schedule civil disobedience, they usually add the spice of drama. Once members blockaded GE's Valley Forge plant by chaining themselves to the doors; another time, four Brandywiners climbed atop the company's six-story test facility at the same site, poured their own blood down the walls and on rooftop test equipment, then unfurled a banner proclaiming "DSCS III (Defense Satellite Communications System) is illegal & immoral; choose life."

Members gathered at the Philadelphia plant on Holy Thursday 1985 for an evening Eucharist and foot-washing ceremony, followed by an all-night candlelight vigil; the next day, Good Friday, they set up the "stations of the Nuclear Cross" around the plant, representing "a corporate Calvary, where GE produces a cross for humanity made of MX, DSCS III and Trident II." Thanksgiving 1984, the group met at Valley Forge two days before the holiday for a religious service, then built a shanty, which they moved into for an all-night vigil. The next day, demonstrators carried the shanty onto GE property, resulting in the expected arrests. The message that time, said Smith, was that "while people are homeless, General Electric is producing billions of dollars of nuclear war preparations."

Bob Smith, the driving force behind this dedicated group, is a mild-appearing, quiet-speaking man who occasionally breaks into delighted, hearty laughter while talking—sometimes offering a joke on GE, sometimes on himself. Now 35, he is a veteran activist. "For the past 16 years I've been involved," he said, "initially in civil rights and then peace activity, on a virtually full-time basis."

He and his wife Beth Centz—a long-time activist, herself—founded Brandywine a decade ago as "an ecumenically Christian, nonviolently-rooted response to preparations for nuclear war." Both husband and wife had grown up with strong religious backgrounds: Smith, Catholic; Centz, Baptist.

"One time a priest asked me how I got involved," recalled Smith, "and I said, well, I took seriously what the church taught me." Smith attended Catholic schools as well as the Catholic church and still considers himself Catholic. Now, however, he believes that while various religions "may have slightly different means of walking, sometimes different rhythms and different paces," they are basically "all the same." Brandywine, he said, is a mix: " . . . Methodist ministers, Methodist lay people, Catholic priests, Catholic nuns, Catholic lay people, Presbyterians . . . ."

Both Smith and Centz have been arrested many times, Smith said; like similar couples, they make sure only one is arrested at a time, so one parent is always available for their two children. Getting arrested isn't seen as anything extraordinary in this family; it's one of those activities they have adopted as a tool of change, although they recognize their actions may affront some others.

"When people sit down and block the White Train or when people go in and hammer on missile components, they're really providing symbols for disarmament and for moral conduct leading to disarmament," said Smith. "A symbol is a very powerful thing if it is a true symbol, and a symbol is always activating; it will always motivate. So, therefore, the most significant symbols will always be very troubling."

At the outset, the Smith family and other Brandywiners lived together in a home loaned by a supporter. But a couple of years ago, the owner moved back in, and the community ended its joint housing arrangement. Since then, Smith, Centz and their daughters, Seonaid (Gaelic for "God is gracious"), 7, and Sarah, 5, have lived under the sloping, jutting roof that forms the ceiling of their third-floor apartment in Media, a few miles outside Philadelphia. The couple support their family on the small stipend Smith receives from Brandywine and the income Centz earns by working two days a week at a peace movement print shop.

The core group of activists who first got together seven years ago is still mostly intact, although they now live apart, said Smith, and hundreds of others throughout the Philadelphia area are supporters.

No, all those years have not changed GE's involvement in military contracts, he said, but discontinuing the efforts against the company "would say that we gave up on them." And Smith does see signs of progress: The Brandywiners are on friendly, first-name terms with some company executives and workers; police react without the old animosity; the local news media now portray both sides of GE. (Just a couple of weeks earlier, the local paper had run a story about accusations that GE had bilked the government on a contract, noting that "GE allegedly cooked its books to bill the government for $800,000 in cost overruns that GE should have absorbed.")

Smith, who dabbled in journalism a bit along the way, said he has great respect for the Philadelphia media . . . although he admitted with a mix of distress and glee that one of Brandywine's wildest episodes resulted largely from a bit of dubious reporting. It all began one day in April 1982, when members of the group noticed four casings for Mark 12A missile warheads in what appeared to be a scrap pile behind a building at GE's Valley Forge plant.

"That night," said Smith, "we went back. One person climbed the fence and lifted them over. It was that simple."

For several weeks, the media yawned over the whole story. The conical casings—each of heavy metal and about waist high—were of no danger in themselves. Brandywiners felt they were significant, said Smith, because they were the means to deliver the bombs; thus, they reasoned, the casings were what suggested—perhaps even more than the warheads, themselves—that the United States was, indeed, willing to fight nuclear war. Brandywiners carted their casings around to churches and meetings, telling their story. They sent releases to the media, but with little response.

Two months later that situation began to change dramatically, after a local investigative reporter contacted Smith for a story about Brandywine. Smith mentioned the casings . . . the writer's ears pricked up . . . and in early fall stories appeared in the Philadelphia Daily News and then Philadelphia Magazine.

Those stories shot Brandywine's mild caper into its own crazy orbit. The writer in some instances referred to the casings as "warheads," and that touched off international media interest; although the group's press releases had carefully called their cones "casings," local, national and international media thought they might have found a small group of activists with four nuclear bombs. Even Pravda got on the line to Smith . . . but the Soviet reporter soon hung up, because Smith, who believes guilt is shared by the two superpowers, "wouldn't say the Soviet Union was the great purveyor of peace in the world."

Philadelphia magazine's story, titled "The Gang That Stole Doomsday," began with a sequence depicting "raiders" who tasted the tang of fear like that "left in the mouth after an old copper penny has been pressed to the tongue" and who, "despite the brisk April air gushing in through the windows . . . found they were sweating." Doors slammed, police cars appeared in the distance. It would have done justice to Steven Spielberg, said Smith, laughing; you would almost have expected to see Indiana Jones hopping the GE fence. The only problem was, it never happened that way.

Repercussions bounced around long after the stories had

appeared, said Smith. Yet, it wasn't all bad: In spite of inaccuracies, there was a great deal of important information about GE presented to the public, he said. And that information, plus that in other stories . . . plus that disseminated by the group, itself, along with its continuing activities . . . has indeed changed the way Philadelphians feel about GE, Smith is convinced.

"I think that goal has been met. I think that generally, at least in this area, when people think of General Electric they no longer simply think of light bulbs, toasters and microwave ovens."

———————————

A Brandywine newsletter in February 1987 announced observation of Brandywine's 10th anniversary . . . with plans to continue opposition to GE. The months ahead would include weekly vigils at both Philadelphia plants, promotion of a GE boycott, a candlelight service and stations of the Nuclear Cross prior to Easter, and civil disobedience in July. In August, said the calender, "like Joshua who circled the walls of Jericho, you are invited to circle the walls of GE's Philadelphia plant and form, on the anniversary of the Hiroshima bombing, a human circle of peace that can resist GE and confront the preparations for nuclear war."

36. SNUBBING THE IRS
George and Lillian Willoughby, Philadelphia

> *To refuse active payment of a tax which our socie-*
> *ty generally paid was exceedingly disagreeable;*
> *but to do a thing contrary to my conscience*
> *appeared yet more dreadful.*
>
> —*Quaker, 1757*

The date is April 15, tax day. George and Lillian Willoughby, both 70, are walking in a no-nonsense manner along the several blocks of downtown Philadelphia streets that will take them from the Friends Center on Cherry to the Federal Building. Lillian has on slacks and comfortable walking shoes; George is wearing his maroon tam. They work their way around the jackhammer operators tearing into the sidewalk and pass the sex "therapy" shop that advertises its wares with tiny, blinking, red lights and provocative wording. The forecast said rain is possible, but for now there is nothing worse than a sky full of somber clouds.

The Willoughbys' destination—the Federal Building, home of the local IRS—will be startup point for a war tax resistance demonstration, and the couple intend to get there at the beginning, 11 a.m. After all, when you've devoted the better part of the last 45 years to working for peace—and have declined to pay taxes for most of that period—you like to join the troops when they gather at Uncle Sam's doorstep.

For many of those years, there was no problem about tax withholding: The couple didn't make enough to even interest the government. But in the mid-60s, when all four of their children were going to college, the couple took money-making more seriously and started to feel the government's sticky fingers reaching into their paychecks. That's when Lillian called a halt: "I quit paying taxes—and I mean all taxes—because I was not about to support the old men's dreams." The old men, she said, were those who were foisting things like military buildups, selective service and governmental secrecy upon the nation. Lillian Willoughby wasn't having any of it.

George was right with her. It's a "myth," he said, recalling those days, "that you can't do anything, that it's impossible and you're trapped. This is the kind of slavery, kind of servitude you get into. We allow ourselves to be enslaved by these shibboleths, these rules laid down on us. You don't need bars and whips to keep people in line; you just need ideas!" Neither Willoughby bows willingly to such regimentation.

Although tax resistance has been just one part of the Willoughbys' personal protest to the nation's military involvement, they did make some fundamental life changes which helped to avoid the tax man. Lillian, who was working as a dietitian in the mid '60s, changed her job status from employee to consultant, thus avoiding automatic deductions. In later years, when the children were through school, the couple reduced their income so no taxes were due; now retired, they live on Social Security. Recently they gave their home and land in nearby Deptford, N.J., to a land trust, so they no longer own property. And they "rent" a car from a friend for $1 a year, remembering an earlier time when the IRS "collected" their VW bug because the couple refused to pay their telephone tax.

But then, their whole lives have more or less been shaped by their commitment to peace . . . plus their willingness to put their necks on the line. Both are native Iowans and both are Quakers: Lillian, a born one; George, a "convinced" one, he explains with a chuckle. Both went through the University of Iowa—Lillian earning a bachelor of science in home economics, George, a Ph.D. in political science—but they met back in Lillian's home town of West Branch, at the Quakers' Scattergood Hostel for German

George Willoughby

Lillian Willoughby

refugees, where Lillian had found her first job as dietitian. They married in 1940. George was a conscientious objector during World War II.

Since then the Willoughbys have lived in Iowa, then in New Jersey and Pennsylvania, as George changed jobs. He started with the American Friends Service Committee's peace education program and moved on to conscientious objector work, then nonviolent social change training. Lillian quit working to raise their children, then found a job to help see them through college. And finally, both retired.

But through those years, the couple—sometimes individually, sometimes together—were involved in a number of incidents, some dramatic enough to provide the stuff of movie plots. In 1957, for instance, Lillian was among 11 volunteers who one day walked onto the Nevada nuclear weapons testing grounds in an attempt to stop

America's continued testing.

"We were met by a tremendous number of police and Pinkerton men," she said. "There must have been 150 or more." The 11 were arrested, but were not sent to jail. She now agrees that there was probably more danger from radiation than from the police. "But we saw the soldiers going in, and they went right up to the testing place . . . which we now know was really treating them like guinea pigs in an experiment."

In 1958, George joined three other men, planning to sail the 30-foot ketch Golden Rule into the South Pacific nuclear test area. They hoped that by sailing right into the no-man's zone of the nuclear weapons testers they could make a statement dramatic enough to halt that testing. George, too, wound up being arrested. The crew had paused en route at Honolulu, where the government got a court order to stop them. The men decided to continue in spite of the order, but were intercepted by the Coast Guard and sent to jail until the tests were completed.

Lillian, meanwhile, decided to do some home support for the Golden Rule and for the Phoenix, another sailboat, which tried to complete the Golden Rule's task (again, unsuccessfully). Lillian and a dozen or so friends demanded a conference with the chairman of the Atomic Energy Commission (AEC). When that was not forthcoming, they moved cots and sleeping bags into the AEC building in Germantown, Md., and proceeded to fast. They were there over Mothers Day, and the AEC lobby blossomed with flowers. The fast lasted for half a dozen days, until the AEC chairman finally agreed to talk with them.

In 1960, as a member of the committee sponsoring a San Francisco to Moscow peace march, George walked with the marchers in this country from time to time, then rejoined the march at the Polish border and walked the rest of the way to Red Square. In 1963-64, he took off most of a year, joining another march. This one was from New Delhi to Peking; its goal was to encourage India and China to settle their differences nonviolently. The march ended when Indian authorities refused to allow the marchers to cross into China. In the mid-'60s, George traveled to Puerto Rico and Panama, attempting to counter American intervention in Central America. Both George and Lillian traveled to India and Asia to strengthen links among nonviolent groups.

Through all of this, the Willoughbys' life at home also was peace-oriented. In the mid-'60s—that period when the couple needed additional money to see their children through college—George set up a center to teach nonviolent social change techniques. Housed at a seminary outside Philadelphia, the center lasted four years, until some of its sponsors became uncomfortable with its activism. While raising their children, Lillian helped organize a local library and a peace center, and she participated in peace marches.

Both also worked in the peace groups that evolved from the original organization that sponsored Lillian's march onto the Nevada testing grounds. Projects included sending a team to Africa to protest French nuclear bomb tests; attempting to set up a nonviolence training center in Tanganyika; sending the Phoenix, the sailboat that had attempted to enter the nuclear testing area, to both North and South Vietnam with medical supplies during the Vietnam War; and organizing a team to begin witnessing in Nicaragua as a nonviolent protest to the attacks by American-supported contras.

In 1971, the couple made another major change in lifestyle, this time moving into a communal living situation; their goal was to develop a better way for people to live together. As part of that, they helped form another group, the Movement for a New Society, committed to a nonviolent way of life. "It called on us to change our own lives, personally, at the same time we were struggling to change the institutions," said George.

Last year the Willoughbys left the community housing in Philadelphia to move back to their New Jersey home and work out their land trust idea; they also wanted to get back into gardening and food preservation, part of their goal of self-sufficiency. They are, however, still active in the Movement. In addition, George is secretary of Peace Brigades International, which is involved in the current Central American situation. Lillian is helping plan a nonviolence and feminist conference. And they still find time to turn out for a tax protest.

So, is it all worthwhile?

"One never knows what one accomplishes in this kind of action," said George. But that's not to be taken as discouragement: The early demonstrations in Nevada, the couple believe, helped jolt the nation out of the McCarthy era; the voyages of the Golden Rule and the Phoenix may have helped lead to nuclear testing restrictions; the later trips by the Phoenix to Vietnam helped arouse Americans to problems of the war there; the pioneering work in nonviolent demonstration surely added power and meaning to the peace movement worldwide; and the example set by the Willoughbys and others like them offered encouragement that "ordinary human beings" can, indeed, fight city hall.

Through all those years, the Willoughbys said, they have maintained their close connections with the Quakers, and they feel good about that, too. Their four children all have turned out much to their parents' liking: Some have been peace activists, themselves; all are supportive of their parents; all are personally successful in their own lives.

You count your blessings as they come along; the world, the Willoughbys know, doesn't change in a day. And this day, as the rain finally starts to mist down, George and Lillian Willoughby have proceeded with the other tax protestors to City Hall. TV crews, radio and newspaper reporters move among the group; photographers and cameramen take pictures of the Halloween-masked "Ronald Reagan" and the gray-faced, khaki-clad "contra" taking part in a bit of street theater. The audience is led through tax-protester parodies of well-known songs.

Lillian is among the speakers here, telling how, back in the '40s, she refused to buy War Bonds, although her employer was pressuring for 100% employee participation; how she stopped paying taxes in the '60s; how she and George turned their property into a land trust. She invites anyone interested in details to see her. But, Lillian said privately, she would never tell anyone to totally stop paying taxes as she did: "We figure we just raise people's consciousness; they have to figure out what they're going to do themselves."

For Lillian and George Willoughby, it would come as no surprise that there was an alternate drama going on almost under their feet this day. TV cameras were there, too, at the city hall underground subway stop, where a group about the same size as that aboveground was gathered. But this group was lined up at a subterranean post office. There was no street theater here, no music, no speeches. The goal of those gathered here this April 15 was the more usual one: as quickly as possible, to send off their taxes.

———————

As Chicago's Renny Golden had found that not all Catholics approved of her challenging activism, the Willoughbys have long realized that some Quakers are uncomfortable with their brand of involvement, believing that social change should be made through an inner journey of the spirit. Other Quakers, of course, find the couple an inspiration.

As the quote from an 18th century Quaker at the start of this chapter suggests, tax resistance is a historically-recognized mode of protest. Not all of today's tax resisters meet the Willoughbys' willingness to stop all taxes; more typical, perhaps, are those who withhold only that portion of taxes that would theoretically go to military support. In some instances, resisters join together to set up a fund where they deposit all taxes they have withheld. Then, when the IRS catches up with any one member, the taxes are paid from the fund; thus, individuals do not face jail or loss of cars or homes. Many other activists express sympathy for the Willoughbys' actions, but admit they are unwilling to face the potential price—financial and personal—of tax resistance.

The idea is one that the average citizen appears to have difficulty even seriously considering. The gathering the Willoughbys attended at the Philadelphia civic center involved a small group of the faithful plus a few straggling people on their lunch breaks—people who mostly hung around the edges trying to figure out what was going on, who laughed with some embarrassment when one of the tax resisters moved up to talk with them, and who then wandered back to work. The Willoughbys understand what they're up against; they're willing to continue against the odds and to adjust their lifestyle as needed. For them, it's a moral imperative. If the government spends money immorally—as they argue it does—they believe it is their duty not to provide any of that money to spend. And so they don't.

X

SPECIAL INTERESTS AND TACTICS

Peace and justice organizations, for the most part, are egalitarian: Anyone is welcome to join if they are willing to get behind the cause. You can be a doctor, a plumber, a professor, an unemployed bricklayer; you can be rich or on welfare. It doesn't matter. The cause is what counts.

But some people prefer to work with others who share their own special skills, interests and knowledge. That way, they point out, health professionals can work together on medical problems; educators can focus on schools; scientists can deal with technical information.

It is a notion that has spawned a large number of groups, with names such as Architects for Social Responsibility, Athletes United for Peace, Business Executives for National Security, Communicators for Nuclear Disarmament, Computer Professionals for Social Responsibilty, Educators for Social Responsibility, High Technology Professionals for Peace, Lawyers Alliance for Nuclear Arms Control, Performing Artists for Nuclear Disarmament, Psychologists for Social Responsibility, and Union of Concerned Scientists. Those, and many more like them, have brought many Americans into the peace and justice process.

The first story that follows looks at one of these groups, Physicians for Social responsibility (PSR). It's the organization Helen

Caldicott revived shortly after arriving in the United States. Since then, with 32,000-plus health professionals now claimed as members, it has become the best known among professionally-oriented peace and justice groups.

Some individuals, of course, incorporate their beliefs into their professional lives without joining any group—and often without considering themselves activists. In the second story, we'll meet a Minnesota judge whose sentencing statement for two young activists gave heart to many peace and justice workers.

And then there are those who combine tactics. Among them is a Northern California minister who has a long record of activism, but who also brings his concerns to his second career as a dream worker. He's become something of a specialist on nuclear nightmares.

37. BRINGING DOWN THE FEVER
Pauline and Richard Saxon, Los Angeles

> *War, to sane men at the present day, begins to look like an epidemic insanity, breaking out here and there like the cholera or influenza, infecting men's brains instead of their bowels.*
> —Ralph Waldo Emerson

Los Angeles' Pauline Saxon vividly recalls one "tiny incident" in 1975 during a visit to Hiroshima: "I saw a black shadow on a piece of stone of a building that was left from the [World War II] bombing. It was the shadow of a person who was, I guess you would say, incinerated at that moment. And that was all that was left of that human being, that shadow on a concrete wall."

The stunned wonder creeps back into Saxon's voice as she remembers. "At that time, I decided I would come back and I would give all my energies to working against nuclear weapons."

That decision may have expressed new determination, but it followed a direction already well-established by Saxon. "I've been in the peace movement since 1962," she said, "when Women Strike for Peace had their first ban-the-bomb march."

Not long after that she left her career. "I have a master's degree; I'm trained to do child counseling." But in the mid-1960s, while working in a Los Angeles program for disadvantaged children, she decided that for those children, as well as the rest of the human race, peace was the most vital goal. Saxon has not held a regular job since.

That early involvement led to her Hiroshima trip, as a member of the United States delegation to the World Conference Against

A- and H-Bombs. It was a conference her husband, orthopedic surgeon Richard Saxon, attended the following year. He, too, came back with new concern.

Before long, both were involved in a newly-reactivated group, Individuals Against the Crime of Silence. It was, said Richard, "based on the Nuremberg principles that people should declare their opposition to nuclear weapons, just as they might have declared their opposition to Hitler's methods . . . . In other words, it's a crime to remain silent."

Although that group is now inactive, the idea on which it was founded continues to inspire the Saxons. "To me, it's still an incredibly important concept: that people have an obligation—not just a right—in a democracy, to tell their leaders when they think something is wrong, and not to say, 'I couldn't do anything about it; I was ordered to do it,'" said Pauline.

Today both Saxons are fulfilling that obligation through Physicians for Social Responsibility (PSR). Richard is president of the Los Angeles Chapter; Pauline was volunteer executive director until a professional was hired recently. Now, she said, "if I had to give myself a title," it would be "sort of coordinator of volunteers and liaison with other peace groups." Richard added, "She's still involved with everything."

For her, Pauline said, PSR is "more than a full-time job, because I get awakened at 7:30 in the morning by someone calling me with something, with some idea, at home." This day the PSR business had begun a bit tardily: "We started on the telephone at 8:30 while we were having our coffee."

For Richard Saxon, PSR responsibilities also are demanding. He often finds himself "interrupting my patients, because I have to talk to somebody about this." It's meant giving up—at least for now—his tennis and the painting which he loves. Pauline thinks some newspaper should do a story punching holes in that old stereotype about doctors spending Wednesday afternoons on the golf course. Now they could tell, she suggested, "how doctors spend their Wednesdays trying to prevent nuclear war."

This morning, the couple have stopped by the Los Angeles chapter headquarters, located in a small complex of offices shared with other peace groups in next-door Santa Monica. With no patients waiting in the room down the hall, the doctor is dressed casually in jacket and slacks.

Their PSR work, the couple said, has continued their international involvements. In 1984, they were among some 50 Los Angeles chapter members who went to Helsinki, where they attended the annual meeting of the International Physicians for Prevention of Nuclear War, and then on to Moscow. The Saxons also visited West Berlin and Great Britain. It was a fascinating trip, said Richard, partly because "we were able to talk to Soviet physicians who . . . were doing research; heads of institutes, things like that." In February 1985, four of those Soviet physicians attended a Los Angeles PSR gathering.

Improved relations with the Soviets would offer a major step toward world peace, the couple believe, and they see PSR as a catalyst in that process.

"We're trying to work at it from the standpoint of showing Americans that there are Soviet people who feel exactly like they do, who don't want nuclear war," said Richard. He cited a related problem: While a majority of Americans want to control nuclear weapons, they're afraid to actually do it because "people are very frightened of the Russians; they think the Soviet Union is very aggressive." If they can just realize, he argues, that "there are people in the Soviet Union who are as concerned as they are," then maybe—in spite of differences—there would be a chance of working with these people.

"At least," said Richard, slipping into a medical metaphor, "we might bring the fever down. If you've got a serious illness, sometimes you have to treat the symptoms, because the symptoms can kill—high fever, or whatever—instead of curing the disease, itself. You give aspirin, alcohol rub, whatever."

When it comes to nuclear war, those untreated "symptoms" could wipe out the human race, said Richard. "Here we have two superpowers, and they can destroy the whole world. Therefore, we have to look at this relationship between the Soviet Union and the United States and somehow find a solution."

"I have to go home at night," added Pauline, "and say to myself, 'I have two children and two beautiful grandchildren. What am I going to do and what have I done to see to it that I prevent nuclear war, so that their lives and their children's and grandchildren's lives will go on?' I just don't think people face the fact that the world won't 'be' any more."

"This is a new world," said Richard somberly, "and with technology and communication and transportation, national boundaries have really become meaningless. Actually our patriotism is to the human species; it has to be to the human species in this dangerous age."

38. WHO IS GUILTY?
U.S. District Chief Judge Miles Lord, Minneapolis

> *Too many of us think [peace] is impossible. But that is a dangerous, defeatist belief . . . Our problems are manmade; therefore, they can be solved by man.*
>
> —*John F. Kennedy*

Mention that you just met Miles Lord, if you're visiting Minneapolis or St. Paul, and there's an instant reaction . . . rather as if you were visiting Los Angeles and casually commented, "Oh, I ran into Paul Newman yesterday" . . . or, in Washington, D.C., "Say, I had lunch with Ted Kennedy."

Lord, you might gather, is one of those folks who have caught the public interest. That fact is of some special note, since Lord's career was not in an area that usually draws intense personal concern: For the past two decades, he has been a judge. Yet, it made top page 1 news in both Twin Cities newspapers when Lord, at 65, announced in May 1985 that he was retiring from his post as chief United States district judge for Minnesota. One thing those reports didn't mention is that Lord has become something of a hero to peace activists.

In almost whatever he is doing, Lord draws intense feelings. Minnesotans revere or reject him with equal fervor, and almost all appear to know some of the stories: how he—a Crosby iron range boy, himself—grew up to successfully challenge the whole Minnesota mining industry when he found carcinogenic taconite tailings were being dumped in Lake Superior; how he made the rulings that gave girls an equal crack at high school sports and women

U.S. District Judge Miles Lord

an equal chance at University of Minnesota faculty jobs; how he upheld federal laws prohibiting motorboating in the Boundary Waters Canoe Areas Wilderness, standing up to special interests within his own state; how he ruled to protect timber wolves when trappers threatened to wipe them out; how he called three top executives of the giant A.H. Robins Co. before his bench, chastising them for their handling of the Dalkon Shield intrauterine device controversy and accusing their company of planting "deadly depth charges" in the wombs of thousands of women.

"He simply has more guts in one of his fingernails than most people carry around," Minneapolis attorney Dale Larson told St. Paul Pioneer Press and Dispatch reporter Jacqui Banaszynski for her front page story on the retirement.

Lord, the center of all this furor, is nothing of the roaring lion in person; in fact, the personality has a touch of Will Rogers—the witty story-teller with a twinkle in the eye and an infectious grin, the easy charmer who stands squarely on the side of feminine rights while enjoying a sort of old-fashioned courtly affection for women.

When a young, foreign journalist asked, "Do you find it easy to detach your emotions from your case and be emotionless?" Lord answered, "No."

"And," he added, "I don't think other judges do either. I think every judge has certain emotional involvement in any case. And those that don't get emotionally involved with things that are supposed to evoke emotion, I think, are not fit to be judges . . . . If you don't have a heart, you don't have understanding, you don't have compassion, how can you make judgments?"

It is not an attitude that has endeared him to all attorneys; some have charged he is occasionally more advocate than judge in a case, and he was eventually removed from the mining suit on that basis. A federal appeals court ordered a new trial in a drug-dealing case in 1983, saying Lord had improperly coached prosecutors.

In 1980, American Lawyer, a New York publication, named Lord one of the 11 worst jurists in the country. But in 1981 the Association of Trial Lawyers of America cited him as the year's outstanding trial judge, and three years later presented him with its first-ever presidential award of honor and merit, recognizing his "judicial independence, courage and integrity of purpose and commitment to our legal system."

By the time he announced his retirement, Lord had been in public life better than 30 years. He had been named assistant United States attorney in 1951, elected Minnesota attorney general in 1954, named United States attorney for Minnesota in 1961 and appointed to the United States district court bench in 1966. At the time of that last appointment, Hubert Humphrey predicted Lord would be "the people's judge."

Minnesotans who would earn national political prominence—Humphrey and Eugene McCarthy among them—had become Lord's friends even while he was attending the University of Minnesota law school, from which he graduated in 1948.

Lord, who has something of a reputation as a practical jokester, especially enjoys recounting some of the gags he put over on Humphrey. There was the time, for instance, when the two men had taken their young sons on a canoeing trip in Northern Minnesota's Boundary Waters Canoe Area. During a four-mile portage, the Lords and Humphreys were in a small van, following a bus filled with other canoers and a truck carrying that group's canoes. When the truck broke down, said Lord, the whole mini-convoy was halted.

"So Humphrey gets out and runs up to the truck; I ran up to the bus," recalled Lord, a conspiratorial grin appearing on his face. "I got in the bus, and I said, 'Howdayado, folks!' There were many people on the bus, maybe 70.

"I said, 'I'm the mayor of this small town up here, and I want to welcome you. You'll enjoy the fresh air and the clean water. The rocks are a bit hard and there are a few mosquitoes, but all in all, I know you'll love it!

"'Now let me point out some local color. There's a fellow running around here who pretends he's a United States senator. He's harmless, but he talks a lot. And frankly, he even looks like Hubert Humphrey.' "

"I said, 'You don't believe me!' . . . they were laughing . . . I said, 'OK . . . Hey! Sen. Humphrey, these people want to meet you. C'mere.' So he did. And while he was coming to the bus, I said, 'Folks, humor him along, but don't lend him any money.'

"So Humphrey gets on the bus: 'Howdayado folks, I'm Sen. Hubert Humphrey.' And one guy says, 'Yeah, and I'm Soapy Williams!' "

Finally, Humphrey caught on, said Lord: "He turned to me, and he said, 'Miles, damn you, what've you done to me now?!?!' "

Another time Lord, Humphrey and their wives were celebrating the Humphreys' 40th anniversary with a cruise down the St. Croix River. Lord was teasing the senator that he had been away from Minnesota too long: The people now were fonder of the judge than the senator. So the two men stepped to the boat's fantail to make an impromptu test.

Lord recalled what happened next: "People called, 'Hey, Judge Lord!' 'Hi, Judge Lord!' from all over. One little boatload said, 'Hello, Mr. Humphrey.' Geez, he was mad."

The two men returned to join the women, and Lord continued to goad Humphrey. They finally decided to try again. It was, said Lord, the same thing: " 'Judge Lord!' 'Judge Lord!' "

"Humphrey says, 'Dammit, what's going on around here!?!?' I said, 'Well, look down below the boat here' . . . where I had a big sign that said, 'Judge Lord's on board. Give him a hail.' "

However, the recognition that comes with being a controversial judge is not all fun and games. "It's not easy to dissent," said Lord in a reflective moment just a couple of weeks before his retirement was to take effect. "You pay a price for speaking your mind. You pay a price personally, professionally. The perception of others reflects on your family. You're questioned by the other judges—the superior judges, particularly—and by some of the lawyers that represent these vested interests."

Two cases that would bring that kind of questioning from some—as well as near-adulation from others—occurred near the end of Lord's tenure as U.S. district judge.

One was the A.H. Robins case, where Lord heard some of the more than 13,000 Dalkon Shield claims filed against Robins nationwide. Robins subsequently filed misconduct charges against Lord, who had accused Robins of foot-dragging and said the company was guilty of "corporate irresponsibility at its meanest," in addition to his comment about the depth charges in women's wombs. The U.S. Eighth Circuit Court of Appeals eventually struck Lord's speech from the record, but refused to punish him.

The second case involved the Sperry Corp. and two Bemidji, Minn., peace activists who had entered the company's plant, smashing computer equipment being assembled for the military. That case, which resulted in another misconduct complaint (again, dismissed by the appeals court), once more saw Lord speak his mind bluntly.

He'd thought a lot about it beforehand, said Lord, especially because he'd had Sperry in his court not too many months earlier, that time as defendant for allegedly overcharging the government—by $3.6 million, according to a federal report. A plea-bargaining deal brought that figure down to $325,000, said Lord, to which Sperry pleaded guilty.

Damages inflicted by the two activists, John LaForge, 28, and Barbara Katt, 25, were set at $33,000. On the day of sentencing, the pair brought toothbrushes with them, according to Dan Oberdorfer's Minneapolis Star and Tribune story; they were ready for jail. But they never got there.

Judge Lord—who said later that he is "a believer in the judge as an educator and in his pronouncements being educational to the public"—had a message he wanted to get across that day.

"The anomaly of this situation here," he said, "—and I must say that this is a very difficult job for a federal judge to do—is that I am here called upon to punish two individuals who are charged with having caused damage to the property of a corporation in the amount of $33,000. It is this self-same corporation which only a few months ago was before me, accused of having wrongfully embezzled from the United States government the sum of $3,600,000.

"The employees of this company succeeded in boosting corporate profits by wrongfully and feloniously juggling the books. Since these individuals were all employees of a corporation, it appears that it did not occur to anyone in the office of the attorney general of the United States that the actions of these men constituted a criminal conspiracy for which they might be punished and imprisoned.

"The government demanded only that Sperry pay back a mere 10% of the amount by which the corporation had been unlawfully enriched. Could it be that these men—who are working to build weapons of mass destruction—receive special treatment because of the nature of their work? Is there something sanctified about this effort to commit national suicide?"

And there was more: "As I ponder over the punishment to be meted out to these two people who were attempting to unbuild weapons of mass destruction," he said, "we must ask ourselves: Can it be that those of us who build weapons to kill are engaged in a more sanctified endeavor than those who would by their acts attempt to counsel moderation and mediation as an alternative method of settling international disputes?

"Why are we so fascinated by a power so great that we cannot comprehend its magnitude? What is so sacred about a bomb, so romantic about a missile? Why do we condemn and hang individual killers, while extolling the virtues of warmongers? What is that fatal fascination which attracts us to the thought of mass destruction of our brethren in another country? . . . How many people in this democracy have seriously contemplated the futility of committing national suicide in order to punish our adversaries?"

Then, toward the end of his remarks, Lord said, "I would here in this instance attempt in my own small way to take the sting out of the bomb, attempt in some way to force the government—though I know it will be futile—to remove the halo—which it seems to hold over any device which can kill—and, instead, to place thereon a shroud, the shroud of death, destruction, mutilation, disease and debilitation.

"If there be an adverse reaction to this sentence, I will anxiously await the protestations of those who complain of my attempts to correct the imbalance that now exists in a system which operates in such a manner as to provide one type of justice for the rich and a lesser type for the poor; one standard for the mighty and another for the meek; and a system which finds its humanness and objectivity is sublimated to military madness and the worship of the bomb."

Guilt—such as that of Katt and LaForge—could bring a 10-year sentence, Lord told the tense courtroom, many persons there to support the defendants. Instead, he sentenced each to six months . . . and immediately suspended the sentences and placed the pair on probation.

There was no applause in the quiet courtroom; Lord had asked that there be no public demonstration. But there was a silent reaction, he recalled: "I noticed that some of the people were crying."

39. NIGHTMARES THAT COULD SAVE THE WORLD
Jeremy Taylor, San Rafael, Calif.

> As human beings, our greatness lies not so much in being able to remake the world—that is the myth of the "atomic age"—as in being able to remake ourselves.
>
> —Mahatma Gandhi

This day Jeremy Taylor is at home and casual, settled into a comfortable armchair. The family's long-haired, golden-beige cat, Owl Fur, is curled contentedly on his lap. The cat's name started out as Oliver, said Taylor, but back then his daughter Tristy, now 12, could not pronounce it. Owl Fur caught on.

The wood-ceilinged room in which Taylor sits is the family kitchen. There are typical domestic items here: a white enamel-finish stove in one corner, a refrigerator, a sink and a small corner of cupboards—white cupboards with green doors and lavendar knobs. But the rest of the good-sized room is an agreeably eclectic clutter: a free-standing iron stove, a round trampoline, a wooden table, a brown rattan daybed. The walls hold cooking tools, baskets, masks, bookshelves, pictures—and, on one shelf, a golden Buddha draped with ivy vines. An old-style record changer is playing a whole stack of records—all flutey, wistful, new age music by Georg Deuter.

This is a setting that would, perhaps, suit someone comfortable wandering about in the land of dreams. And that description neatly fits Taylor, for it turns out that dream work is one of the intense interests he has brought to the peace process.

The Taylor home is in Marin County, just north of San Francisco. From here, Taylor offers counseling to both children and adults; he also commutes to Berkeley, where he teaches dream work at Starr King School for the Ministry, the Unitarian Universalist West Coast training center.

Starr King is part of the Graduate Theological Union, which has the status of a graduate department of the University of California at Berkeley. Taylor's classes routinely entice a majority of their enrollments from other theological schools and the regular Berkeley campus. Taylor has written a book, "Dream Work" (Paulist Press). As a Unitarian Universalist minister, he occasionally fills in for other pastors, but currently has no church of his own.

Dreams, Taylor is convinced, have a great deal to say—and can offer a great deal of hope—about many of humankind's problems, including the nuclear threat. He has come to believe, in fact, that people's dreams—especially the shared ones that many of us touch into—are signalling the evolutionary change in humankind that could lead to a new world order . . . and peace.

"My experience," said Taylor, "is that all dreams come in the service of wholeness and healing . . . and that nightmares, in particular, tend to be the result—the cumulative result—of messages of wholeness and healing that have come in a less dramatic and less gripping form and have been ignored."

That, he said, holds true for children no less than their parents. "There is a tremendous reservoir of resentment among young children these days about having been born into this world that is so unsafe," he said. "We are experiencing an increase in child suicide, and my sense is that it's directly related to this phenomenon—directly associated to the kids growing up with a sense that they may not make it into adolescence."

When children have nuclear nightmares, "I will encourage them to draw pictures, put on a little play or make a mask or something like that, and in the process of that creative work, we'll talk about the feelings that come up and give a safe arena for the negative feelings to be acted out."

But more than that, Taylor helps children—and their parents—understand that even childhood dreams of death are not necessarily negative.

"Childhood is characterized by nightmares—even happy childhood—because of the deep archetypal association between death and growth. Little children are achieving developmental milestones every couple of weeks or every couple of months, and every time they do that, the little person that they were before has to die, metaphorically speaking, in order for the little person that they're going to become to have a space to live in." As is true for their parents, Taylor is convinced, children's nightmares can be signs of growth.

Three or four versions of the nuclear nightmare have become relatively common now, for a variety of ages, Taylor has found: "One where the bomb is going to fall . . . one where it's seconds away and the dream ends with the flash . . . the dream of immediately afterwards, walking through the ruins, stunned at the horror of it . . . and then the [dream of] long-term dying from nuclear radiation and nuclear winter and other sickness."

While all those dreams can be terrifying, the people who recall them may have an advantage over those who don't, Taylor proposes: "My guess is that many more are dreaming them than are remembering them, and that the ones who aren't remembering them are victims of a sense of helplessness . . . that because they really believe they can't do anything about it, the dream memories disappear, and they're left only with the sense of having had an awful dream."

"My experience is that nobody ever remembers a dream if the main point of that dream has to do with something which you can't do anything about," said Taylor.

He's worked with psychotics—and observed that they almost never dream about their own illnesses, presumably because their problems are too great to deal with. But when they do dream about the psychosis, he's found, it is a sign they are ready to accept treatment and to improve.

"In other words," he said, "if you dream about something, it means—from my point of view and my experience—ipso facto, that there is something positive and creative that you can do about it. So the fact that so many people are dreaming about the nuclear menace at this point is, from my point of view, an indication that solutions are at hand; that it is not an insoluble problem. My experience is that if this were an insoluble problem, we would not be dreaming about it."

Concern about solving the world's problems is nothing new for Taylor. While still a high school student in Buffalo, N.Y., he became a conscientious objector and eventually joined "an underground railway movement to smuggle AWOL servicemen who didn't want to go to Vietnam out of the country."

He also organized friends to picket a local Cadillac dealer who had constructed a fallout shelter display in his window and "hired Miss Niagara Frontier Tomato Crop to live in the fallout shelter and to prove to everybody how neat it was." That McCarthy-era incident, he recalled, "was a baptism of fire": "We provoked a lot of very negative response in the community . . . . We polarized opinion in the city, and we were definitely in the minority . . . . We got physically attacked a couple of times."

He moved on to the University of Buffalo (which was renamed State University of New York at Buffalo while he was attending) as a young man concerned about "the perpetuation of the war in Southeast Asia . . . racism, economic inequality, sexism and ageism, and all general sorts of institutionalized brutality."

He came to the conclusion that all of them, ultimately, were motivated by unconscious factors. "It was not sufficient to demonstrate rationally the uselessness of any of those activities," he discovered. "You could demonstrate how any number of these activities were not producing health and safety for the very people who were supporting them, that they were counterproductive and dangerous and stupid—and it made no difference." That led Taylor to study irrational motivations . . . and dreams.

But now Taylor believes it may be the bomb, itself, that could spur dramatic improvement in the way we live and relate to other people. In fact, he said thoughtfully, "I think it's already happening." Because people now are recognizing the potential for nuclear holocaust, and even a nuclear end to the world, he argues, "the direness of our circumstances has penetrated into the deep unconscious." As a result, the archetypes—those deep, subconscious wellsprings of knowing shared by all humankind—"are moving," as clearly evidenced by those shared dreams, he believes.

Taylor is convinced that the result—if we manage it—will finally be world recognition that "we are one folk, that we are one species, that it doesn't matter who's right and who's wrong, or who's smart and who's stupid, or who's rich and who's poor; that the reality of the nuclear technology makes us all one."

"Prior to the nightmare of the nuclear menace," he said, "that was an opinion and a perception that was limited to saints. But it's certainly not new: The world's great religions have been pedaling this notion for at least 4,000 years. But prior to this development, the direct perception of the unity of humankind was limited to a few relatively developed folk, and it was considered to be beyond the grasp of ordinary people.

"What the nuclear menace has done is to just eliminate that. It's now not beyond the grasp of ordinary people at all, that idea. It's a fundamental necessity for our thinking now. And I suspect that that is not accidental, that the collective nightmare is serving the same function that the individual nightmare serves: to force us to pay attention to things we otherwise might not pay any attention to."

The changes that are required, he said, "are of such an order that they are analogous to the ways in which society has changed in our imagination and speculation after the bomb falls: The institutions are wiped away; what is left of human society must be reconstructed on a face-to-face basis.

"My suspicion is that that's a negative metaphor of the scope of change that is required of us if we are to survive, and that the only thing that is in our hands at this point is how we are going to negotiate that change, how we are going to accomplish it. Either we accomplish it by dropping the bomb and wiping the slate clean in that fashion, and the few remnants starting over again, and maybe not surviving at all, or we accomplish a change of similar magnitude by conscious choice.

"We're like the ancient Mayans: We walk away from the institutions that don't work anymore and let the grass grow over them, and start over with new institutions that are based on different principles."

Answering those who think such an idea may be beautiful, but impossible, Taylor draws on the analogy that inspires many peace activists—the end of slavery: "There were a large majority of folks who thought that slavery was a bad idea, but who were convinced that it was never going to be abolished, because it had been part of human history forever—that there was no way we were going to live in a society without slaves: 'It's a wonderful, utopian ideal, but it's never going to happen.'

"That's exactly what people are saying now. And I think they are as ill-informed as the people 100 years ago, who thought that slavery was an inevitable human institution."

XI

REACHING ACROSS NATIONAL BOUNDARIES

It's no longer good enough to see this world as "us against them," say most peace and justice people. This is one world and we're all in it together. If nothing else, the bomb has taught us the lesson, for it doesn't matter much who drops the first one on whom; when those nuclear warheads start flying, we'll all bow out together.

Big business in this country already has gone international, although not necessarily for altruistic motives. That fact of life was exposed with great embarrassment during the Iran-Contra hearings, revealing incidents where loyalty was pledged only to the dollar signs, where national ethics had become incidental—fine when they fit in, dispensable when they didn't.

The average American, however, does not live on that pragmatic plateau. Loyalties that have grown since elementary school still count. We hesitate to trust old enemies—even when our own lives may depend upon it.

But, say the peace people, the time is now and we've got to grow and change. And that means we must learn to work with all the world's varying cultures, including those we may still distrust, for there is one basic interest we all share: We all hope to survive. Cultivating such relationships is another thread reaching among peace and justice people. Some groups and individuals have made it a primary goal.

40. BUILDING BRIDGES
Howard and Alice Frazier, Woodmont, Conn.

> *The often very deep differences between cultures should not be seen as divisions between people. Instead, cultures should be interpreted for what they really are: the ultimate declaration of belonging to the human species. We are one people; and we can all strive for one aim: the peaceful and equitable survival of humanity.*
>
> —*Richard Leakey, "Origins"*

There's a story they like to tell at the Woodmont, Conn., headquarters of a group called Promoting Enduring Peace. It's about their founder, Dr. Jerome Davis, for many years a Yale University divinity professor . . . and how, as a young man, he got caught in the Russian revolution; how he clambered through a Russian bank's basement window while trying to save his funds; and how he wound up a friend of Lenin and Trotsky.

It all began, said the group's current director, Howard Frazier, when Davis went to the Soviet Union in 1915 or 1916 under auspices of the YMCA; his assignment was to work in the czarist prison camps in an attempt to improve conditions.

But while he was there, the revolution broke out in full force. Long lines grew in front of the banks as people tried desperately to get out their money; Davis had visions of all his YMCA funds disappearing. That's when he discovered an open basement window in the bank, slipped inside armed with a note from the minister of war, raced upstairs and jumped to the front of the line. Sorry, the bankers told him; to get out the YMCA money he would need an official signature from the revolutionary leader, Lenin.

That led him to Lenin and Trotsky, who were speaking at the Smolny (the revolutionary headquarters) that night. He not only got the signature and saved the YMCA funds, but also told the two revolutionaries that he would like to remain in Russia, continuing his work to improve conditions for soldiers. He got permission (he would later travel the Volga, starting libraries and clubs in the villages), and the result was a friendship with Russia that outlasted the two revolutionaries, even outlasted Davis' own life, and continues today.

Now, of course, Davis' work is carried on by Promoting Enduring Peace (PEP). But that basic Davis idea—citizen diplomacy—remains fundamental to PEP operations, and has been picked up by other peace and justice organizations, as well.

Davis had begun encouraging others to join that effort even as he settled back into the United States and went on to earn the title of professor of social ethics at Yale. Occasionally, he would invite a few friends to travel to the Soviet Union with him.

During the post-WWII McCarthy era, when Americans were "seeing communists under every bed," Davis added a new technique: trying to counteract what he saw as a national paranoia by clipping and reproducing articles presenting a different view of the Soviet Union, then sending those articles out free across the country.

Such activities, of course, did not endear Davis to those running the country at the time, and he soon realized government "plants" were joining many of his journeys. That finally stopped, Frazier said, when government officials realized they might as well save their money, because Davis, a prolific writer, was distributing reports on everything that went on.

In 1969, Frazier was among those joining a Davis tour. Frazier had just retired from a government career that began during Franklin Delano Roosevelt's New Deal.

On the tour, "We came back through Rumania, and Davis was given a reception with the president," Frazier recalled. Frazier

Howard and Alice Frazier

admitted to an embarrassing moment at that reception: Noticing a man near him who was wearing a fancy uniform of some sort, Frazier asked, "Do you work here?"

"Yes," the man responded, "I'm the foreign minister."

It turned out, said Frazier, that the man also had served as president of the United Nations for two terms. But in spite of the social gaffe, the man soon posed happily for photographs with Frazier's sister and her friend, both of whom had accompanied him on the trip.

Davis did not limit his travelers-outreach idea to the Soviet Union; he also rounded up groups to visit other countries—again, mostly those that weren't necessarily favorites of the United States government at the moment, those that ordinary tourists might even have trouble getting into.

Frazier joined another trip—that time to China—in 1973. During that journey, Davis invited Frazier to apply for the post of executive secretary of PEP.

For Frazier, the timing of that offer was right. He had completed not only the 34-year government career that began in 1935, but also a pair of related assignments that followed. He had begun his career with four years at Tennessee Valley Authority, followed by 15 with the Department of Labor's wages and hours division (broken by World War II service as a major in the Army Air Force). He had then joined the Office of Economic Opportunity, eventually moving to the White House staff, where he worked on consumer affairs with Esther Peterson and Betty Furness. Finally, after his 1969 retirement from government service, he was named president of Consumer Federation of America and then accepted a post with another consumer group, located in Philadelphia. The move to PEP felt like a natural progression.

Besides, there was another major change in Frazier's life about that time. A widower, he had visited a yoga camp in Canada during another of his travels. There Frazier, a tall, lean man, was challenged to learn to stand on his head. Help came in the form of a small, bright-eyed, energetic yoga teacher, Alice Zeigler, who would recall later that a mutual friend from Washington, D.C., asked, "Alice, would you look after Howard? He's never done yoga." Smiling at that memory, Alice added, "I have ever since." Howard and Alice were married a week before he began his new job with PEP.

The couple moved into the turn-of-the-century oceanfront, Woodmont, Conn., house that Jerome Davis had bought in 1958 as headquarters for the organization and home for the director and his family. Today, the downstairs is definitely a nicely comfortable private home's living quarters, although the Fraziers do a good deal of organizational entertaining there. Upstairs, there are offices where the couple and their two assistants do the hard work of running an organization with international involvements.

Although the tours to other countries continue as the group's most eye-catching activity, the nitty-gritty is getting out those articles, said Howard.

"We spend about $30,000 a year just on printing," he said, "and $8,000 on postage." The reprints are sent out to churches, schools, peace groups . . . anyone who asks for them, and they're sent in packages of hundreds or even thousands when requested. All the groups are asked for in return is the postage, although many send a little extra, he added. The costs are helped by those "little extras," a few bequests left the group, donations from a number of regular givers, and annual mild letters inviting supporters to send money. But the major funding still comes from investments built on money left by Jerome Davis. "We're very fortunate," said Howard Frazier.

Today, Alice, now 63, and Howard, 73, operate as a team: He's executive director and she's associate. Alice left a 39-year education career as teacher, counselor and school psychologist about four years ago, taking on more responsibilities with PEP. One of her special skills is producing and presenting slide shows about the group's activities. Howard accepts no salary; however, the couple live at the house at no charge, and when they travel, costs are picked up by the travel agency, since the Fraziers are trip organizers.

Those tours, said Howard, are the group's "second main activity." March 1985 saw the group's 11th high school trip to the Soviet Union—this one led by a Quaker teacher of Russian language from Baltimore; 35 students participated. The organization has sponsored five groups that visited China, studying topics such as communal life and adult education, as well as three trips to Cuba, several trips around the world and many tours to the Soviet Union.

They now also offer what they call their Volga Peace Cruises. "We take over the Alexander Pushkin, a river boat, for 10 days," said Howard. "We have speakers from the Soviet Union and the United States speaking on peace issues. Following the talks, we have had a United States-Soviet Union peace rally for the past two years."

One of the problems, Howard added unhappily, is that the United States media either fail to report such activities or pooh-pooh them. American media refuse to believe that peace demonstrations are allowed in the Soviet Union, said Howard, "but we've known in the peace movement that Soviets have been demonstrating for years."

In 1983, the Fraziers decided to challenge that situation: They would force media attention by holding a big joint rally in Gorky Park. The result? "Prime news on Soviet TV," said Howard, "but not one United States medium turned up, although many were invited." The next year, one reporter from Los Angeles skipped the rally, but did show up at a later press conference, only to write scathingly that "you're dupes, you're dupes," said Howard, and that "you're being used by the Communist government."

The Fraziers are used to that charge of being dupes; they're used to hearing that even if individual Soviets want peace, that won't affect the "evil" government; even that they, themselves, may be communists. They could get all the headlines they want if they would say something critical of the Soviet Union, Howard believes.

"But our experience has been that the people in the Soviet Union are seeking peace," he said. "They lost 20 million people during

World War II, and it's been our observation that they're really conscious of the need to work with other groups for peaceful solutions to the world's problems . . . . The Soviet Union lost more people in the siege of Leningrad than we lost in the whole World War II."

That doesn't mean they think everything is dandy in the Soviet Union, said Alice. For instance, she explained, when they get asked about the Soviet gulags, "I don't try to answer that, because that's out of my experience. I wouldn't try in any way to characterize that as being blameless. I guess what we say is sort of this: We know that neither of us is blameless; both of our countries have things of which we should be ashamed . . . but we can't put that as a condition! We can't say to them, 'Straighten up all your internal affairs or we're not going to talk with you.' We have to start from where we are, and do what we can."

In addition to the trips and their reprint distribution service, PEP also sponsors an annual Gandhi Peace Award. It's a tradition that was started by Jerome Davis. The first recipient was Eleanor Roosevelt.

And with all the activities, the hope remains the same. As Alice expressed it, without even finishing her sentence: "If we could melt the iceberg of the cold war even a little . . . ."

———————

The idea of actively seeking friendship with the Soviet Union—of offering our faith and trust—is still a tough go for many Americans. Maybe that's why some proposals about how to encourage such friendship have seemed fairly off-the-wall.

A St. Paul Pioneer Press writer came up with one notion shortly after attending a Soviet-American citizens' peace conference in Minneapolis.

"On the scale of megabucks and megarubles being sluiced into defense budgets," he suggested, " . . . it would be peanuts monetarily to arrange a broad scale swap of, say, 10,000 or so citizens a year from all walks of life. [Such an exchange] would . . . tend to sweep away the dangerous overburden of myths and misinformation which are so valuable to rabble rousers on both sides. In time, Americans and Soviets could do their disagreeing without interpreters. And we would hope they could keep on disagreeing and have a future to disagree about."

Another proposal some months later suggested a similar exchange—this time presuming those exchanged citizens would be volunteer hostages. As a result, the reasoning went, neither country would be willing to blast apart the other, since it would mean wiping out so many of its own citizens in the process.

Yet another plan was offered by a World War II vet—one who lost a leg to a land mine and who through the years has bragged about being a hawk. Today, however, he shakes his head with frustration and asks, "Why don't they just get a bunch of American vets together with a bunch of Russian vets. You'd better believe we could find solutions." It's not a matter of trusting the Soviets; he still doesn't. But, for him, the bottom line threat has changed from "red or dead" to "apocalypse now." He's willing to believe the Soviets are as concerned as we are about that ultimate peril.

Alice Frazier added an update on Promoting Enduring Peace's projects in an enthusiastic note a couple of months after our visit:

"We leave for USSR on July 13 for our fourth annual Volga Peace Cruise. Plans are now being firmed up for the Mississippi Cruise, summer of '86. We will take over the Delta Queen with 50 Russian guests and 130 American peace activists. The one week peace cruise from St. Paul to St. Louis will be the first of its kind. We're anticipating great things from it. Howard has just returned from Moscow where he discussed plans with peace committee and friendship organization officers. They are very enthusiastic."

Alice included a quote from one of PEP's latest reprints, "Losing Moral Ground," by Richard Barnet, which originally appeared in Sojourners magazine:

The injunction to love your neighbors is a call to create and affirm a social order. The only alternative to getting along with co-habitants of the planet, to seeing them as human beings, to empathizing with their needs, their fears and their dreams, is fratricidal war, social decay and personal despair . . . . The sick hope that God will soon blow up the world to rescue us from the moral duty of growing up and figuring out how to coexist with the people of the Soviet Union and 150 other countries offers a theological justification for human-initiated holocaust—there are no moral ends to be served that can spell the death of everything."

The quote, wrote Alice, "says so well what we mean."

41. THE PERSONAL PRICE
The Rev. Sharna J. Sutherin, Bozeman, Mont.

> *When I was a child, I spoke like a child, I thought*
> *like a child, I reasoned like a child; when I*
> *became a man, I gave up childish ways. For now*
> *we see in a mirror dimly, but then face to face.*
> *Now I know in part; then I shall understand fully,*
> *even as I have been fully understood. So faith,*
> *hope, love abide, these three; but the greatest of*
> *these is love.*
>
> —*I Corinthians, 13:8-13*

For Sharna Sutherin, the day had started early. She had agreed to substitute for a preacher who spoke each Sunday at two small churches about 200 twisty miles north of Bozeman, in Stanford and Geyser, Mont. Sutherin had gone to Stanford the night before, spent too much time that evening talking with her hostess—the minister's wife, Sherri Field—and gotten up early to work on her sermon. Her contemplation, sitting there "out in the middle of nowhere," was broken by the sound of helicopters.

"Who's flying helicopters at 9 o'clock on Sunday morning?" she asked her hostess.

"Oh, they're moving a missile head," was the reply.

"So," recalled Sutherin, "on my way to Geyser, as I came out to get on the highway at Stanford, there were two helicopters landing at the little airport in Stanford. About five miles down the road, first came the blue Blazers—the Air Force must have hundreds of blue Blazers—then two [more vehicles] . . . . Sherri called them armored cars, but they looked like fast tanks to me. They had these little thin windows and there was a machine gun mounted on top

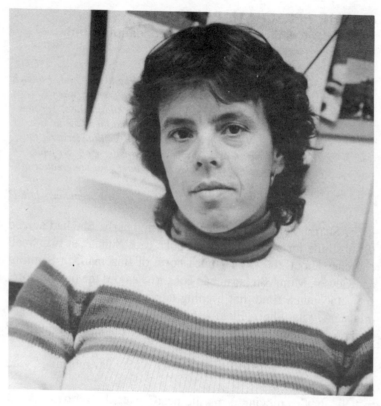

The Rev. Sharna J. Sutherin

of each. Then a semi that had the missile head in it. Then three more armored cars and five more Blazers.

"It was like, this is Sunday morning, people! I'm on my way to church to preach. I can't believe you guys have got to move these instruments of death on Sunday morning!"

Driving to Geyser—just 15 miles from Stanford—"I must have passed five or ten missile silos on the way; they're all over," said Sutherin. "For me, having grown up in Cleveland, that's not something I'm used to. But for the people in that area, it's . . . they've resigned themselves to the fact that that's part of the way they're going to have to live."

"If Montana and North Dakota seceded from the union, they'd be the world's largest nuclear power," said Sutherin, pronouncing each word with emphasis.

Montanans may be resigned to that situation, but Sutherin is not. Her brain, her heart, her soul demand action. There are Christians, she admits, who feel it may be a waste of time to fight nuclear weapons—that they are just one sign of the impending Armageddon. "To me," she said forcefully, "that is the theology of Christian irresponsibility. If God is going to end the world in my life, God can end the world. He—or she—doesn't need anything we have created to destroy the world . . . . I don't think God calls us to wait for him to destroy the world; he calls us to try to make the world a place that's grounded in love with every last breath that we have."

For Sutherin, that call has taken her to the Soviet Union, as well as to Central and South America. It has encouraged her to speak out for causes that still make many other citizens uncomfortable—things like removal of those missiles, plus friendship with the Soviet Union and an end to United States meddling in Central America. It has made her a controversial personality in Bozeman.

But for Sutherin, recognition has come at a heavy price. Many Montanans are not sure they want to get rid of those missiles . . . not convinced the Soviet Union could become a friend . . . not ready to disengage in Central America. And not ready to put up with an outspoken, opinionated, sometimes abrasive, 29-year-old female preacher. The result is that Sutherin has seen her own life and dreams threaten to fall apart.

Two and a half years earlier, when Sutherin first arrived here, Bozeman had seemed full of opportunity for a can-do sort of young woman who dared to dream big. Several months before her arrival, Sutherin had been ordained—the first woman ever so recognized by her home state's Cleveland Baptist Association, as far as that organization's 150-year records show. Bozeman offered her first chance at a full-time ministerial job: She was to be United Campus Christian Ministries pastor at Montana State University.

Sutherin went to work developing a strong program. Before long, she was offering Sunday services and counseling for the campus. She began speaking on both women's spirituality and Central America; she joined the university's AIDS task force and the search committee for a professor of religious studies; she served on the Women's Resource Center advisory board; she worked with New Genesis, a Christian outreach singing group; she joined the Bozeman Central American Advocates.

That kind of involvement had its roots back in her childhood, spent in the Cleveland suburb of Bradford. Although she lived in a working class neighborhood, with parents she considers conservative, Sutherin's early years provided a solid basis for her later activism. It was the family's church, First Baptist Church of Greater Cleveland, that provided one of the first windows to a bigger world out there: The church sponsored a medical missionary who worked in Central America, and he would come back and tell about his experiences. Sutherin was a good listener.

While Sutherin was in eighth grade, she was confronted with another world trouble spot: "I had a friend whose brother had been killed in Vietnam. He ran over a mine. He just drove over a mine, and they didn't really know whether it was our side or their side that set the mine . . . . That started not to make sense to me."

Still, she added, "I believed in the domino theory; I was sure the communists were taking over Southeast Asia, so it was all right for us to be in Vietnam . . . . I believed the experts must know what they were doing."

"Then," she said, "Kent State came along." The Sutherins lived just 20 minutes from the university that made international headlines during the Vietnam protests. "I couldn't understand why the National Guard was shooting students who were protesting the war . . . . The line to justify killing in Southeast Asia didn't seem to fit in the United States." The reaction in her neighborhood, she recalled, "was eerie; our whole area just got quiet. Nobody quite knew what to do . . . . And I didn't understand."

In 1973 the family welcomed an AFS student from Argentina to their home for the school year. "That was right after the coup in Chile," said Sutherin. "Lilly said to us that the United States had been involved in that coup. I was a junior in high school and believed in America and knew we stood for democracy and freedom and would never ever do such a thing in another country."

"The year after she went home, it came out that the CIA had, indeed, orchestrated that coup in Chile," said Sutherin. Her concern grew, and it continued growing when Martin Luther King Jr. died.

By the summer of 1974, Sutherin had graduated from high school. She decided it was time to put her concerns into action and signed up with a youth group the church's medical missionary took each summer to work in Central America. That year they headed for Nicaragua, where the 18-year-old Sutherin participated in a medical program, fought rats that were stealing community food supplies, and helped dig wells and build latrines.

But even that experience eventually brought confusion: Three years later, while sitting in a women's studies class at Dennison University, she would be stunned into close attention. The subject of the day was birth control. Back in Nicaragua, Sutherin had given birth control shots, using something the doctors called Depo-

Provera. At Dennison, she heard her instructor saying "that we don't use Depo-Provera in the United States for birth control, because of the high incidence of breast cancer, and other kinds of cancer and difficulties . . . and that it's illegal. Although it's manufactured here, it's illegal for use in our own country." Sutherin thought back to the trusting women who had allowed her to sink needles into their arms. Even today, she said, "it sort of gives me nightmares sometimes."

At Dennison, Sutherin started in pre-med, but switched to religious studies. She went on to Union Theological Seminary in New York City, earning a Master of Divinity degree.

During those school years, she continued to enlarge her knowledge of Latin America. She visited Puerto Rico, helping set up a student exchange . . . got a job as a Caribbean and Latin American research specialist at the United Methodist Church's United Nations office . . . returned to Puerto Rico, then went on to the Dominican Republic with a seminary group . . . flew to Argentina to visit Lilly, the AFS student. Sutherin became a founding member of CISPES (Committee in Solidarity with the People of El Salvador), of the Inter-Religious Task Force on Central America, and of the Puerto Rican Information Center, which lobbies at the U.N.

Then, shortly after her ordination in the spring of 1982, Sutherin reached out to another part of the world: She joined a group of 50 travelers for a two-week visit to the Soviet Union, sponsored by the Baptist Peace Fellowship of North America. The fellowship, she said, "felt that part of the reason for the tension between the United States and the Soviet Union is ignorance . . . and part of the way to counter that is to meet people face to face." Sutherin came back convinced that was true.

And, although the common notion may be that religion is dead in the Soviet Union, it's quite the opposite, said Sutherin. For instance, "there are three-quarters of a million to a million Baptists in the Soviet Union," she explained. "The church is just growing like wildfire."

During their first stop, in Moscow, Sutherin and her group attended Easter Sunday services (in May, the Russian Orthodox Easter date that year) at Moscow Baptist Church. "There must have been 2,000 people at the service we were at . . . and it was the first of five services for the day," she said.

Her tour continued to Siberia, Uzbekestan and Kazakhstan. In all, the group visited five Baptist churches. Sutherin preached at two of them, in Novosibirsk and Tashkent. Without much doubt, she was the first ordained Baptist woman to do so. Both times Sutherin spoke of peace.

In Tashkent, Sutherin recalled, she didn't know she was to speak until the service had begun. Another speaker preceded her, so she took that time to pray for guidance. "I opened my Bible and turned to the 13th chapter of Corinthians, the love chapter," she recalled. When it was her time to talk, she aimed her message at the women sitting before her.

"I said, 'You, just like women in the United States, have sent your sons and fathers and brothers and uncles off to war. And just like the women in the United States, far too many of your loved ones never returned.'

"At that point, much to my amazement, the congregation was just in tears. I said that the kind of love that I thought Paul was talking about in First Corinthians 13 was a love that could forgive the loss of loved ones and move beyond all conflict that might exist between human beings, to be more loving to each other, and that that could be the more important thing."

"I think," Sutherin said, recalling that incident, "for me it was a real experience of being moved by the spirit, and not anything I can explain any other way than that God used me in that time to speak to those people. After the service, the women, one after the other, came up, talking a blue streak to me in Russian and hugging me and crying." The whole trip, she said, "was quite an experience."

On her return, Sutherin attended the American Baptists' biennial meeting in Cleveland. She was elected to the steering committee of the Baptist Peace Fellowship and named a contributing editor of the Baptist Peacemaker magazine. And then it was on to her job as campus minister in Bozeman.

And although the record she put together here would look impressive on a resume, the good things began to fall apart less than five months after she arrived. She thinks that mostly relates back to another trip she tried to make to Central America. The destination was Honduras, where 150 American women, including Sutherin, planned to join Central American women for several days of constant prayer for peace.

The North Americans planned to leave from two airports, Miami and New Orleans. The Miami group got as far as Tegucigalpa, the capital of Honduras; they were not allowed off the plane. The New Orleans group, which Sutherin had joined, were not even allowed to board the Honduran airliner on which they held tickets.

"We all just kind of fell to our knees and prayed and started singing," said Sutherin. Then they went to the Honduran embassy in New Orleans seeking answers, but got neither help nor information; they tried to call the United States embassy in Tegucigalpa, but "there didn't seem to be anyone there."

Eventually, both groups of women decided to meet in Washington, D.C. There they held a press conference and contacted their congressmen. In spite of the failed trip, there was international press coverage, said Sutherin. "There was a statement made." There was daily front page coverage in the Bozeman Chronicle, as well. "I had a friend who was the religion writer," said Sutherin. "I was calling her two or three times a day to let her know what was up."

But when she got back home, Sutherin found that—at least with some of the readers—all that page 1 coverage had backfired. "Letters to the editor started appearing, saying that I wasn't Christian, and that my ordination must be a fraud, and that if I were a Christian, being a woman I would know to keep my mouth shut, and that I had simply gone on a kiss-a-commie mission."

The letters kept appearing for several weeks. There were a few letters supporting Sutherin, but, she admitted, "I felt kind of frightened." And in the end, "it effectively silenced me . . . it really was devastating."

Feeling silenced and devastated is not something Sutherin can accept. Maybe she's part of the problem, she mused. "Maybe there's somebody else out there who can do this better than I can."

"Even my Christian friends I don't think understand that my faith and my knowledge of God call on me to do justice and"—reading from a poster on her wall—" 'to wage peace like war is waged.' "

She sensed, unhappily, that she would not be able to do that in Bozeman. The Rev. Sharna J. Sutherin would soon be moving on.

XII

WOMEN TAKE RESPONSIBILITY

One male activist expressed a serious concern about this book: He hoped there would be at least a sampling of women included in the stories; from his experience, it was once again men who were taking the leadership roles.

He needn't have worried. Today's peace and justice leaders, as well as the workers, have at least equal representation among women—the Sharna Sutherins, Helen Caldicotts, Edi Ironses and many others.

It is not exactly a new role, of course. Tales of women demanding peace go back into antiquity. It was the Greek dramatist Aristophanes who offered the story of "Lysistrata" in 411 B.C., during the war between Athens and Sparta.

Aristophanes, who longed for peace, himself, wrote a tale in which the women of Athens gathered while their men were still asleep and agreed to withhold love until there was peace. More than that, they invited the women of Sparta to do the same. Eventually, the men agreed to a conference of the warring states . . . and Lysistrata provided all the wine they could drink. Soon everyone was happy and a treaty was signed. The play ended with a paean to peace.

Today, many men are recognizing women's essential role in the peace process—not just their participation, but the special gifts they may bring. Men like Bill Caldicott are calling on men to learn from women—to learn how to nurture the world, as the best hope we will all survive.

Women play a variety of roles in the stories that follow: leading national and local groups, moving among different causes, working to bring other groups together. All are women who are making a difference.

42. SPEAK NOW OF PEACE . . . OR BE FOREVER SILENT
Betty Bumpers, Washington, D.C.

> *During the wars of old we bore with you . . . .*
> *But we observed you carefully; and oftentimes,*
> *when we were at home, we used to hear that you*
> *had decided some matter badly. When we inquired*
> *about it, the men would answer, "What's that to*
> *you? Be silent." And we asked, "How is it, hus-*
> *band, that you men manage these affairs so*
> *foolishly?"*
>
> —*Lysistrata*

Take the Washington, D.C., metro to the Eastern Market stop. Cut across the small mall and turn down Eighth Street. Pass the spiritualist palm reader, a couple of thrift shops, the sidewalk jewelry salesman and a sprinkling of store-front centers for good causes. Four or five blocks down, across from the suddenly spit-and-polish Marines Barracks, is the national headquarters for a group called Peace Links.

Pass the folded-back night grate, climb the stairs, take a quick right and you will have found Peace Links. And—if she happens to be in town—Betty Bumpers.

Bumpers is a Senate wife; her husband is Dale Bumpers (D-Ark). She is also a full-time activist: founder and president of Peace Links, a group she organized in 1982 with the specific purpose of pulling women into the political process—especially those women already involved in traditional women's groups, the clubs and organizations.

Today, close to 100 groups across the nation have "linked" with

Bumpers—35,000 to 40,000 women, and some men, Bumpers reported proudly. If this country does make a turnaround toward peace, it's going to be women who make it happen, she is convinced.

"What I'm trying to do is to erase the intimidation that women have always felt about getting involved in national security issues and foreign policy . . . and to say, you have every right—in fact, you have a duty—to be involved in it," she explained.

While talking, Bumpers sat in a large, upholstered desk chair that had been "inherited" by the office. She had on a casual red jacket and a black-on-white striped dress—the kind of outfit that travels well.

Bumpers is on the road a lot these days. She had just come back from California, where she had made a presentation to the YWCA; her schedule for the next few days included a workshop for congressional wives, a talk before the Little Rock, Ark., Junior League, and visits to other Southern cities. "It's very difficult for me to be away from my husband, who travels a lot, himself," she said. "I'm gone almost as much as he is; we just kind of meet each other coming and going. The only reason I do it is because I think there's hope. And it's activism that has given me that hope."

Women have a couple of blocks when it comes to getting into peace work, said Bumpers. For one, "Peace still has bad connotations in many places." So, women are "scared . . . scared somebody's going to call them a communist or question their patriotism or look at them like . . . they're one of those 'crazies.' " Second, there's that problem of women thinking they don't know enough. Not true on either count, argues Bumpers.

She tells of a discovery: "I found out that women know more about national security issues and the arms race than many men do. We just thought [men] knew all about arms, knew all about foreign policy. They're all busy making a living, busy with their careers, busy trying to carve out a little piece of free time." Sometimes, in fact, "it is more difficult for men, with their career and business concerns, to question authority on this subject," she

Betty Bumpers

added. But "women will question, question, question . . . especially when it comes to the welfare of their children or their families."

Moreover, she believes, women grasp the situation intuitively. Every woman she's talked to, said Bumpers, "somehow had her sixth sense tuned in to the fact that her children—and indeed her home on this planet—are in jeopardy." They don't need to be experts on missile-ese—they don't have to use terms like MIRV and SLBM and throw-weight—to realize that something is wrong, said Bumpers, when "the current superpower arsenals have the capacity to virtually destroy each other 17 times, which is a little ridiculous. Your common sense tells you that; you don't need to be an arms expert!"

"My idea is, if we put the same kind of time, energy, money, expertise, commitment and know-how into finding ways to coexist on this planet that we spend on finding ways to destroy ourselves . . . don't you know we'd come up with an answer?"

Once women firmly grasp the situation, Bumpers believes, they will move to change things: "Women are not going to stand and wring their hands and gasp and moan. They'll do anything that will protect their children and their homes. Women are mean, viscious spiders in those areas."

What women—and men—need to do, according to Bumpers, is to jump into the political process. "People feel powerless, because we've been shut out of the process for so long," she said. But democracy "is we, the people, ruling and calling for the leadership to take us . . . where we want to go."

"What Peace Links is saying," she continued, "is that we know the leadership is out there to lead us out of this dilemma if we, the people, call for it. Now how much more patriotic can you be, than to say it's within our country, it's within the leadership that we have. But we, the people, have to set the tone and direction . . . . That's what democracy's about: our electing and holding accountable our elected officials."

Bumpers likes the story of a West Coast woman who sat down to call the White House one morning to state her opinion on an issue—a tactic recommended by Peace Links and other groups. The woman's 15-year-old "was just horrified," said Bumpers. "He said, 'Moooooother! You're NOT going to call the White House!' " But she did, "and before he could get to his carpool out front he was bragging, 'Hey, my mom just called the White House!' What better role model could she be?"

Bumpers admitted she has not always been so involved politically, herself. There were earlier years when she would simply "vote for whom my dad and then my husband told me to vote for." But she's always been active in her community, and at one time organized an Arkansas drive for immunization against polio and other childhood diseases—a drive that she then helped introduce on a national level.

Bumpers made the shift to political activism after a particularly unsettling conversation with her daughter Brooke, then 19—a story she has told and retold. The way it happened, said Bumpers, is that "we were on our way back to Arkansas after her freshman year in college." The summer before there had been a frightening accident involving a Titan II missile in Arkansas, and during the school year there had been that Three-Mile Island incident. Brooke asked "how we'd know where to find each other in case of a national disaster," Bumpers recalled.

"I mentioned, well, we'd just go back to Arkansas. Then she really let me have it, saying, with all of the silos we have there, plus a lot of other things—a nuclear power plant right in the middle of the state, the manufacturing and storage place for toxological warfare, two SAC bases, several other things—she said, 'You know they're all triple-targeted; Arkansas would be at the bottom of the crater.' "

"I mean," said Bumpers in soft, Southern accents, "it just blew my mind." And that's when Bumpers—drawing on the organizational techniques she had used in the immunization drive—pulled together Peace Links.

Now, "what we're trying to do is to get this on the agendas of other clubs and organizations—not other peace organizations, but civic and professional and social groups," said Bumpers. In the early days of Peace Links, she added, "I thought we would be on the agenda of every woman's club and organization in this country in three years. And I could quit." She would go back to her gardening and quilting and knitting; maybe even back into teaching. "But it hasn't worked quite that fast," she said, laughing.

So, for Betty Bumpers, it is a continuing commitment "to charge women with the responsibility [of participating in this democracy], taking it as an important part of their citizenship, and passing it on—charging their children with being responsible citizens, charging themselves and their neighbors."

"It's the only hope we have of we, the people, shaping the quantity and quality of our own future," she said. "It's not going to happen to us otherwise. I just think that it's a time in history when women's voices must be heard. Or they will be forever silenced."

43. OF POLICE CHIEFS' WIVES, AND JUDGES' WIVES, AND . . .
Polly Mann, Minneapolis

> *The woman earth is angered, mourning, receiving
> the terrible death. She will appear with us, that
> mother energy.*
> —Meridel Le Sueur, *"Woman Earth Is Angered"*

Another group committed to making women's voices heard is
located in Minneapolis. Its name is Women Against Military
Madness (WAMM), and its best known member is Erica Bouza—
who just happens to be wife of the chief of police. People magazine
was one of those introducing her to a national audience in 1984,
choosing a provocative headline: HOUSE ARREST WASN'T FOR
HER, SO POLICE CHIEF'S WIFE ERICA BOUZA TRIED
POLITICAL PROTEST—AND JAIL.

Above the headline was an equally provocative picture: Bouza,
in a "NO NUKES" shirt and casual pants, gripping her jail cell
door while kissing her nattily-dressed husband, Minneapolis Police
Chief Anthony Bouza.

Erica Bouza had been arrested twice in the previous year on
charges of trespassing during demonstrations at Honeywell, Inc.,
the nation's 16th largest defense contractor, People reported. Now
she was starting a 10-day sentence at the Hennepin County
workhouse.

"I didn't want to make life difficult for Tony," she was quoted
as saying. "I don't like breaking the law. But this is something I
feel very, very strongly about. You have to be your own person
no matter whom you're married to." The chief, himself, was

brusquely, but determinedly, supportive.

When I first reached Minneapolis, there was Bouza, a media star again as Saturday's top-of-the-page story in the Star and Tribune. This time the headline promised more fame to come: "Erica Bouza's life may be the stuff of which TV movies are made." A script already was in the works for ABC-TV, the article declared. Mariette Hartley was the choice for the role. Bouza had been arrested a third time that May, the article reported, when she once more went over the fence at Honeywell. The Star and Tribune had not been able to get a comment on this latest episode from Bouza, herself: "Bouza, 54, could not be reached because she was at a crafts show displaying jewelry she makes."

But Bouza is only one of the gutsy, determined Minnesota women who make up WAMM, and the one I found at the Minneapolis headquarters was not Bouza, but director Polly Mann.

While Bouza might get the headlines, Mann, too, had been arrested recently at Honeywell. For her, the date had been Good Friday, in April. She had chosen to spend a day in the county workhouse rather than pay a fine—it probably would have been $100, she thinks. The day in the workhouse "wasn't very eventful," she said wryly. "The food was good and I was not badly treated. I'll probably get arrested again."

It's not that she enjoys it, but she does believe her willingness to put up with arrest makes a couple of important statements: "I think civil disobedience is important because it shows how serious you are and because I think the society has to be disrupted before it is going to change."

With that spunky manner and her choice of dress this day— chunky, pink, dangling earrings and a boldly-printed, long tunic top over white slacks—it would be hard to know Mann's age if she didn't matter-of-factly mention that she is now 65. Her office is decorated with a WAMM poster, children's drawings and other artwork. Mann's voice still carries a slight, soft Southern accent, dating back to her Arkansas childhood. There is, however, a hard edge

Polly Mann

to the words. Polly Mann means business. And most of that business these days involves WAMM.

WAMM, Mann believes, is a unique group of strong-willed women. They—and she—are proudly feminist, she said. "If there is any hope [of saving the world], the women will have to do it," she declared . . . even though "it isn't women who have made these decisions that are sending the world right down to hell."

"Women," continued Mann, "do not hold positions of power in the three institutions that run this country: the government, the corporations and the military." And, she added, "we don't propose that women should try to get into these things."

Unlike Betty Bumpers, Mann dismisses politics as the route to power: "That isn't where the changes are made. The politicians are chessmen on a board, and they get pushed by the forces this way and that way. What we want to be is one of the forces that pushes. I don't want to waste time urging good people to be chessmen on a board. I want 'em to push . . . to push the world toward peace."

Toward that end, Mann sees WAMM's role as that of a catalyst—"to provide support for women who have ideas, and at the same time to encourage women to do this action." WAMM does not tell its members what to do, she said; it does support them in projects they develop themselves. Members have organized anti-nuclear vigils at freeway offramps, put out brochures and flyers, formed a committee opposing intervention in Central America, started a speakers bureau.

One thing they have not done as WAMM members has been to endorse or partcipate in acts of civil disobedience. WAMM, as an organization, could lose its tax-exempt status if they did; direct political action is forbidden. Yet, a number of members have followed the model of Bouza and Mann, individually taking their turns at clambering over the Honeywell fence.

Their approach has brought the group its share of criticism, Mann admitted. She recalled a recent discussion with Erica Bouza: "Erica talked to a Jewish group the other day—she's Jewish—and she told me, 'It was the worst group I've ever talked to; they said we were funded by the KGB!' " At that point, said Mann, Bouza set them straight on the group's funding, which comes from their own money-making efforts, including memberships, fundraisers, subscriptions and community canvasses.

WAMM now has about 1,200 members, said Mann, with another 300 on the mailing list. Raising the money to keep it all going is a challenge. But that is OK with Mann; she never yet has found life to be particularly easy. Both she and WAMM are survivors.

Mann grew up as a member of a proud Arkansas family caught in the depression. Her mother, divorced, took her two children to live with their grandfather. When he died, they went to stay with a great aunt. College was out of the question for Polly; her paychecks were a family necessity as soon as she finished high school in 1937.

World War II brought Polly her first decent-paying job, as a civilian employee of the Army. She began as a secretary at Camp Joseph T. Robinson in Little Rock and wound up in charge of the rail transportation section that supervised travel of some 30,000 men leaving the base by rail. During the latter part of the war she spent a year and a half with the lend-lease program in South America, working in both Ecuador and Peru.

During her time in Little Rock, she also met a young lawyer assigned to examine contracts in the same building where she was working. She and Walter Mann were married in 1942.

It's a marriage that has lasted, though not always easily. Walter brought his Southern bride back to his home turf, Windom, Minn. The small town seemed to offer nothing challenging for Polly: "I wasn't doing anything that was fulfilling for me, not really."

Thinking back on those early days, Mann again gave her wry laugh. "I used to go to bed and wonder what I had done that was so bad that I had ended up where I was." She had no skills to earn money there; Windom was conservative, in the way of small towns, and Polly was used to some merriment: "putting on a big-brimmed hat and having a drink and going out to lunch." Soon there was a child . . . then two children . . . eventually a total of four to care for. "I loved my husband and I loved the children," said Mann, "but I was really discouraged."

Then she found politics—the progressive brand of Minnesota's Democratic Farmer Labor Party. She worked enthusiastically for Hubert Humphrey in the early years, and for Orville Freeman, who would become Minnesota's governor. She left politics in 1960, when her husband was appointed a district judge and the family moved to a larger town, Marshall. At that point, Polly switched to volunteer work—the United Nations Association, the governor's Council on the Aged, groups for mental health and handicapped children.

But before that, said Mann, one simple event had "totally changed my life." It happened when she picked up a Society of Friends (Quaker) publication, "Speak Truth to Power." The tract identified the causes of war as "greed, self-righteousness and love of power," and suggested that "to combat these things, you apply the principles of the Sermon on the Mount." Mann did not become a Quaker, but did join a fellowship group sponsored by the Friends. And that seemed to start a chain reaction of activities that would eventually lead to WAMM.

In the early '60s, she helped set up a local peace committee in Marshall. After the United States became involved in Vietnam, she began reading about that conflict. When she got a job in 1967 as bookstore manager at Southwest State University in Marshall, she soon became a rallying figure for college war protestors, she recalled. The college president "would get calls every month or so, [saying] that they should fire me, because I was too radical and I was agitating the students. And I did."

She stayed in that job "until the first class graduated." Then she quit, as a different part of her life began to pull apart. "My middle daughter," she said, her voice faltering, "at 25 . . . was found dead of an overdose . . . in Omaha on her way home from California." In reaction, Mann wrote a novel, "The Years of Destruction," about young people and the traumas they were going through in those years. It was never published.

Life has not always been easy for the other children either, although they seem to be making it through. One daughter, now nearing 40, is a typesetter and activist, living in California; the other, 33, was a dropout at 14, but now is studying pharmaceutical medicine at the University of California at San Francisco. The youngest child—a son, 28—is working as a carpenter.

Sometimes, said Mann, she worries that if she had been different, that if she hadn't brought quite so much of the world into the home, her children would have had an easier time of it. "Maybe it would be better to be ignorant," she said quietly. "I had years that I never knew the things that I know, and they knew it from the time they were little, because it was such a part of my life."

In 1980, Mann finally moved to the Twin Cities—by herself. She'd gotten a job with the Nestle boycott; her husband stayed in Marshall, where he is now a state district judge. Their marriage became one of weekend visits. WAMM began the following year, with Mann as one of the founders. She became the paid director in 1984.

Fairly often now she is the one called on to explain WAMM's position toward the threat of war. She's found it's best to touch people's emotions. "I can talk facts," she said, " . . . but the end of the world is an emotional issue! And none of us is going to deal with it without talking about the end of the world: the fact that the trees aren't going to be there, the animals are going to go blind." And, suggests Mann—in spite of the pain that touches her when she thinks of problems faced by her own offspring—the ultimate issue may be the future for children: "We're going to talk about what it's like for you not to have a world for your granddaughter."

44. DARING TO CHANGE
Esther Pank, Long Island, N.Y.

> *Knowledge is power, and knowledge entails respon-*
> *sibility. Preventing nuclear war is the greatest*
> *ethical priority of our age . . . . We must assume*
> *the responsibility to make great changes in our*
> *nation and our world, even though it will require*
> *us to change our lives.*
> —*Eric Markusen and John B. Harris*

It's funny, the things that can turn a life around. For Esther Pank—Long Island homemaker and mother, solidly-conservative Republican, Irish Catholic, corporate wife—it was a picket line at a supermarket.

The year was 1968, and Pank had realized she was becoming disenchanted with the war being fought in Vietnam. But no one else seemed to feel that way, so she pushed her own feelings aside. Then one day she went to the supermarket . . . and there was that picket line.

"It was a vigil, actually," recalled Pank, "being sponsored by the Women's International League for Peace and Freedom. The picket signs said things that I had been thinking. I walked up to the picket line and just asked if I could join them." Remembering that day, she laughed. "They were as surprised as I was!"

For Esther Pank, things were never again the same. In following years, the proper suburban housewife would become a radical organizer and a feminist, her politics would do an about face from right to left, she would leave the Catholic church for the Catholic left, she would leave her husband . . . and eventually, she would

Esther Pank

leave her upscale suburban home, moving into a nearby group living home for peace activists, accompanied by one of her daughters.

Yet, life has never been more meaningful, she will tell you today. Finding those women with their signs—finding that there were "other people who thought what I thought . . . was an empowering thing . . . an enormous moment for me," she said. "That was my open door into this thing called the movement."

Esther Pank, recently turned 50, curled a leg under herself comfortably as she talked, sitting on a sofa at Smithtown House on Long Island, where she and daughter Jennifer, a college student, live with three others. Her gray hair is cut in a casual bob; she has gray-blue eyes, an easy smile. She had been doing some spring housecleaning this April Saturday, she explained. She was barefoot, dressed in tan pants and a summer blouse. She reached frequently for a Salem.

Before that picket-line incident, she said, she had been "totally non-activist."

"I'd been an active PTA mother, but the closest I'd ever come to organizing anything was, I'd been a cookie mother for the Girl Scouts and I had been a class mother in the PTA."

For the first few years, Pank's newly-burgeoning activism would be intimately involved with her church, and would send a few shock waves through her conservative parish. It turned out that a couple of the women pickets that she met belonged to the church—a newly-forming parish on Long Island—where they were organizing a Justice and Peace Committee. Pank joined them, realizing that "this was the first time I had found anybody who also challenged the war in Vietnam."

At the time, Pank, who had four youngsters, was studying to become a religious education teacher at the church and had read the pope's letter on human life, issued shortly after Vatican II. That letter, said Pank, "challenged the whole 'just war' theory. That was when I began to realize that it was perfectly OK as a Catholic to be opposed to war. I very quickly became deeply immersed in the

Catholic left . . . and very quickly got into trouble in my local parish."

With Pank assuming a leadership role, she and other members of the Justice and Peace Committee attempted to set up a parish draft counseling service—a move that "ran into enormous opposition." Then, as the Harrisburg Nine activists went on trial in Harrisburg, Penn., the women joined other Long Island activists to attend. Next Pank helped organize a Justice and Peace Coalition among various groups on the Island and started planning a series of educational talks on "what it meant to lead a Christian life in the 1960s," to be held at her church.

One of the speakers, as that series developed, was a young man who had been a draft card burner. "Our parish was not too happy with that," admitted Pank. But when she invited Elizabeth McAlister, the controversial former nun and radical activist who had married Philip Berrigan, "all holy hell broke loose, and within a short period of time, I went from being someone in a position of leadership within the parish to someone the parish council was attempting to censor."

"They actually held a hearing to see whether or not I should be censored, publicly censored," she said, and a group of men in the parish marched on the rectory, challenging the pastor who was supporting Pank's right as a parish member to hold educational forums. That situation was especially trying, for Pank's husband was on the parish council at the time; because of his own beliefs, he offered only lukewarm support for his wife.

However, the pastor held his ground and the forum went on as scheduled . . . ironically, without Elizabeth McAlister, who sent a last-moment message that she was too ill to attend. And that got Pank in even more hot water: "Immediately," she said, "we just put together a rather serendipitous program" featuring guests who happened to be there that evening from the United Farm Workers. That program turned out to be "far more radical than we might have had, had McAlister shown up" . . . and brought Pank and the committee under more pressure within the church.

But the women went ahead, and even added a new project: "We rededicated ourselves to opposing the church's silence against the war, and we began a series of actions throughout all the churches on the Island," said Pank.

The women would go to a church on Sunday, join the congregation and stand silently through the whole service. In addition, "we held a large demonstration at the ordination services [being held on the Island]," said Pank, "and directly affected a number of the young priests who were coming into being at that time, many of whom became anti-war activists."

"I didn't make things a whole lot better," said Pank, "in that I was also beginning to become a feminist, and I forced the issue of becoming a woman lector within the church." The lector, she explained, is someone who stands at the altar with the priest, does some of the readings and helps lead the congregation. Women had not been allowed in that role prior to Vatican II, and still were not, within her parish. "They finally let me," she said, but it was only after she "stacked the liturgy committee and called for a vote."

Eventually, Pank parted ways with the parish, although, she said, "I still consider myself a Catholic. But I express my Catholicism through the actions of the Catholic left, not through the institutional church. It is too patriarchal, too confining, too rigid."

Meanwhile, Pank's marriage also was pulling apart, as her husband, she said, "became more and more involved with Republicans, and I became more and more involved with radicals."

It was Esther, however, who went off to the 1972 GOP convention in Miami Beach—but no longer as one of the Republican faithful. Instead, she "stayed in the park with all the other activists and was teargassed." Her husband, who remained at home, had plans for an evening out when she returned: The couple were to attend a dinner meeting with corporate friends—people who were friends of the Nixons. "That was absolutely impossible," said Pank. "I'd just been teargassed by the man!" Pank spent summer weekends

that year at workshops for activists in New Jersey, where "I totally intensified my own commitment."

As the Vietnam War finally ended in 1974 and the spunk seemed
to dissolve out of the movement, she and other Long Island activists
jumped in to encourage "the remnants of the peace movement."
They began holding workshops on nonviolence; they started an alternate newspaper.

But at home, Pank was running out of inspiration when it came
to her marriage. The growing philosophical gap between Pank and
her husband was mirrored in the ways they spent their money: "He
wanted to buy all these new gadgets. But part of my re-evaluation
was that middle America cannot live like that and have justice in
the world. I didn't want dishwashers and Cadillacs; he did. By 1976,
we were divorced."

Pank remained in the family home while the children were growing, but moved in 1984 to the group home where she and Jennifer
now live.

"It was for me another step in integrating what I really believe,"
she said, "which is that of sharing, of not owning . . . . It was
important for me to strip myself of a lot of trappings of suburbia,
which frees me up to be able to do more activist things." Like Beth
Centz in Pennsylvania, she is now a typesetter, working closely
with a small peace movement print shop. That job, said Pank,
"allows me to earn my living in a way that I can be at peace with."

Since 1977, Pank has added new pages to her activist file. That
year, she joined the Mobilization for Survival and helped plan the
spring mobilization in 1978. In 1979, she was a leader among a small
group of Long Island activists who set out to stop a multi-million-
dollar nuclear power plant; their actions seemed to have an effect,
even though their target—the Island's Shoreham plant—was by then
already 80% complete.

Their initial Shoreham action made headlines, as Pank and the
others climbed over the power plant's fence and got arrested . . .
an action that Pank believes made many Long Islanders realize

"for the first time, that Shoreham was even being built here on the Island." Along the way, the activists formed the SHAD Alliance, and in the summer of 1979, shortly after the Three Mile Island incident, they held a demonstration that brought 20,000 people to the plant; 700 were arrested during a civil disobedience action.

The Alliance sought to stop the plant through political means, as well. They threw in a legal monkey wrench, based on a law requiring that an area evacuation plan must be approved before a nuclear power plant can go on line. SHAD convinced county legislators that no evacuation plan could quickly get everyone off Long Island. As a result, the county declined to work on the required plan. And Shoreham—"it's fully built; the fuel has been loaded"—was not on line.

In 1981, the local electric company, bristling under SHAD's continuing provocation, filed suits seeking $2 million each from Pank, Riley Bostrom, who owns the home where Pank now lives, and six others. The company finally settled for an injunction, requiring that the activists stop any activity at the plant. "Riley and I have since both been arrested at Shoreham and continued to organize demonstrations," said Pank, smiling. "They've never moved on it; it was just a scare tactic."

In 1984, Pank added another task, helping with nonviolent civil disobedience training for close to 300 Long Islanders who signed the Pledge of Resistance, promising to commit civil disobedience on the group's summons as a protest to United States actions in Central America. By that year, Pank had switched her major efforts to the War Resisters League, and soon found herself serving on their national executive committee, helping plan the 1985 April Actions for Peace, Jobs and Justice, held in Washington, D.C.

Those April Actions, which included a march, rally, religious convocations, lobbying and nonviolent civil disobedience, were planned through the joint efforts of many groups and many races—a fact that gave Pank some special hope. The actions were "the first time that the issues of peace and justice were really combined . . .

with equal treatment throughout," she said. Pank fervently believes that pulling together all peace and justice movements, all racial groups, is the next big, essential step toward reaching peace . . . the one that could make peace happen. "They're not going to get peace by stopping weapons," she said. "We're only going to get peace when the reasons that wars are fought are addressed."

Esther Pank—the one-time Girl Scout cookie mother—is committing her life now to making that happen. Winning that kind of peace, she knows, would mean big changes in the world: People caring for each other, rejecting injustice, sharing the world's riches.

Pank already has some personal knowledge of making change and taking chances. Today, she dares hope it is coming together.

Many married women made major changes during the '60s, '70s and '80s. For some, the wrenching turn came in adding a new title—job holder—to the roles of wife and mother. For others, it meant going back to school, tackling books and degree requirements. News stories told of women donning caps and gowns for the same graduation ceremonies honoring their own children. It was an era that redefined women's roles . . . and demanded accomodation from children and husbands.

Yet, Esther Pank went further than most—leaving church and marriage . . . rejecting the comforts of a corporate lifestyle . . . adopting both activism and feminism . . . changing her politics from Republican to what she now describes, with some hesitation, as anarchist democratic socialist. That political description doesn't neatly fit her beliefs, she admitted. What she really wants is equal opportunity and justice for all; she doesn't see that happening with our system—or with the Soviet's. She's not sure what you'd call a system that would do that. But she does have some ideas about how she gained the courage to put those beliefs into action.

"I've always harbored a real sense of being offended at injustice," she said. Even back in high school, she had gotten in trouble by writing in the school paper about an injustice she saw then. This time, she said, "I think I took the leap when I found other people who thought what I thought and gave me permission to think what I was thinking, and then, in effect, gave me permission to act on it . . . .

"Perhaps it was just all there, waiting to be released. But it was the time in my life, too: My children were all in school; it's a time when women look for something else more fulfilling." Other women went back to school or found a job; Esther Pank became an activist.

45. ONE WOMAN, ONE COMMUNITY
Betty Richardson, Madison, Wis.

> *Of course prayer helps. And knowing that we are
> one with the power that helps the blade of grass
> break through the asphalt. Wishing helps, and
> dreaming, and talking together, and having a
> vision, and communicating that vision in our
> actions.*
>
> —Dorothee Solle, *"A Few Ears of Corn"*

Link House is one of those marvelous, old Midwestern homes.
It was built by Elizabeth (Lisa) Feldman Link and Karl Paul Link,
two bright, dedicated individuals.

Karl was a biochemist at the University of Wisconsin and involved
in research. He was, among other things, the scientist who
developed Warfarin after the Department of Agriculture asked him
to help farmers battle rats that were devouring their grain.

Meanwhile, Lisa, who held a master's degree in German, was
active in the Women's International League for Peace and Freedom.
She also became a member of the Soviet-American Friendship
Society; her parents were Russian-born Jews, and she hoped to
help bridge the gap between cultures.

Karl died before his wife. Later, when Lisa found she had cancer,
she tried to make sure the family home would continue serving
its community, as its occupants had tried to do. When she died
in April 1982, Lisa left instructions that the home—plus one and
a half wooded acres around it—should be put in the hands of a
good candidate, to be chosen by her attorney and her son.

What followed was an intriguing bit of inter-religious cooperation:

The Links' son and attorney chose the American Friends Service Committee to manage the home, and AFSC, seeking a director, selected a Catholic nun.

Thus it was Betty Richardson—nun, musician, teacher, administrator, artist—who opened the door when I arrived at Link House. The smiling Richardson was wearing a blue, long-sleeved turtleneck layered with a white T-shirt tie-dyed with a dramatic design of navy and lavendary purple, plus lavendar sweatpants and matching Jordache jogging shoes. The welcoming party included Jenny, a Weimaraner—the kind of dog that barks as you come in the door, then trots up for a scratch behind the ear.

Now 51, Richardson has been at Link House for two years, arriving some three decades after entering the Sisters of Mercy of the Holy Cross as a 17-year-old.

A career in education had begun quickly. As soon as she had a year of college behind her, she was given an extra assignment: to begin teaching at a local Catholic elementary school. "They were desperate," she explained, laughing. But she continued her own education, as well, and eventually attended eight institutions, taking 14 years to get her first degree. That degree was in English, with close to a second major in music, and it was followed by a second bachelor's in art and a master's in art education.

With her first degree in hand, Richardson moved into college teaching . . . then to campus ministry . . . and then returned to Merrill, Wis., her order's United States headquarters, where she helped found a center for spiritual growth. At Merrill, part of her goal was to broaden cultural perspectives and direct people toward social justice. But after a year and a half, Richardson said, "I began to see that if I wanted to really move this forward, I should move to a larger locale."

The connection with Link House at that time was serendipitous. Richardson had begun looking for work, either in Madison or Milwaukee, hoping to earn enough to support her social justice efforts. She'd thought of a job as a part-time choir director or

Betty Richardson; her painting, "Birth of the Androgynous Self"

organist, or perhaps a spot as a parish peace minister, but nothing was happening.

Then on one trip she stopped in Madison to talk with Quaker friends living in an ecumenical lay community. "Just at my whim," she recalled, "I said, 'I would just love to own a house in this city and do some ministry for struggling artists or musicians or people who want to work for social change.'" One of the friends looked at her for a moment, then exclaimed, "We've got a house!" Sure enough, the Quakers had just been given Link House. By that fall, 1983, Richardson had her house—although, of course she didn't own it—and the title of Link House director.

Since then much has happened, both for Madison and for Richardson. "I have just had some discoveries about myself—that I am becoming an administrator," said Richardson, sitting on a couch in the sunny living room whose windows opened to the trees beyond. She's learned to recruit and manage volunteers; she's learned to let go in areas where others can handle important tasks; she's learned that she can pull together a growing, meaningful program. And it's been exciting.

"About four years ago, I went through what I'd call a midlife crisis," she said, "but now I'm past it. I know who I am and I know what I've done, and I know what I've got to do yet."

"I'm a Jungian," she added, "and I firmly buy Jung's whole analysis that all of us have a shadow side. We develop one side of ourselves very well first . . . you can't do it all simultaneously. But if you live long enough, inevitably your shadow side is going to come out, and, Jung says, out of the shadow also comes the child. And the child is the most creative, has the best ideas, and is the most exciting part of you that's going to emerge." That, she senses, is what is happening for her, and the sparkle in her eyes tells how she feels about it.

Meanwhile, Link House has developed—not as a drop-in activist center, which would be prohibited in its R-1 residential setting, but as a networking hub for Madison. "I handle a lot of phone calls," said Richardson. She also directs development of some special projects and encourages communication among the various activist groups throughout the city.

As part of that latter task, Richardson shepherded production of the city's first justice and peace network directory. The final product showed 65 groups—everything from Alliance for Animals to World Federalist Association.

That first group, Alliance for Animals, turned out to be something of a special jewel, she is convinced. She'd learned of it a few months earlier when "somebody called me and said, 'We're thinking of getting a conference started on nonviolence.'" The caller explained, "We're just a few people, six or eight, and we just don't think that animals should be mistreated. But we think it's a bigger issue." They envisioned a "whole conference on people and reducing the level of violence in our society."

Richardson put them in touch with other groups that could add expertise . . . and the conference, complete with workshops, panel discussions and mime, would be held in November. It was a satisfying example of how the networking process can succeed. Richardson convenes representatives from various groups once each month to make sure just that kind of interaction can occur, and to make up a calendar, so groups don't trip over each other's projects.

Among other Link House-sponsored events are workshops titled "Transforming the Nuclear Dragon," inspired by Joanna Rogers Macy's book, "Despair and Personal Power in the Nuclear Age." The idea, said Richardson, is to get people to consciously own up to the human cost of nuclear confrontation and to deal with it on a personal basis. Each workshop closes with empowerment exercises, showing how individuals can indeed be involved in the process of change. "All go out of here stronger than when they came in, and they know that somebody else cares," said Richardson.

In spite of such solid satisfactions, the post of Link House director is not without its problems. One of those is finances.

"Elizabeth left a small sum, and I mean small—$12,500 a year," explained Richardson. That must cover taxes, upkeep on the property and Richardson's meager salary. She's paid as a part-time employee, but willingly admits she knew before accepting the post that she would be putting in 60-hour weeks. There is a fundraising drive planned now to raise money for some part-time help, and Richardson does receive supplementary support from the Holy Cross Sisters, who still consider her part of their community.

But the pluses outweigh the minuses. And there are many unexpected pluses—like the opportunity Link House offers to host visitors from foreign countries who are active in the peace and justice movement. Richardson has had guests from West Germany, the Union of South Africa, England and the Philippines. She makes sure their information is shared with Madison.

"What it's doing," she explained, "is making us one world. It's helping us to say that governments are not the only ones responsible for making us one world. Scientists are, doctors are, ordinary people are. It's people to people, it's music uniting us, it's art uniting us, it's all of these languages that are so human. It's one human voice crying out, wanting to be itself, wanting to be united."

"We have only one planet, we all live on this one, and war is obsolete."

46. CHALLENGING THE BOMB—AND LOTS MORE
Jean Bernstein, Laguna Beach, Calif.

> *No great improvements in the lot of mankind are*
> *possible until a great change takes place in the*
> *fundamental constitution of their modes of thought.*
> —*John Stuart Mill*

When Jean Bernstein bought her Laguna Beach home, the town was famed as an artists' hideaway, where struggling painters and potters could find inexpensive housing, as well as an artistically-inspiring setting.

But since then, growing chic has sent prices skyward, squeezing out the new, unmonied talent. Classified ads began to offer a "2 BR. home with cozy fp., wood floors & story book charm"—which almost surely translates out to "tiny and old"—for $225,000, or "A light & bright country home w/oodles of charm & warmth" for $1,600,000.

Jean Bernstein admits she's lucky: "My mortgage payments are $110.15 a month, and I'll have the house paid off (knocking on wood) in September. I regard myself as rich."

She also calls herself "rich" because she has been able to spend most of the past 20 years on matters she finds important. Her basic financial needs—"no luxury"—have been covered by income from a small family business. And there are some special pleasures: the ocean view from the front door, for instance; Bernstein keeps binoculars handy to watch the boats go by, or the whales on their migration to Mexico. This chilly day, she breaks wood from a tree that fell in her yard last year, feeds the crackling fire, puts her feet up and sips steaming mint tea from a large, hand-thrown mug.

Her activism, Bernstein recalls, began better than four decades ago, when she was a freshman at UCLA. There, just before the start of World War II, she was introduced to the heady brew of campus political debate by a young intellectual, Sanford Bernstein, who would become her husband. Before long, she helped found an alternative campus paper to fight for the rights of Japanese-Americans and for those of the black servicemen who attended UCLA but "couldn't get a haircut unless they went all the way to downtown Los Angeles."

School, however, soon ended. Following Pearl Harbor, when friends were getting drafted, she recalled, "the study of esthetics and astronomy and Latin and Spanish, all of which I loved—I wanted to become a linguist—became meaningless to me and I left. I never went back." Instead, she signed on at Lockheed, "building B17s." Before the war was over, she left to work with an alternative Hollywood newspaper; when that folded, she moved to a film group that supported liberal Henry Wallace's presidential campaign.

Her first child, John, was born in 1952, and for some years she concentrated on raising the couple's children—eventually, four of them. But when the marriage broke up in 1962, Bernstein resumed the old activism. During the Vietnam era, she joined the Women's International League for Peace and Freedom, and participated in their weekly vigils. In addition, "I went to the big rallies, we went to San Francisco for the big marches there, and I went to Century Plaza [Los Angeles rally] and was chased away by the police," she said.

After Vietnam, she moved into the anti-nuclear power movement. That was when the Clamshell Alliance was making headlines with its occupation of the Seabrook, N.Y., power plant, and when Abalone Alliance gained notoriety for its opposition to the Diablo Canyon, Calif., plant. Bernstein recalls "the ferment that existed then, the kind of fizzing that was going on among the youth, the great hallelujah enthusiasm for those big sit-ins."

Jean Bernstein

"It was within that psychological and emotional context" that Bernstein and a few others, in 1977, formed the Alliance for Survival, a group that would dominate local peace and justice activities for the next several years. Since then, Bernstein has led Alliance delegations before the Orange County Board of Supervisors, protesting involvement in civil defense; she has held up signs at freeway offramps; she has demonstrated against the storage of nuclear weapons at the Seal Beach Naval Weapons Station; she and friends have held weekly vigils on the beach, faithfully showing up every Saturday from noon to 2 p.m. for the past 7 1/2 years.

Those actions do more than just get publicity, said Bernstein: "Ordinary people [begin to feel] that they matter and that their beliefs and concerns matter, and that by coming together and sharing their ideas and their convictions and their energies and their intelligence, they can effect change. When people come together and stand on a street corner—holding up signs together, singing songs together—they're deriving a tremendous amount of value and nourishment from that activity, itself."

However, her own assessment of the future is guarded: "I feel that the probabilities of some nuclear catastrophe are pretty big," she said. "I don't know why my predictions are valuable, but I have this sense that there will be a nuclear catastrophe. I have strong hope that it will not result in total, global nuclear war . . . . I don't have to tell you, I think nuclear weapons can destroy civilization as we know it."

"The consequences of the use of nuclear explosives are so widespread that they actually render war, as a useful exercise, obsolete," she said; there would be nothing left to win or capture.

Yet, Bernstein added, "that is not really why I oppose nuclear weapons." Like many others, she believes the real challenge is a larger one: changing society so that both war and nuclear weapons are deemed unacceptable.

"If we're concerned with the preservation of our species, we're going to have to direct this consciousness with which God has blessed us to creative, productive, loving goals, and in order to do that, we have to build cooperative and loving societies, while at the same time overcoming ancient, outlived, purposeless exercises like war. The destructive capacity of nuclear explosives has brought this so clearly into focus."

"I think the most important way of thinking that needs to be changed is that we have to learn to share. We have to be willing to sacrifice individual privilege, and be willing to re-examine the nature of our wasteful lifestyle. You can't pick up a paper without reading about the decay of this society: all the drunkenness, all the murders, all the widespread, deviant sexual practices—you know, this frenzied seeking for some reason for living." And that sharing, she said, would have to be world-wide, seeing other parts of the world as belonging to our own families.

The changes she is proposing, Bernstein admits, are profound.

"If we manage to forestall a global nuclear catastrophe, it's going to be generations before ways of living together without violent conflict become the general modus of human society," she said. "But I think human beings will find a way. They have to."

XIII

THE MEDIA CURTAIN

Media in this country are fickle: overly solicitous when they love you, unapproachably aloof when their interest lags. They can make a national hero one day, forget him or her the next; move—complete with star-quality reporting teams and truckloads of gear—to cover an event in some small, stunned foreign land, then drop the country as if it had never existed.

When it comes to peace and justice groups, media occasionally move in for some event—a demonstration here, an arrest action there. But otherwise, nothing—no recognition that there is a continuing movement with the potential for causing change.

That is a situation with multiple implications: For the general public, it may mean we are unaware of a movement we should know about—one in which we might wish to participate. For some news people, it means they are unable to cover a story they believe desperately important. For groups, it means a tough challenge to get the coverage that brings both members and the clout to get things done.

The stories that follow look at the last two of the above: first, a reporter who became so frustrated that he quit his job and turned to writing the stories he believed had to be told; second, a young woman in Cleveland who is trying to build support for the nuclear freeze in spite of media disinterest.

47. DIFFICULT CHOICES
Larry Shook, Spokane, Wash.

Of all the problems that demand priority today, the nuclear threat to humanity is, by all odds, the greatest . . . the greatest moral problem that has ever faced humanity.
—Father Theodore Hesburgh, 1983

Winter had already arrived when I got to Spokane in mid-November. The evening news featured shots of vehicles playing bumper tag on slushy, frozen roads.

But Larry Shook opened his door to the kind of scene that makes northern living seductive: An enclosed fireplace, one that heats the entire house, was sending out flickering light; wooden paneling caught the fire's glow. Kids—two of Larry and Judy's own, plus a couple of their youngest daughter's friends—wandered through, carrying games and dragging blankets; crayoned drawings were on the wall, and children's toys and games shared the room's bookshelf space.

Judy Laddon was not home when I arrived, but her current project—a heavy, fuzzy, grey and white Norwegian-pattern pullover—was lying on a small table, with knitting needles in place. While her husband and I were talking, she arrived home, sat down quietly and picked up her knitting. Occasionally, she joined the conversation.

Shook, an investigative reporter who has written for San Diego Magazine, Newsweek, the Washington Post and New York Times— and who, with Judy, founded and then ran Spokane Magazine from 1977 to 1982—seemed at peace in this scene. When son Ben, "just about 8," or daughter Katie, 6, tried to whisper in his ear, he shooed them away while we were talking; but when Ben came back to lean his chin on his father's shoulder and listen pensively, Shook let him stay. When Katie brought the tiny book she was reading, Shook lifted her onto his lap, where she read quietly. One of the family's three cats, long-haired, orange-colored Sampson, also had a turn in the lap.

Yet, Shook is a man living with a grave concern: a firm, well-researched, documented vision of a world that he sees may be ahead of us—a world where cozy living rooms and happy, healthy kids may be things of the past.

That future, his journalist's analytical skills and research have convinced him, is one immutably tied to nuclear weaponry. There are steps that could turn the world away from that vision if we would move soon enough, he believes . . . but he fears that those steps may not be taken in time.

Like many others, Shook does not see the media getting the story out. And so, he has accepted more of that responsibility, himself—leaving high-calibre, mainline journalism, with all its potential for plump paychecks and automatic prestige, for the role of advocate.

"What I've committed myself to," he said, "is to understand that information, myself, [about what nuclear weapons development and production is doing to our country and world] and to be a conduit for the rest of our society: to do everything I can to force the public to come to grips with it."

As it turns out, it was one of his own stories that turned Shook, himself, into a fully-committed activist. At the time, Spokane Magazine had closed, a victim of the recession. Shook was working as state editor for the Weekly, which describes itself as "Seattle's Newsmagazine."

"I started reporting on the Hanford Reservation in the central part of our state, which is where the plutonium that destroyed Nagasaki was produced," Shook recalled. "The Hanford Reservation is the oldest and one of the most important plutonium

Larry Shook, Ben and Katie

distilleries on earth."

"I decided I wanted to focus on Hanford full time. Obviously the paper I was working for couldn't justify having a fulltime Hanford reporter, so I quit." Besides, Shook had recently done a big Weekly feature on Jim and Shelley Douglass, and the local Ground Zero battle against the Hood Canal Trident Base and the armored trains that bring hydrogen bombs for those submarines to Bangor, Wash. The Weekly, a successful "lifestyle" publication catering to young professionals with stories on the good life, was not enthused about running more stories prophesying potential Armageddons.

With three children to support—Ben and Katie, plus Judy's 16-year-old daughter, Michelle—moving into advocacy journalism was a financial gamble. Initially, Shook and a colleague won a grant from the Fund for Investigative Journalism in Washington, D.C., enough to support preparation of a four-part series on Hanford's PUREX plant. PUREX, in this case, stands for Plutonium Uranium Extraction. "It is not a bleach factory," Shook said, laughing; then, more seriously, "It has nothing to do with cleanliness."

When that funding ran out, Shook signed on as staff researcher with a new, small citizens group, HEAL, the Hanford Education Action League. But research still required grants, and Shook finally decided his family responsibilities called for a stable paycheck. He took a job as a management communications consultant, while continuing to work with HEAL and to research Hanford on his own time.

By now, Shook and his colleagues believe they have compiled a picture that should, indeed, shake Americans awake. Shook offered some of their findings:

—At Hanford, "where the plutonium has been reprocessed for almost 40 years, the contamination is almost as great as it was directly under the bomb in Nagasaki . . . ."

—"Three-Mile Island, the worst nuclear accident in history, released 15 curies of iodine 131, which goes to the thyroid and is particularly lethal to women and children . . . . In 1959, Hanford released an average of 10 curies of radioiodine every day; some days it was over 20 curies."

—"As members of the public, you and I aren't supposed to have more than half a rem per year of radiation. The government's health physicist did a paper, which we now have, that said workers walking around the outside of the PUREX facility, where they make the weapons, would get 10 rems a day of plutonium to the lungs."

—Hanford's nuclear waste already is getting into the Columbia River . . . a river that area agriculture depends on for irrigation water. Then those chemical and radiological elements "concentrate in the food chain." One example: "When they were dumping the most radiation into the Columbia River, they stopped because they got caught. Zinc 65 and a number of constituents like that were concentrated in goose eggs, millions of times greater than they were in the environment [farther from the plant] . . . . So if you'd eaten one of those goose eggs . . . ." More than that, there is the strong potential for mutations in the goslings produced by those eggs . . . and, both Larry and Judy said, quietly observing their own youngsters, the potential for permanent mutation in future generations of human beings.

The findings—which Shook and Allen B. Benson, a Spokane Falls Community College teacher who holds a Ph.D. in chemistry, published in a 1985 HEAL report, "Blowing in the Wind"—were based on the government's own records, said Shook. "We did no original research; we used government documents that have been published for 30 years. It was a very compelling indictment." Yet, he added, the government has denied responsibility, claiming that the plutonium found in the ground is from some source other than Hanford.

"If it is not Hanford plutonium, there is a very simple test for determining it," said Shook. And that is one of the steps that he and his colleagues believe is essential if we, as a society, hope to deal with nuclear danger: In situations like Hanford, the government must order those tests. Then, if weapons production has, indeed, deposited plutonium, the government must face up to its responsibility to clear up the problem. Beyond that, he said, there must be health studies by independent agencies to determine plutonium's effect on workers and on citizens living near the plants.

In some other areas, citizens have filed court suits demanding the government take responsibility, said Shook. At Rocky Flats, outside Denver, government contractors actually paid damages to property owners who had filed the suit, rather than go to court, he added. But, he said, "the government is now throwing every resource it's got into defending these cases, and it's winning some of them. It's very difficult for citizens to successfully prosecute—not because of the issue of merit, but because of the issue of expense. And the government knows that it cannot lose these cases, that it could get sued right out of the nuclear weapons business."

Shook intends to keep putting on the pressure. He and Benson already have begun research on another situation—this time around the Nevada Test Site. Again, indications are ominous: "They have contaminated an area equal to the size of the entire state of Nevada," said Shook, "with hundreds of times more plutonium than we've found here." Results of that study, he believes, may be shocking enough to cause—nationally—"a kind of pandemonium in the public." And, eventually, the nation as a whole may demand responsiblity from its government. "As long as the public response is just the peace movement," he said, "it will never have the scientific horsepower to hold the government's feet to the fire."

Yet, as Larry Shook now sees it, even the proof of nuclear danger will not be enough to bring peace to the world. Although he continues his search for answers as an investigative journalist, Shook now expresses some of his conclusions in terms that mix hard facts with a personal philosophy touching the realm of theology.

"I do not believe nuclear weapons are moral," he said. "I don't believe that they should be used under any circumstances."

"I don't believe in violence," he added. "I wish our country would take its chances, resolving our differences nonviolently."

That distaste for violence goes back to his own days as a Vietnam volunteer in 1967-68, said Shook. He had signed on between his sophomore and junior years at California's San Diego State University. "I thought that if America was at war, we should all be at war, and some of us shouldn't be hiding out under a deferment in college." Shook was assigned to duty as a helicopter door gunner.

By the time that tour was over, he said, "I had become just devastated with what we were doing . . . . I came away from Vietnam with a very strong sense of the futility of violence. Apart from philosophical considerations, violence does not work."

He recalled one action involving a small local community that took place while he was there. "There were VC in the village. We hit the village all day long with everything we had, and it didn't make any difference. They called it an air strike. [We used] Phantom jets. It was just an astonishing display of weaponry. They hit it with 500-pound bombs and 250-pound bombs, and then cluster-bomb units, which are little bombs that go off, and then 20 mm cannons, which are bullets that are this long (indicating 8-10 inches) and would just make a huge streak of dust on the ground when they would hit it. And then finally napalm.

"They waited for 30 minutes or so before they tried to bring the American troops back in. And the American troops couldn't go in, the ground commander said, because the soles of their boots were melting, the ground was so hot. So we finally flew back over it to reconnoiter it from low levels. And some little guy stood up with a little carbine and took shots at us . . . . The government must have spent a million and a half dollars on that air strike; it didn't do anything."

Today, Shook observes the contemporary situation with a mix of hope and dismay. The dismay centers on the continued use of nuclear technology.

Recalling his Hanford research, Shook said, "I think what the evidence indicates is that you cannot make nuclear weapons and you cannot own nuclear weapons without poisoning your own society . . . . My instinct is that what this data supports is a very sublime, poetic revelation, which is that you cannot perpetrate this dimension of evil—or even the thought that you would do it under any circumstances, against other creatures and against the creation—without perpetrating it against yourself in the same way. If that's true, then America, the Soviet Union, France and Great Britain are going to spend the rest of eternity, literally, cleaning up what they already have done to themselves."

Part of that effort, he said, will be economic. Cleaning up the environment—just what we have done so far—will put an almost unbearable burden on future generations, he fears, and the costs will run forever. The half-life of plutonium 239, Shook said, is 24,000 years, meaning "250,000 years of biological hazard."

Yet, said Shook, "I think there is a solution." That solution, he added, will likely be "a process rather than an outcome."

"I think if the human race starts living in the truth, we will find our way out of this labyrinth . . . . If we get facts in front of the world community and we stop behaving as though we're living out an idyll of the caves, saying we can't look at this information . . . because the answer may be too terrible . . . I think a lot of solutions will occur to us."

Among those solutions, he believes: "Very early on, we're going to see that we're going to have to abandon nuclear weapons. And you can't abandon nuclear weapons without abandoning war." That recognition will be the result of an intellectual process, Shook suggested . . . but will lead to something more: "a kind of spiritual conversion."

"And once that conversion has taken place, then I think the human spirit, the human creativity will have full sway in the universe. And I think human beings can resolve any problem they can create."

Already, said Shook, there are those theorizing that a special nuclear reactor could be built—one that could speed up the decay process, getting rid of radioactive danger quickly. That could be part of the solution, if that were where we put our priorities.

"I hope and expect," said Shook, "that our raised consciousness will stimulate human genius; that human beings will come together to do what they have done for three million years every time they are under the gun. And that is, figure out new ways to cooperate, which were unthinkable prior to crisis."

Hanford popped into the national news half a year after I'd talked with Larry Shook, as Russia's Chernobyl nuclear reactor disaster jolted the world. Writing a week after Chernobyl, Lynn Simross reported in the Los Angeles Times that Hanford, "ironically, houses a nuclear first cousin to the Soviet Union's Chernobyl reactor." Later in the story, Simross continued:

> Today, Hanford is the largest nuclear facility in the world, covering 570 square miles. It is owned by the Department of Energy and operated by United Nuclear Industries Inc. Hanford has a total work force of about 14,000 people and is located about 200 miles southeast of Seattle, and 120 miles east of Mount St. Helens volcano.
>
> The Hanford reactor similar to the Chernobyl one is called the "N" reactor, which, like Chernobyl, is not covered by a containment structure—the concrete dome—to limit the release of radioactivity in case of a nuclear accident.
>
> Hanford's "N" reactor does have something called a "confinement structure," which is supposed to allow no pressure buildup. It is not known if the Chernobyl reactor has such a structure . . . .
>
> Also like the Chernobyl plant, Hanford's "N" uses a water cooling system and graphite to moderate nuclear reaction inside the core. It is the graphite that scientists say ignited, causing the severe fire at the Soviet plant, estimated to have reached heat of 5,000 degrees.

The Hanford reactor is the only one in the U.S. that has
a dual role—it manufactures plutonium for nuclear weapons
as well as generating electricity.

Another Times story, shortly before Christmas 1986, continued
the Hanford story. Larry B. Stammer reported that the reactor was
being shut down for six months to deal with significant safety defi-
ciencies. The Department of Energy, announcing the closure, had
added that the aging reactor would have to be decommissioned as
early as 1990. Two plutonium processing plants at Hanford already
had been temporarily closed that October following disclosure of
lapses in nuclear safeguards and security.

Time magazine picked up the story Jan. 12, 1987, pointing out
that the N reactor "dates back 23 years—and was designed to last
only 20."

"The parts are worn, the pumps and wiring often fail, the whole
reactor conks out 20 to 25 times a year," Time added. "The graphite
casing that holds the nuclear rods is swelling by nearly an inch
a year, and will collide with the overhead shielding by the middle
of the next decade." Time also recognized the problem of waste
disposal, noting that "500,000 gal. of nuclear toxins have leaked
into the ground from storage tanks over the years."

None of that, of course, was especially new to Larry Shook.
When sending him a draft of his story to look over, I'd used the
word "nightmare" to describe his reaction to the nuclear threat.
But he wrote back that he was uncomfortable with that word, for
his true sense of the future is hopeful: "I feel as though I live with
a constant sense of blessing and God's pleasure in the world . . . .
I just think we're going to have to work like hell. But I'm convinced humanity is equal to its challenges."

48. FAITH IN THE FREEZE
Monica Green, Cleveland, Ohio

> *Our minds and hearts cannot grasp the meaning of*
> *a million Hiroshimas or the possible deaths of*
> *hundreds of millions, if not billions, of human*
> *beings, so we turn away in a kind of benumbed*
> *horror and address ourselves to problems of more*
> *manageable scale.*
> —*John E. Mack, M.D., Harvard University*

For Monica Green, the first sturdy shoots of activism had sprouted early. "I can remember being a very young girl and having heated arguments with my grandfather about women's rights," she said. Her grandfather, whom she remembers as "a very traditional person"—the kind who felt a woman's place as wife and mother was in the home—would tease the child, "and I would get very emotional and upset about these issues that I felt very strongly about but was too young to be able to articulate."

But Green, whose parents both were activists, soon learned how to make her opinions known. While still in elementary school, she sometimes skipped lunch on Tuesdays to join her mother, a longtime member of the Women's International League for Peace and Freedom, at weekly vigils protesting the Vietnam War . . . went doorknocking with her mother to promote the presidential candidacy of George McGovern . . . and joined student protests at Wellesley College (where her father was teaching) after the invasion of Cambodia. In junior high, she accompanied her father, a theologian, to a Washington, D.C., rally opposing the re-inauguration of President Richard M. Nixon; she found herself "getting knowledge of that power and helping them reach the point where they can use that power to make a difference . . . . The message I focus on is individual empowerment . . . what we as citizens, as citizens of the globe, can do to end the arms race."

It's a message Monica Green is determined to get out—preferably with some help from the media.

The freeze was one campaign that seemed, for a while, to have changed the pattern of media indifference. During the early 1980s, it had turned to the ballot referendum, a gutsy sort of grassroots tool that caught the interest of reporters. Suddenly, the freeze sailed giddily across TV screens and newspaper front pages; press coverage seemed to be there for the asking. Media enthusiastically covered the 1982 referendums; they turned out for House debates at the start of 1983.

But just two years later, in the June 1985 issue of Mother Jones magazine, writer Mark Hertsgaard remarked, "You don't hear much about the nuclear freeze movement these days, do you?" Although a major pollster had recently told freeze leaders that their movement had made an enormous impact, said Hertsgaard, "that progress has been rendered all but invisible . . . by a virtual blackout in national news media coverage."

"Popular movements become worthy of serious coverage only when they produce an effect within the formal political system," he wrote. For the freeze, neither referendums nor debate changed national policy, and media moved on. That hurt, for as Hertsgaard added, "In the American political culture, things that do not get media coverage simply do not exist."

There was a brief flurry of media attention some months later when the Freeze combined forces with another major national group, SANE, taking the shared title, SANE/Freeze. Meanwhile, some media did seem to be trying to do a better job of covering peace and justice stories. During the Soviet-American peace walk to

Moscow, for instance, on-the-spot reports by staff writer Kathleen Hendrix were carried by the Los Angeles Times. Small steps, perhaps, but the kind that offer encouragement to workers like Monica Green.

XIV

EMPOWERMENT

"Empowerment" has become a big word in today's peace and justice movement. Groups know that before individuals will act, they have to know how to do it, and they have to have hope that their actions will have results. Peace and justice groups try to respond to those needs as they reach out to the rest of us.

Yet, it is hard to touch Americans with their messages. Most of us already are aware of the awesome nuclear threat; we realize uncomfortably that war between the superpowers could mean the end of everything. But the complexity of the whole situation confuses and overwhelms us; we feel powerless to confront all the governmental/military/industrial might behind the arms buildup. We don't especially want to hear more warnings of disaster when we can't do anything about them.

Convincing us that we can, indeed, do something may be the biggest challenge facing the movement as it tries to get the rest of us started.

Yet, it happens. It has happened for those we've met so far within this book, although to different degrees and in different ways. The three stories that follow relate to that process. The latter two are about individuals who already feel empowered. But the first tells of a Texas woman who is not in the peace movement—not even, really, aware of what movement is out there. Yet, she recalls a personal visit to Alamagordo as a vision of the disaster that could afflict this world and realizes that she shares responsibility for peace. She is, perhaps, at the beginning of empowerment.

49. THE WAY IT BEGINS
Ann Harrell Boone, El Paso, Texas

> The journey of a thousand leagues begins with a
> single step. So we must never neglect any work of
> peace within our reach, however small.
> —*Adlai Stevenson*

Ann Boone and her husband Daniel are bed and breakfast hosts
in El Paso. They're perfect for the role: friendly, eager-to-please
people with a nice home. When they found that their very first
bed and breakfast guest—me—knew next to nothing about El Paso,
they pulled out the family car, scooped up their aging poodle, and
improvised a moonlight tour.

Dan, a property manager, proudly pointed out turn-of-the-century
structures being restored, buildings going up, and other improve-
ments underway. He parked briefly on a hill overlooking both El
Paso and next-door Juarez, Mexico, and enthusiastically described
El Paso's attempts to make international relations work on a city-
to-city scale. He told tales of old-time El Paso, when the likes of
Bat Masterson cut their trails through the history of the West; he
showed how Fort Bliss takes a huge bite out of the middle of the city.

Looking at that sprawling military establishment brought back
an incident that occurred during World War II. Dan was 10 at the
time, and he and some schoolmates visited the Fort Bliss hospital.
Rows and rows of wooden temporary structures spread down the
foothills below the hospital then to care for wounded coming in
from the Pacific.

"My class was supposed to help entertain the patients," Dan said.
But for him, the memory that returns is not one of entertainment;

it is a 10-year-old's sudden, horrified recognition of war's toll on human beings.

Another wartime memory is shared by both Boones, and Ann told me about it the next morning during breakfast. Both she and Daniel grew up in this town, and when the first atomic bomb test was held in Alamagordo, N.M., "the light was seen even in El Paso," said Ann. "But people didn't know what it was, because no one knew about such a bomb."

Now, four decades later, the test site is open to the public just one day each year, in October. Five or six years ago, the couple decided to visit the site, a trip they'd been thinking about for some years. From Alamagordo, "it's a whole day's trip," Ann recalled. "You have to assemble on the lot of K-Mart, or whatever; everybody who's going has to be there. It leaves at like 9:30."

The year the Boones went, there were maybe 40 or 50 cars convoying to the site. Before the group left, the military men accompanying them checked to make sure each car carried plenty of gas, food and water. "They caution you not to touch anything, not to pick up anything, not to try to take off a souvenir," said Ann. "They tell you that it is still radioactive to some extent."

The Boones never saw a hole in the ground at the explosion site. "It went off in the air," Ann said. "I don't know if there is any hole." But the Boones did see some of the results: "All the rocks look like jade, kind of a crystal jade, like bath crystals," Ann recalled. "There are no weeds growing there, nothing growing there."

"We wondered, 'Maybe it's even worse than they're telling us,' " Ann said. "But they only allow you to stay briefly, like 40 to 45 minutes. You're in and you're out."

"It was hair-raising; it was awesome," she said. "It was the kind of thing where you aren't sure whether you're glad you went or not."

Today Ann describes herself as someone who tries to "stay away from politics." Her concerns center around her family, her home and her neighborhood. The couple's three daughters all have turned

Ann Harrell Boone

out wonderfully, she said. The family home is the fulfillment of a dream: an older house, built in 1916, one they renovated with mostly their own hard work and then filled with Ann's quilts and other handiwork. The couple have forged good relationships with the Latino neighbors they moved in among.

Yet, what goes on in the world bumps into the serenity of Ann Boone's private life and causes her to flare with worry and frustration. Like that visit to Alamagordo. Like skyrocketing taxes. Like moral decay. Like the arms race.

"I get real discouraged about our world and our country, the morals and some of the values, and things that as a child I grew up to know were wrong. It makes me wonder what kind of a world we'll have maybe 20 years from now—maybe not even that long."

Meanwhile, Ann tries to make sense of today's bundle of problems—like the money questions, personal and governmental, that frustrate her.

"I'm just one little person, living here in this little town, minding my own business, while during the day millions of dollars are being spent that I have no control over," she said.

Ann would like someone to take note, really pay attention to how much it is hurting middle-class El Paso families to pick up their share of the bill for the Palo Verde nuclear power plant that serves them; the El Paso newspaper had just reported that local electric bills soared 347% in the last 10 years, an increase blamed largely on cost of the plant. Besides, said Ann, "I think it's dangerous and I'm afraid of it." And there are other things: "chemicals being dumped . . . even some of the medicines, drugs and things . . . what they do to people. That's all experimentation, and people have to pay the price."

Ann, a genealogist, took a history course at the local college to learn more about how societies developed. Along the way, she said, she learned that "it's economically 'important' to have wars; people make money." But the small people come out on the short end of that bargain: "Lives are lost and families are shattered because of war."

So Ann Boone tries to deal with that problem within the world she knows. For instance, "My husband and I try not to fight, because neither of us feels good when we're upset with each other. This is just like a little tiny grain of it—and if that's what it's like, war and peace, then we all know a little taste of it from just living with one person or with one family or in a neighborhood."

Ann didn't know if there were any organized peace groups in El Paso, and maybe she wouldn't have been comfortable in most of them if there were. But she did know that peace—personal and global—was important to her.

Reflecting a few moments on all that she had talked about, Ann Boone crossed her hands just above her heart—and admitted to a catch in the throat, because the statement she was about to make seemed so important to her. It might not be a statement that was dramatic or daring, or even especially new. But it was where many Americans seemed to be beginning the process, and it carried its own deep challenge:

"I think that peace begins in the home, and peace begins with me."

50. IMAGINING THE WORST
Dorothy Baker, Birmingham, Ala.

> *The mind resists involvement with horror as, in a*
> *normal person, it resists preoccupation with death.*
> *And in consequence we leave the issue of nuclear*
> *arms, their control and their consequences, to the*
> *men who make horror their everyday occupation.*
> *It is reckless, even fatal, delegation of power.*
> —*John Kenneth Galbraith*

If you've got something that needs to be done in Birmingham, the person to call is Dot Baker.

She's one of those people who keep things moving, drawing on a personal style that combines Southern warmth with well-organized, effective action. There's no fence-jumping or blockade-breaching here; this is the kind of activism that evolved through work to support schools, help the physically handicapped and improve the criminal justice system—work done through established community organizations.

As the wife of a South Central Bell engineer and the mother of three children, Baker has long been active in community service. "Ever since I didn't have to spend my full time with the children when they were little, I did volunteer work," she said.

While talking, Baker was sitting on the living room sofa, with her back to a large window that looked out on Vestavia Hills, one of Birmingham's nicest suburbs. Blooms were just now appearing on redbud trees across the way; leaf buds were swelling on other branches. This Tuesday morning Baker was wearing a lavendar spring suit, with a white, short-sleeved sweater. Her gray hair was

Dorothy Baker

carefully waved. She was ready to head for an American Association of University Women (AAUW) luncheon as soon as our talk
was over.

At different times through the years, she's been president of the
AAUW; she's worked with the PTA, her church and the Greater
Birmingham Ministries, and she's served with the local Criminal
Justice Organization and the Organization for the Physically
Handicapped.

But a couple of years ago, Dot Baker's volunteer work suddenly
began narrowing. That happened in 1982, mostly because of her
daughter, Suzanne, then a nursing student at the University of
Alabama and a creative dancer. Suzanne had picked up Time
magazine's issue with the picture of an atomic explosion on the
cover, announcing a story on "Thinking the Unthinkable" inside.
That article was a catalyst for the Bakers, daughter and mother.

Among other information, the article gave the phone number
for a Washington, D.C., group dedicated to educating on the dangers
of nuclear war and ways to prevent it. To cut a fairly long story
short, Suzanne called the number . . . was referred to the organization's Alabama contact person . . . helped put on a week's
educational program at the University of Alabama . . . and was
invited to attend a national march and rally that June in New York
City.

Dot got involved when the contact person who was taking Suzanne
to New York backed out. Suzanne, she recalls, "was so disap-
pointed." So the mother made a quick decision, offering to go with
her. And that's what they did. Mother and daughter set off for the
New York City rally, which had been called to support the United
Nations session on nuclear disarmament.

"We went up early," said Baker, "in time to go to the interreligious
convocation they had at the Cathedral of St. John the Divine. There
were 10,000 people there from all over the world—[even] a Japanese
contingent. If you were not there, you cannot imagine how impressive that was." The next day they joined the march. It was, all in

all, quite a weekend, said Baker: "To be involved in that huge march and rally! I see different figures: 500,000, 750,000, a million. There were a lot of people. Yet it was very peaceful."

That fall, as Suzanne became a student organizer for the United Campuses to Prevent Nuclear War, Dot Baker began cutting back on her own activities so she, too, could begin working for peace. Before, said Baker, "I think I was like the majority of the people—not paying that much attention to the buildup of nuclear arms and not really thinking about what that really meant. And when I did think about it, I'd think, 'Well, there's nothing I can do about it. So I guess there's no point in my worrying, because it's the leaders who are doing it.'"

Now, however, Baker acted. "I've always been interested in causes," she said, reflecting on the shift. "And I decided that this was the ultimate cause." In February 1983, she accepted a post as Sixth Congressional District coordinator for the Nuclear Freeze, the organization that seeks an end to the arms buildup. "I really didn't know what I was taking on," she says now, with a laugh. "It just snowballed!"

Since then Baker, utilizing skills honed in club and volunteer work, has attended two national freeze conferences; she and Suzanne have put on a fundraising freeze walkathon; Baker has organized seminars and workshops, and started a local newsletter. One forum she helped put together brought Dr. Helen Caldicott and Admiral Noel Gayler, two peace movement superstars, to Birmingham.

In addition to all this, Baker has maintained close contact with other local peace-oriented groups through her newsletter. She has joined vigilers waiting for the White Train, which occasionally passes through Birmingham as it carries nuclear weapons across the country. She participated in the local Jobs, Peace and Freedom March on the 20th anniversary of Martin Luther King Jr.'s "I have a dream" speech, and she helped register voters for the national election.

When she thinks about the world situation, Baker said, "I always feel like I can never do enough." With all the potential for nuclear disaster—by accident as much as intent—"it's just a miracle that it hasn't already happened," she said. Yet, she knows it is difficult to really come to grips with the situation. "It's hard to think that [those weapons] are sitting out there by the thousands when you don't see them, you know."

"Look," she said, turning impulsively toward her front room window, "it's just gorgeous outside. It's spring, the sky is blue. It's hard to think you could go from this—in half an hour—to destruction of the planet, really."

"Somebody said," Baker recalled, "that you cannot really be involved in this movement unless you have a good imagination, and I think that's probably true. If you can't imagine that it could happen, then you won't make yourself get involved."

Dot Baker, clubwoman, volunteer and activist, has a good imagination.

A letter some time later confirmed Baker's continuing involvement: She participated in the August 1985 peace ribbon celebration in Washington, D.C., and took her own banner as one of the thousands made by women across the country—enough to circle the Pentagon and then some; at home, she took part in a Paper Lantern Observance marking the 40th anniversary of the Hiroshima bombing.

Just in the month of November that year, she was her congressional district's delegate to the Sixth National Nuclear Weapons Freeze Campaign conference in Chicago, she helped put on a National Issues Forum for the Birmingham Domestic Policy Association, and she organized an Interfaith Candlelight Vigil and Walk supporting the summit meeting between Reagan and Gorbachev. In the spring of 1986, she was heading for the Gerald Ford Library in Ann Arbor, Mich., as a citizen delegate to a

Presidential Libraries Conference, where she would join a panel of experts and citizens to discuss U.S.-Soviet relations.

That Dot Baker who once said, "Well, there's nothing I can do about it," had changed. How does an individual shake that sense of impotence? Somehow, she and others like her had made the jump; somehow they feel empowered, they believe that they can call government to task and get it to listen. I called Dot Baker back to ask how that occurred with her.

"I think that at some point something has to happen to cause you to feel that you, as a citizen, can have an impact," she said. For her it began with her daughter's involvement. Then she started listening to speakers who came to Birmingham. "What I learned was that that's why we're in this predicament—why the survival of the planet is at stake—partly because citizens have been leaving it to the experts," she said. "Then I found organizations I could plug into, that were enabling us to have some effect. And the more I heard, the more interested I became in being involved."

After three years as an anti-nuclear activist, Baker admitted that "some days are better than others." She's realized there is no quick fix available, "that we're in this for the long haul." Yet, she expresses her continuing hope through a favorite expression: "Every pebble you throw in causes a ripple, and every ripple counts."

51. CHALLENGING TRIDENTS AND TRAINS
Shelley and Jim Douglass, Poulsbo, Wash.

> *I say with a deep consciousness of these words*
> *that Trident is the Auschwitz of Puget Sound.*
> —*Seattle Archbishop Raymond Hunthausen*

When I first reached Shelley Douglass by phone from Seattle, she caught me by surprise: Would I like to come out the next day, stay the night at their home just outside the Bangor Trident base on the Kitsap Peninsula, and join them for a pre-dawn demonstration in the morning?

Members of the Ground Zero Community, including Shelley and Jim, would be at the nearby Puget Sound Naval Weapons Station in Bremerton, Wash., as workers arrived for their shift. It would be the day before Thanksgiving, and the demonstrators would hand out 1,200 small loaves of bread. I would be welcome to go along.

Although I'd never met the Douglasses before—never even talked to them on the phone—I accepted.

This was a couple I was anxious to meet. If the subject at hand was empowerment, this pair had gone the route. Their entire lifestyle had become a double commitment: to their opposition to violence in this world, especially nuclear weaponry, and to the religious faith that calls them to this kind of dedication. Theirs is a life that mixes prayer, study and activism.

It's the activism, of course, that has brought the headlines:

—When the first Trident submarine, the USS Ohio, arrived at Bangor in August 1982, Jim was among 50 protestors who took small boats—a "Peace Blockade" of 15 rowboats, a trimaran, a sailboat and three motorized boats—out into the Hood Canal, daring the huge sub to bully its way through the tiny flotilla. It did, of course: "They had 99 Coast Guard boats ranged against us—big Coast Guard cutters. And they had machine guns on the decks with belts of ammunition in them," Jim recalled.

—Just four months later Jim and Shelley discovered that the White Train—the one that carries nuclear weapons across the country—was passing their own front door on its way into the Bangor base. With that, they encouraged vigilers to be ready along the tracks all the way to Amarillo, Texas, where the train started its journeys. When the train headed north on its next trip, news pictures showed determined Coloradoans meeting the train in a snowstorm.

—Earlier, during the fighting in Indochina, Jim and two other men had slipped into Hickam Air Force Base, Hawaii, to hand out

Jim Douglass

Shelley Douglass

leaflets protesting American involvement in that conflict. Two of them, including Jim, had gone further, managing to actually enter Pacific Air Force headquarters. The two were seeking confirmation that civilian facilities such as schools and hospitals were among targets selected by the Hickam strategists. When they found files that seemed to do just that, they poured blood on them.

But those incidents, and others like them, give a lopsided view of the Douglasses. You also need to know that Shelley is just one semester away from a master's degree from Vancouver School of Theology, and that Jim holds a master's from Notre Dame University and studied two additional years at Gregorian University in Rome.

Also, that neither has held a full-time job for better than 10 years—not because they're lazy, but because they believe the work they are called to is their opposition to war and weaponry. The gospel, explained Jim, dictates that believers should "seek first the kingdom of God and then everything you need will be provided

. . . that you should not worry about livelihood, but worry about what you are called to do." Jim laughed and added, "It may not mean you'll be sustained in the way that you want to be, that's not the law; it's that you'll be sustained in the way that God wants you to be."

Indeed, the Douglass lifestyle is a simple one. They do have some income from lecturing, the books Jim has written and gifts, but it is obviously spread thin. Home—by choice—for Shelley, Jim and their son Thomas is the boxy, faded, orangish-red house that used to belong to the Bangor stationmaster. Heat is from a woodburning stove. There is just one bedroom upstairs, so Thomas' room is below—a space reached by entering a closet, pulling up a trapdoor and feeling with a toe for the ladder built into the far wall. Thomas' bedroom could have been where the stationmaster once stored wood for the stove. Furniture throughout is comfortable, but the kind that may already have been handed down through a succession of owners.

There's no real street address here, because the front steps don't lead to a street—they go straight down to the railroad tracks. And that's the way the couple like it. It means they can monitor every train entering the base—exactly how they first saw the White Train.

That happened on Dec. 8, 1982, after a phone call from a local reporter. "He said that a train had gone through Everett, Wash., north of Seattle, the day before, and it was a train carrying nuclear weapons for the Trident base," Jim recalled. "He asked if we knew anything about that, because he knew where we lived."

By then the Douglasses and their "house on the tracks" were widely known because of their protests against materials the rail lines brought to the Bangor base. Soon after moving to the house, they had developed a group of vigilers, the Agape Community—named, said Jim, for "the love of God operating in the human heart"—to witness along the tracks between Bangor and Salt Lake City, where missile engine shipments originated.

"We knew that Trident materials came by rail, but we did not then think that any nuclear weapons came by rail," said Jim. "We thought they came other ways." But, he added, "We felt that if we lived in this house, our eyes would be opened to things."

And that's how it went following the reporter's call. The train described by the reporter did not sound like one of those from Salt Lake City, Jim said. "I went outside after the phone call, and there were more security cars than I'd ever seen before in the area across the tracks. They were all just outside the gate. I came back in and got a camera, and as I was going down the steps, a train was coming in. That was the White Train."

"After the two engines, the first car was a huge thing, all white and heavily armored, with a turret on it like you'd see on a tank, and with slits in it, like you'd see on medieval armor, that clanked open and shut. That's where the guards are for the Department of Energy. They have machine guns and hand grenades and all kinds of weapons to protect the nuclear weapons. Then there were the longer, lower white cars, again all heavily armored." This, Jim decided, was "the most concentrated symbol we have of the hell of nuclear war."

Soon, with the Douglasses' encouragement, the volunteer network opposing arms shipments was extended all the way to the train's starting point in Amarillo.

Between the submarine protest, the tracks campaigns and other, related activities, Jim and Shelley Douglass have earned national reputations as the pair who have dared to look the Trident system straight in the face and try to do something about it.

Although they, themselves, had no idea of it at the time, the Douglasses' path toward their Poulsbo "house on the tracks" began as a result of that earlier Hickam action in 1972. They were living in Hawaii then, while Jim taught religion at the University of Hawaii.

The three men who entered the base at that time had been arrested after two of them found their way into Pacific Air Force headquarters and poured blood on the documents they discovered. During the trial that followed, however, the government refused to produce the bloodied files, so charges against one man were dropped, while Jim and the third man were found guilty of misdemeanor and freed on probation.

Meanwhile, support for the three men was offered at a series of public forums. Among those scheduled to speak one night was Robert Aldridge, an aerospace engineer who had helped design the Trident missile system. Before his turn, Aldridge had listened to an earlier talk by Mary Kaufman, formerly a United States prosecutor during the Nuremberg trials of Nazi war criminals. "Mary was talking about how at Nuremberg she had prosecuted people for doing the same thing that we [in the United States] were now doing," Shelley recalled.

When it was his turn to speak, Aldridge looked distraught, stammered a few words and sat down. It was only much later that the Douglasses learned why: Aldridge, with his insider's knowledge of the Trident potential, had decided that Kaufman's talk had branded him, too, as a war criminal. Although Trident was sold to America as a deterrent weapon, Aldridge knew it had first strike potential, Shelley said. With that knowledge, he reasoned, if he continued to help build the system and refrained from speaking out, he shared the guilt.

Soon after that, Aldridge quit his job and began fighting the weapons system he had helped design. It was in that role that he approached the Douglasses several months later.

By then the couple were living in British Columbia. Shelley had entered Vancouver School of Theology; Jim was working on a book. But Aldridge brought urgent news that pulled them back into activism.

"He asked us if we knew where the Trident system would be home-ported," Shelley recalled, "and we said, 'No.'" It would be Bangor, he told them . . . "only like 100 miles from Vancouver," said Shelley.

In the months that followed, the Douglasses quickly learned a great deal about Trident. For instance, that by the time installation was complete, Puget Sound would house 10 Trident submarines; each would initially carry 24 MIRVed (multiple independently-targetable re-entry vehicles) Trident I missiles—meaning, since there would be eight warheads on each missile, "192 hydrogen bombs on each of those 10 submarines," Jim said. Eventually, Trident II missiles would be installed—"the same number, but . . . much more destructive and much more accurate."

Aldridge put it in more graphic terms, estimating that each sub's destructive power equals "6,500 Hiroshimas." In other parts of the country, Helen Caldicott had picked up the message, telling audiences that "there are enough bombs in one Trident submarine to destroy every major city in the northern hemisphere . . . . It could kill hundreds of millions of human beings within half an hour."

The Douglasses' response was to gather other activists from Seattle and Vancouver in January 1975 to discuss not just nuclear weaponry, but the whole role of violence in contemporary society. They soon formed a group, the Pacific Life Community, where they talked about "all the different forms of violence: the sexism and the racism and ageism and consumerism and all the 'isms,'" said Shelley. They also studied "our own, personal violence," she added. "That meant looking at the way we worked together in a group . . . looking at relationships."

"It was kind of exciting," Shelley said, "because it showed where we were tied into the problem. And if you're tied into the problem, then you're also tied into the solution."

The group concluded that "nuclear war was kind of a culmination of those [other problems], and [that] to resist the one, you had to be dealing with all the others in some way," Shelley said.

"So, the question became, how can we learn how to live as nonviolent people, ourselves, and by doing that, counter the violence in the larger society . . . . We figured out that it wasn't going to do any good to stop the funding for Trident, because they'd just fund something worse; that the real problem was with ours and everybody else's mentality."

That didn't mean giving up activism, they decided; activism was needed to shake the American conscience awake. "We didn't think you could only address the mentality, because the issue was too urgent—you couldn't just [instantaneously] convert people's minds and hearts."

"So the thing we were really trying to do was to learn how to do all of that at once."

As far as the Douglasses are concerned, "that's still what we're trying to do," Shelley said, although the Pacific Life Community dissolved two years after its founding. But by then, the Northwest had become aware of the first Trident's planned arrival at Bangor; as many as 5,000 people showed up at demonstrations.

By the fall of 1978, the Douglasses decided it was time for them to move to Kitsap County, home of the Trident base. They already had established a meeting center there, the Ground Zero Center for Nonviolent Action, in an old farmhouse (the name chosen because it was so close to the Bangor base, an obvious "ground zero" target for a nuclear weapon, should an enemy attack). They spent their first three years in a rented trailer, moving to their "house on the tracks" in July 1981.

Today there are eight adults in the Ground Zero "core community," which coordinates both the Trident and tracks campaigns. The core group meets each week to discuss plans, to pray and to accept their own responsibility for both causing and stopping the arms race. Among traditional events on their calendar is the Thanksgiving distribution of bread which Shelley had invited me to join.

That particular Thanksgiving, it would turn out, would break the pattern. The day I arrived at Poulsbo was a chilly one. An early winter storm had just passed through, and the white blanket of snow in front of the Douglass home was broken only by the parallel black lines drawn by the tracks. More snow was forecast, and the Ground Zero Community had canceled plans to distribute bread the next day, although they still hoped to hand out leaflets.

As we talked that evening, Shelley curled up in a well-worn easy chair, knitting small white kitten figures for Christmas gifts; Jim poked wood in the fire or worked on papers spread on a small table.

The next morning, I found Jim already up and warmly dressed at 5 a.m., but looking worried as he listened to the radio. It had been snowing all night . . . schools were closing . . . even Boeing was shut down. Jim called the Highway Patrol. Driving, he was told, would be "extremely dangerous"; especially so, he knew, because the trip to Bremerton would be made in pre-dawn darkness. Jim thought about safety . . . about whether there would even be any workers arriving at the plant . . . and decided to talk it over with other Ground Zero members. After a series of phone calls, the decision was "no"; this would be one of the rare times when there would not even be leafleting.

For me, it was a disappointment, of course. But it brought a consolation: more time to talk with Jim and Shelley, while waiting for the sun to come up and the weather to clear enough for my trip back to the ferry and Seattle. With these two, talk takes time, because it often involves discussions that are both philosophical and theological.

Jim, for instance, quotes Dostoevski, Gandhi and Jesus as he explains a favorite theory—that one about how all of us share responsibility for problems of the world, including nuclear weaponry. In "The Brothers Karamazov," said Jim, Father Zossima expresses it when he says "that if we see deeply enough, we see that evil has its beginning in ourselves; and if we can make the connections deeply enough in our own lives, we see the way in which we are responsible for all the evil in the world."

"That is, I think, the basis of the doctrine about Jesus dying for everyone in the world," Jim continued. "It is a basic insight about the way evil in one particular person is tied in with the evil in everyone."

"That could be a hopeless doctrine," said Jim, "because, how can I deal with all the evil in the world. But you turn it around and it becames extremely hopeful . . . and that was Gandhi's idea of nonviolence: The way to deal with all evil in the world is to deal with yourself . . . .

"The most difficult process of change is in our own lives. That's the basic insight or hope of the Trident campaign and the tracks campaign. If we can change . . . if our community can change . . . if Kitsap County can change . . . then anything is possible."

52. WHAT IT MEANS

> *What is rational and what is decent and accords with my understanding of God's will, is for all of us to wage peace in the name of love and children. What is rational is to conceive of a different world, to offer every American a vision challenging far beyond what is being served up by either political party.*
>
> *—The Rev. William Sloane Coffin*

So, how does it all add up, this peace and justice movement that encompasses Peter DeMott, who launched a one-man attack on a Trident submarine; Betty Bumpers, who draws America's clubwomen into the process; Larry Agran, who pulls in local politicians; Marge Roberts, who moves back and forth between Rocky Flats and Nicaragua, who is at home at weapons protests or a soup kitchen; and all the many more.

There is no simple answer to that question. This is a movement that is everywhere and nowhere, one that is trying to do everything and often appears to be accomplishing nothing. Although there are those who have earned superstar status among activists—Helen Caldicott, for instance—they are largely unknown by the general population.

And so, the "movement" seems amorphous . . . something that many would argue does not even exist. What's needed, it seems, is some way of getting a handle on all of this, some way to identify with it.

That's tough, when the movement, itself, reaches toward so many different goals. Especially so when some of those goals, such as weapons reductions, are clearly measurable—the kind a good business manager could break down into rational steps and stated objectives—while others breathe the heady, hard-to-quantify air of philosophy, ethics and morality. All gather under that general heading, peace and justice, but they don't fit together neatly, like pieces of a jigsaw puzzle, to produce a recognizable whole.

And that presents a major problem. For without broad recognition and a comprehensible plan, the peace and justice movement has difficulty pulling other Americans into its dream for a better world or influencing political power centers.

So, what needs to be done? Many observers and activists have have come up with suggestions—often urging that all those involved rally around one goal, pulling the large mass of truly-concerned, committed Americans behind a single, winnable cause. There's real power already out there, they argue, but it's dispersed. If all those individuals put their shoulders behind one goal, they could be unstoppable.

Understandably, the cause proposed most frequently is weapons reduction. It's a hard one to argue with, when such weapons could, indeed, mean the end of the world, and when peace and justice workers, whatever their primary causes, all support such reductions.

Another good case can be made for improving relations between the United States and Soviet Union. Fear of the Soviets is the hobgoblin threat behind most problems identified by activists. It's why we "need" so much nuclear weaponry, "had to" send money, weapons and expertise to Nicaragua, "have to" chop human services budgets. But new winds are blowing. Governments of the United States and Soviet Union already have taken steps toward negotiation and cooperation. If enough of us would enthusiastically support such change, the two superpowers might more quickly recognize their shared interests and responsibilities. And then both nations—and the rest of the world—could begin the healing process.

Others, of course, argue that the ultimate goal is still that seemingly ethereal one: an evolution of consciousness. Sure, we applaud those other goals, they will tell you. We, too, want to get rid of the bomb, for instance. But let's say we actually reach that goal. What happens the next time there is a major flare-up? By then, every Third World country will have neatly-drawn plans for nuclear bombs and missiles hidden away in some bottom drawer. We'll soon be right back to where we were before—or worse. What really counts is to turn this world around so that we truly begin caring about what happens to other people, so we begin taking responsibility for them. If that were to happen, nuclear weaponry—all weaponry—would become obsolete. That is the only way to handle the problem permanently.

For me, one of the big surprises turning up in this study was the number of people who accept that last position. They include Larry Shook, the investigative journalist; David and Louise Smith, the Beyond War workers; Dan Hirsch, the UC Santa Cruz instructor, and many others like them. At the beginning of my research I— like many others—would have responded "nice, but impossible." Now, although I still have difficulty imagining all of that happening—in my own life as well as in the rest of the world—I believe they are right. It offers a challenge on a level of both difficulty and urgency never before placed before humankind.

It's worth noting, however, that even those individuals now actively accepting that challenge are putting their time in on more substantive projects. They are in among those working to decrease weaponry, lessen the dangers of nuclear power, feed and house the hungry, lobby the politicians, improve international relations, or whatever else.

They are, in effect, following the process proposed by Lynn Greenberg, the Santa Monica psychotherapist (Chapter 15), and the Thursday Night Group in the SAFE plan: Share, Accept, Fact Find and Formulate, and Encourage.

That idea, to review briefly, is that no matter what the ultimate goal is, once you have shared and accepted each other's concerns and fears, it is necessary to define the task and formulate logical steps toward completing it. Thus, Greenberg explained, all of us need to ask: "What are the manageable steps to create [the world we want]? What are the concrete steps? How do we make it short-term, small, measurable, achievable? What is our first step?"

Perhaps it doesn't matter so much if her first step is not the same as mine, Greenberg suggested. What matters is the sense that everyone does something. If everyone feels part of it, even in a small way, then the world we want would have a chance to evolve.

Larry Shook had offered a similar idea: It may not be any one cause that's most important; what now appears essential is the process. It's an idea closely bound up in that word, empowerment. It would not require converting the mass of citizens to any one position—weapons reduction, friendship with the Soviet Union, or whatever, although it would validate all of them. What it would ask is that each person face the reality that humankind today is confronted by problems more perilous than ever before. And that each of us shares responsibility for solving those problems.

That's not to suggest that this idea would be easier to bring about than any of the others. In fact, it would probably be tougher, because "process" suggests something that keeps happening, that doesn't have a nicely-marked stopping point. It means opting for change and growth on a permanent basis. There's no neatly-packaged objective at the end of the tunnel, one that we could tie up and declare "done." Perhaps, if empowerment were the mutually-approved "goal" of the peace and justice movement—and it already does rank high on the list for many groups—it would actually make the whole movement appear even more amorphous than it does today.

Yet isn't it, really, the basic notion upon which our country was founded two centuries ago? The one we all paid homage to as students in civics, history or political science classes—that idea that each citizen shares the goal setting, decision making and responsibility? Empowerment anticipates that not all of us would agree. But it also presumes that an informed, concerned, involved citizenry would eventually make the right decisions.

For those willing to give it a try, peace and justice workers with whom I spoke seem to agree on the first step: Just start. That's not being facetious; it means that once you begin with one small step, the next, possibly larger one will be easier, and that along the way, the result will be empowerment. It can begin as an individual, of course, but most suggest finding a group that matches your concerns—one that encourages sharing of thoughts, feelings, goals and activities. With that comes a new vision of self as someone who can, indeed, make a difference in this world. It may not be a big difference, they say. But it matters.

That, of course, mirrors Lynn Greenberg's fourth step, encourage. Her expertise and experience both indicate that continuing group support keeps individuals optimistic and active. For many, it's where they make their best friends and discover the deepest meanings within their own lives.

Indeed, the greatest danger may be isolation. Alone, it often seems that no one cares, and that problems such as nuclear weaponry are beyond the average citizen's ability to even comprehend, let alone to offer solutions. Besides, there are so many major problems demanding to be solved. We can't tackle all of them, can we? That's when we shake our heads and say, "Leave it to the experts."

But that's also when we abdicate our role as citizens, when we give away our inheritance as participants in the process. That's what happened in Nazi Germany, when basically good, well-intentioned citizens turned their heads to knowledge of what was going on in the death camps. Even when we decline to "know," we must live with the consequences.

Maybe, after all, it's not the peace and justice movement that needs a clearer self identity; maybe it's the rest of us.

All of this, of course, is challenging stuff for a nation that has gotten as big as ours, as committed to personal pleasure as ours, as overwhelmed by the issues as ours. And equally challenging for individuals who have felt cut out of the system. But the payoff could be an inestimable gift to people today and to future generations.

It could be life, itself. And peace.

EPILOGUE

There is a major frustration in writing a book like this: the impossibility of including all of the groups and ideologies that are involved. Even some of the major groups are not here, except, perhaps, for incidental mention: Jobs with Peace, Women's International League for Peace and Freedom, Greenpeace, for instance. And there are many, many more, both large and small.

Likewise, some four dozen people can do little more than represent the thousands of Americans who have joined the peace process at one level or another. Laguna's Jean Bernstein spoke eloquently of those unable to participate with the same intensity as those in the preceding stories:

> For each of them who are identified as peace people there are thousands who cannot or will not give a major part of their lives, but who cannot just do nothing. They go to demonstrations, they give money, they call in to radio talk shows, they put stickers on their bumpers, they open their mouths on the job, they tell their kids' teachers to teach issues, they join church social concerns committees, they subscribe, send in their dues, occasionally come to meetings, and—bottom line—they vote (or even, very consciously, they DON'T vote). Apathetic they are not. They are the stuff of the movement, and their support, their faith, their need and their demand are what make possible a movement and justify and invigorate its leadership.

All the preceding stories tell of people I would like to follow as they move on through life. Glimpses come in letters they write or in secondhand reports. Mostly they tell of new accomplishments, changes in focus, additional challenges. These are people who tend to move around as they see new demands and new opportunities.

Sometimes there is sadness. One letter came from a friend of Marge Roberts, the woman who had been my guide in Denver, Colo. Marge, it turned out, had left out one critical part of her story when we talked: While she told of her daughter's cancer, she had failed to mention her own. Her friend's letter included a folded, mimeographed paper: "Memorial . . . Marge Roberts, August 3, 1928—March 25, 1986 . . . special friend to many." Apparently Marge knew well of her own illness while we were at Rocky Flats, but chose to concentrate on life and goals and hope.

Marge was among those drawn to action. When she was concerned about the poor, she worked at the soup kitchen; when she worried about nuclear weaponry, she joined vigils and demonstrations; when she disagreed with intervention in Nicaragua, she went there.

Excerpts from her letters written during the 1984 visit to Nicaragua were included in the memorial program. Marge wrote:

> I went to a campesino mariachi mass in Managua. The music was stimulating and the words superb. God is with the people. The earth is for the poor. Life and love will triumph over death . . . .
>
> The contras are outside of Esteli' . . . . There is tension even as the streets are full of children playing . . . . The scene is sobering and yet life goes on and people smile . . . .
>
> I am not feeling afraid. Mostly I am feeling what I came to early on with the cancer thing, where I came to know that while I am not invulnerable, the essence of me is. I will be okay with whatever happens to me. If something happens to me, it is still time that I am where I need to be.

It is to Marge Roberts—and to all the others who are committing their lives to bringing peace and justice to the world and the people who live in it—that this book is dedicated.

APPENDIX

HOW TO GET INVOLVED IN A GROUP

Los Angeles psychotherapist Lynn Greenberg remembers the incident that jolted her into getting involved: listening to a taped talk by Dr. Helen Caldicott.

"[Caldicott] said, 'You know, you have no right to sit there feeling hopeless and helpless and overwhelmed'—which was, of course, exactly what I was feeling. She said, 'Unless you've tried everything and failed—and how many of you have tried anything? . . .' She got to me. The next thing out of her mouth was, 'And now you're going to ask me what you should do. Just think what the world would be like if every person did one small thing.' "

What Greenberg decided to do first was simply to share the tape she had heard with some friends. One of the women who heard it said she was interested, too. Together, they invited friends to join them, and eventually started the Thursday Night Group.

Greenberg's tactic—starting your own group, or simply beginning to discuss your concerns with friends—is, of course, one way to get involved. Joining an existing group is a more usual choice.

According to one estimate, there already are some 12,000 peace and justice groups in the United States today. That's a lot of groups, involving lots of members. So, it should be easy for an individual to find a group . . . and not just a group, but one that matches his or her interests and personality, right?

Not necessarily. While those who already are active usually know about lots of other groups and how those groups operate, some of the rest of us haven't a clue about how to even begin finding them. Some of the larger groups will be listed in the telephone book, but that does not always work. In Los Angeles, where I live, there are many groups. But with their headquarters in other parts of the city, there is little chance of finding their listings in my directory. However, don't give up. There are other ways:

—Through churches and synagogues. If your church or synagogue does not have a social concerns committee with its own activities or with numbers of other groups, ask the pastor or rabbi; if that still does not work, try the district office—or the district office of another denomination. Ask about ecumenical as well as denominational groups, plus non-religious organizations. Friends (Quakers), Brethren, Mennonites, Unitarians, Catholics, synagogues and most mainline Protestant churches should have the numbers or know how to get them.

—Through other groups or individuals. Your doctor may know about Physicians for Social Responsibility, for instance, and PSR is usually aware of other organizations. Your school district may know Educators for Social Responsibility. Any college's political science department should have contacts. If there is an American Friends Service Committee nearby, they should be able to give a good rundown of groups in the area. If no AFSC is listed in the phone book, get the number through the nearest Friends (Quaker) church.

—Through stories in newspapers and magazines. True, the peace and justice movement is not the A-1 topic for the media, but stories DO get in now and then. Pick the name of a group or individual mentioned in the story, get the number from the phone book or operator, and call.

—Through numbers listed below. You'll find information about most groups that are featured in this book, as well as a number of others. If you do not find a group listed near you, call or write a national office asking for a local reference.

The groups, you will find, are eager to hear from you. They will welcome your attendance at a meeting. Best of all, if you listen to those already involved, a group will offer a community of shared concern, and will help you realize that you, too, are important in the peace process.

NATIONAL OFFICES

American Friends Service Committee (AFSC)
1501 Cherry St.
Philadelphia, PA 19102
215/241-7000

American Peace Test
(Nuclear test site demonstrations; see also, Nevada Desert Experience)
333 State St.
Salem, OR 97301
503/371-8002

Beyond War
222 High St.
Palo Alto, CA 94301
415/328-7756

Bridge the Gap
1637 Butler Ave., Suite 203
Los Angeles, CA 90025
213/478-0829

Catholic Worker Houses
St. Joseph House
36 E. 1st St.
New York, NY 10003
212/254-1640

Center for Defense Information
1500 Massachusetts Ave. NW, Suite 24
Washington, DC 20005
202/862-0700

Clergy and Laity Concerned (CALC)
198 Broadway
New York, NY 10038
212/964-6730

Coalition for a New Foreign and Military Policy
712 G St. SE
Washington, DC 20003
202/546-8400

Committee in Solidarity with the People of El Salvador (CISPES)
PO Box 12056
Washington, DC 20005
202/265-0890

Computer Professionals for Social Responsibility
P.O. Box 717
Palo Alto, CA 94301
415/322-3778

Educators for Social Responsibility
23 Garden St.
Cambridge, MA 02138
617/492-1764

Federation of American Scientists
307 Massachusetts Ave. NE
Washington, DC 20002
202/546-3300

Fellowship of Reconciliation (FOR)
Box 271
Nyack, NY 10960
914/358-4601

Greenpeace USA
1611 Connecticut Ave. NW
Washington, DC 20009
202/462-1177

Institute for Defense and Disarmament Studies
2001 Beacon St.
Brookline, MA 02146
617/734-4216

Jesuit Social Ministries
1424 16th St. NW, Rm. 300
Washington, DC 20036
202/462-7008

Jobs with Peace
76 Summer St.
Boston, MA 02110
617/451-3389

Mobilization for Survival
853 Broadway, Room 418
New York, NY 10003
212/995-8787

Nevada Desert Experience
(Faith-based nuclear test site demonstrations)
PO Box 4487
Las Vegas, NV 89127
702/646-4814

Nuclear Free America
325 E. 25th St.
Baltimore, MD 21218
301/235-3575

Peace Brigades International
4722 Baltimore Ave.
Philadelphia, PA 19143
215/724-1464

Peace Links
747 8th St. SE
Washington, DC 20003
202/544-0805

Physicians for Social Responsibility
1601 Connecticut Ave. NW,
Suite 800
Washington, DC 20009
202/939-5750

Pledge of Resistance
PO Box 53411
Washington, D.C. 20009
202/328-4040

Promoting Enduring Peace
Box 5103
Woodmont, CT 06460
203/878-4769

Sanctuary
c/o Tucson Ecumenical Task Force
for Central America
(or see Chicago Religious
Task Force)
317 W. 23rd St.
Tucson, AZ 85713
602/628-7525

SANE/Freeze
711 G St. SE
Washington, DC 20003
202/546-7100

Union of American Hebrew Congregations
Religious Action Center
2027 Massachusetts Ave. NW
Washington, DC 20036
202/387-2800

Union of Concerned Scientists
26 Church St.
Cambridge, MA 02238
617/547-5552

United Campuses to Prevent Nuclear War
309 Pennsylvania Ave. SE
Washington, DC 20003
202/543-1505

War Resisters League
339 Lafayette St.
New York, NY 10012
212/228-0450

Witness for Peace
511 Broadway
Santa Cruz, CA 95060
408/425-3733

Women Strike for Peace
145 S. 13th St., Rm 706
Philadelphia, PA 19107
215/923-0861

Women's Action for Nuclear Disarmament (WAND)
New Town Station, Box 153
Boston, MA 02258
617/643-4880

Women's International League for Peace and Freedom (WILPF)
1213 Race St.
Philadelphia, PA 19107
215/563-7110

LOCAL AND REGIONAL GROUPS

ALABAMA

Alabama Nuclear Freeze Campaign
2512 Glendmere Pl.
Birmingham, AL 35216
205/822-0855

ARIZONA

American Friends Service Committee
745 E. Fifth St.
Tucson, AZ 85719
602/623-9141

CALIFORNIA

Alliance for Survival/Orange County
200 N. Main St., Suite M-2
Santa Ana, CA 92701
714/547-6282

Immaculate Heart College Center
10951 W. Pico Blvd.
Los Angeles, CA 90064
213/470-2293

Local Elected Officials Project
17931 Sky Park Circle, Suite F
Irvine, CA 92714
714/250-1296

Center for Economic Conversion
222C View St.
Mountain View CA 94041
415/968-8798

Physicians for Social Responsibility/ Los Angeles
1431 Ocean Ave., Suite B
Santa Monica, CA 90401
213/458-2694

Resource Center for Nonviolence
515 Broadway
Santa Cruz, CA 95060
408/423-1626

Southern California Federation of Scientists
3318 Colbert Ave., Suite 200
Los Angeles, CA 90066
213/390-3898

The Thursday Night Group
1431 Ocean Ave., Suite B
Santa Monica, CA 90401
213/395-4123

COLORADO

AFSC: Rocky Flats Project
1660 Lafayette St.
Denver, CO 80218
303/832-4508

ILLINOIS

Chicago Religious Task Force
59 E. Van Buren, Suite 1400
Chicago, Ill. 60605
312/663-4398

IOWA

Beyond War
506 Locust St.
Des Moines, IA 50309
515/282-2727

MARYLAND

Gray Panthers, and SANE/Freeze, Prince George's County
7F Crescent Rd.
Greenbelt, MD 20770
301/474-6890

MASSACHUSETTS

Underground Railway Theater
21 Notre Dame Ave.
Cambridge, MA 02140
617/497-6136

MINNESOTA

Women Against Military Madness
3255 Hennepin Ave. So.
Minneapolis, MN 55408
612/827-5364

OHIO

SANE/Freeze
1468 W. 25th St.
Cleveland, OH 44113
216/861-7999

PENNSYLVANIA

Brandywine Peace Community
PO Box 81
Swarthmore, PA 19081
215/544-1818

SOUTH DAKOTA

South Dakota Peace & Justice Center
PO Box 405
Watertown, SD 57201
605/882-2822

Black Hills Steering Committee
PO Box 19
Manderson, SD 57756

UTAH

Utahns United Against the Nuclear Arms Race
c/o Haley & Stolebarger
175 S. Main St., 10th Floor
Salt Lake City, UT 84111
801/531-1555

WASHINGTON

Ground Zero Center for Nonviolent Action
16159 Clear Creek Rd. NW
Poulsbo, WA 98370
206/692-7053

Hanford Education Action League
S. 325 Oak St.
Spokane, WA 99204
509/624-7256

WISCONSIN

Computer Professionals for Social Responsibility/Madison
1046 Jennifer St. #1
Madison, WI 53703
608/251-7925

Link House Peace Center
1111 Willow Lane
Madison, WI 53705
608/233-6979

INDEX

You may order additional copies of PEOPLE WAGING PEACE direct from the publisher. Send $19.95 for hard cover, $13.95 for paperback, plus postage and handling of $2.50 for one copy and $1 for each additional copy (plus sales tax for California residents), to:

Alberti Press
P.O. Box 5325
San Pedro, CA 90733
(213) 548-0260